10 Years On The Line:
My War On the Border

Second Edition

Mike Ligon

DEDICATED TO THOSE OFFICERS AND AGENTS WHO
KNEEL AT THE ALTER OF FREEDOM ENFORCING THE
LAWS THAT PROTECT AMERICA

VERITAS ET INTEGRITAS

ACKNOWLEDGMENTS

It was difficult writing this book. Despite having literally hundreds of documents in five boxes in the bottom of my closet for a few years I put off writing it because it was just too emotionally painful to relive. However, as I've seen the social entropy of my beloved nation continue its' downward spiral I'm reminded of a quote I've since posted in my office:

"If Ever A Time Should Come When Vain and Aspiring Men Shall Possess the Highest Seats In Government, Our Government Shall Stand In Need of Its' Experienced Patriots To Prevent Its Ruin"
Samuel Adams

I want to especially express my gratitude to those peers who stood beside me against management, their sycophants, and others who exerted so much pressure to compromise principle, integrity and our oath of office. May there be a special place in heaven for you…..and a special place in Hell for them.
Strength and Honor!

CONTENTS

Introduction

"The Immigration & Naturalization Service (INS) is *the* most corrupt organization in the federal government – and Douglas is its' most corrupt Port of Entry".   So said the Ethics Representative from INS headquarters in Washington D.C. as he began his lecture.   This was a stunning admission in 1997.   As I looked around at many in attendance in the conference room of the Douglas, AZ Port of Entry I could see why.   I was still only a "proby" but had already run afoul of the "Douglas Clique" for trying to enforce the law.   By the time I left CBP I had witnessed the de facto dissolution of the international border.

If you are an American citizen concerned about the nation's border security this book will enrage you.   The American public is well aware of the problems associated with our porous southern land border and the election-year promises by politicians to increase the number of Border Patrol agents to deal with the tidal wave of illegal aliens entering America.   What is not well known is what occurs at the more than 327 official land, sea, and air Ports of Entry where every person entering the United States is required to apply for admission.

For ten years I tried to enforce the law at the Douglas, Arizona Port of Entry.   I was harassed almost every day for doing so.   The local clique considered the Port of Entry "theirs" and "administered" immigration law as they thought it should be – not as the law required.   Douglas is not an anomaly.   Most Ports of Entry are fiefdoms manned by locals with divided loyalties (at best) who enforce the law – or don't – as they please.   They hide their subversion under the rubric of being a "service-oriented" organization.

If you are an American citizen contemplating becoming a Customs & Border Protection Officer (CBPO) at our nation's Ports of Entry (POEs), this is a "must read".   I'm not advising against working on the border.   Despite my experience I encourage honest, conscientious Americans to do so – in such numbers as to take back control of our border POEs.   Securing our national borders is important work.   I took my job personally.

I also hope politicians who are sincerely looking for ways to secure our borders read this. I describe in detail where many of the holes in our nation's border policy exist. We could have a fifty foot high wall ten feet thick the entire length of the southern border and still not secure it as long as management believes their job is to "facilitate" aliens' entry into the United States. Unless the mind set is changed from "service" to law enforcement at the highest levels, unless the politically subversive, demographic gerrymandering of our population and voting base is ended by both major political parties, the flood will continue unabated at the Ports of Entry. If it is not the unique and special American culture and freedoms we now enjoy will disappear.

Finally I hope this effort provides some advisory information for prospective inspectors and training benefit for new inspectors. CBP officers are now journeymen GS-12s. This means an inspector can be hired at a GS-5 or 7 (based on qualifications) and be promoted each year up to GS-12 without having to test for it. When one considers shift differential, holiday and overtime pay plus medical benefits it adds up to considerable income. They've also received "6C" (law enforcement) coverage which means 20 year retirement. As discussed further, one need not speak Spanish in order to be hired as a CBP officer. And, as with any government job, getting fired is nigh impossible. Believe me. I put that to the test. I worked on the southern land border with several fine men and women under difficult circumstances. They are still working under the duress of a subversive "service" oriented management that refuses to enforce the immigration laws. I dedicate this book to those enforcement-minded officers in the hope it will bring them some relief.

Chapter 1.

ENTRY

There is a nation-wide lack of knowledge about how people can legally and illegally enter the United States. This naivete' has a significant impact on the political debate about immigration policy.

"The general provisions of laws enacted by Congress are interpreted and implemented by regulations issued by various agencies. These regulations apply the law to daily situations. After regulations are published in the Federal Register, they are collected and published in the Code of Federal Regulations, commonly referred to as the CFR. The CFR is arranged by subject title and generally parallels the structure of the United States Code. Title 8 of the CFR deals with "Aliens and Nationality" as does Title 8 of the U.S. Code. (U.S. Citizenship and Immigration Services, U.S. Department of Homeland Security)

Federal law dictates that any alien physically present in the United States is presumed NOT to be a U.S. citizen unless there is specific information to the contrary. That is why aliens are required by law to carry their U.S. government-issued documents authorizing their presence with them at all times. The legal burden is on the alien to prove he is here legally. The burden of proof is also on the alien to prove he is eligible for admission into the United States. These federal requirements were reversed on a daily basis by Douglas Clique "local policy".

There are two basic statutory categories to legally enter the United States: as an immigrant or as a non-immigrant. An immigrant enters the U.S. with the intention of staying regardless of the basis for their petition to enter (i.e. refugee status). The non-immigrant enters with the intent of visiting or conducting temporary business and returning home. Annual immigrant numbers and categories are set by Congress and implemented by the State Department. Historically, immigration into the United States was tightly controlled with an eye toward the needs of America and time for assimilation. A significant number of certain categories of persons were selected from the world's population. Based on American economic requirements and the country's ability to assimilate that population immigrants were allowed to enter the country with the intent of becoming U.S. citizens in both legal status and state of mind.

One of the oft repeated mantras regarding immigration is that America has always been a nation of immigrants. That's not exactly true. Congress in the early 20th century routinely ceased immigration entirely for decades at a time to provide the current influx of immigrants time to assimilate into American society and culture. If it hadn't imposed some periodic restrictions we most certainly would have Chinese as our official language soon after our transcontinental railway was built. It was primarily for the purpose of keeping illegal Chinese out that the U.S. Border Patrol was established. Since the Immigration Reform Act of 1976 (heavily pushed through Congress by Ted Kennedy) that the principle of limited immigration was turned upside down. It was said at the time that every social scientist who testified before Kennedy's commission on immigration told him and the other senators that if they implemented the changes the senators were proposing it would destroy the American culture and bankrupt the nation. It was passed anyway. Basically the new immigration law reversed the priorities of classes of immigrants from those with professional and technical skills from industrialized nations to those with no skills from Third World countries. In the '90s homosexuals with AIDS were moved to the top of the list of applicants as "refugees from persecution". Ted Kennedy inserted one class of people as an exception to the new law – the Irish. So began the demographic subterfuge by our political representatives.

The "Oath of Allegiance" found in the 8 C.F.R. (Code of Federal Regulations) often referred to as the "oath of citizenship" is required by law to be taken by all immigrants at their citizenship ceremony. It states:

" I hereby declare, on oath, that I absolutely and entirely renounce and abjure all allegiance and fidelity to any foreign prince, potentate, state, or sovereignty of whom or which I have heretofore been a subject or citizen; that I will support and defend the Constitution and laws of the United States of America against all enemies, foreign and domestic; that I will bear true faith and allegiance to the same; that I will bear arms on behalf of the United States when required by the law; that I will perform noncombatant service in the Armed Forces of the United States when required by law; that I will perform the work of national importance under civilian direction when required by law; and that I take this obligation freely without any mental reservation or purpose of evasion; so help me God."

Taking the oath of allegiance was a significant event for my Okinawan step-mother. Shigeko was 12 years old when the Americans landed on Okinawa in 1945. Historically, Okinawa had been the "Sicily of the Pacific" on which China and Japan tested their military might against each other. These foreign occupiers banned the possession of weapons for native islanders resulting in a unique style of karate for unarmed self-defense. The Japanese occupiers were cruel and sadistic. The Japanese commander on Okinawa had pressed many of the teenaged Okinawan high school girls into service as nurses. Shigeko was sick and had stayed home from school the day the Americans landed. She and her grandmother hid in one of the thousands of caves on the island during the battle. Okinawans had been propagandized by the Japanese to believe the Americans would rape, murder – even cannabalize them - if they were caught.

My step-mother still vividly remembers the first American she ever saw. He was a tall, red-haired soldier with the letters "MP" on his shoulder. He was holding a German Shepherd on a leash at the entrance to their cave. When they didn't respond to his entreaties to come out he unleashed the dog. It immediately went in, grabbed my step-mother by the shoulder and dragged her out of the cave. Oba (grandmother) came running out after her. Shigeko still has large scars on her right shoulder from the K-9's bite. When she married my dad they applied for her and her son's Resident Alien cards and

3

eventually became U.S. citizens. My stepbrother served twenty years in the navy aboard the USS Midway and Constellation. They did it the right way. I don't have much sympathy for those who don't.

As evidence of the increasing lack of loyalty to the United States consider the increasing number of "dual citizens". The United States government does not recognize "dual citizenship". It's implicit in the oath of citizenship. Yet for several years the Mexican government has increased their efforts to recruit "dual citizen" Hispanic, American citizens. Our neighbor to the south has been allowing Hispanic American citizens to not only claim Mexican citizenship but to vote in Mexican elections since the late 1990s. The Mexican government has exponentially increased their efforts to create Mexican "cultural centers" in the United States where they encourage Hispanic- americans to "stay Mexican". An adjunct to this effort is providing "cedulas" or Mexican "targeta de votar" – voter registration cards to illegal Mexicans in the U.S. to give the appearance of legal presence. I talked to a contract background investigator who interviewed newly hired CBP officers for their security clearances. She told me the law prevented those holding dual citizenship from becoming CBP officers. She was amazed at how many Hispanic CBP inspectors held dual citizenship when it came time to renew their secret clearances. In an agency that is over 70 percent Hispanic, this guarantees that our borders are manned by some who have declared their affinity for the country directly across the border rather than for the country they swore to defend. It is not unique to Hispanic officers. In my immigration academy a classmate belonged to a religion that did not believe in borders. How well is *she* enforcing the law? CBP / DHS routinely ignores this breach of oath of office.

The effectiveness of this propaganda assault is further reflected in the emergence of "sanctuary cities". We received the following from Headquarters, INS:

"**Malfeasance within Starr and Cameron County, Texas Offices**: The Texas Vital Records Offices of Starr and Cameron County are having "internal control problems." [my quotes] A recent investigation revealed that issuance of **_all_** birth certificates issued by the Office of the County Clerk for Starr County, Texas and Cameron County, Texas are to be considered "Suspect." The security paper is good the information is fraudulent. **Do not verify these certificates with the issuing office.** These certificates need to be verified by the Austin Bureau of Vital Statistics, Fraud Prevention Program at 512-458-7395 by calling either Josie Pardo or Anthea Rodriguez. A sample of a Cameron County birth certificate and Starr County birth card is attached for your information."   My note: These two counties are certainly not the only ones by far. Someone in local and state government is making a lot of money selling birth certificates nationwide. I think we are in a crisis situation when elected officials prefer to ignore this subversion to avoid "alienating" the electorate. I'm curious as to what, if any, criminal action was taken against those issuing the Starr and Cameron County documents.

It appears the black market for documents is flourishing on both sides of the border. This is demographic subversion pure and simple.

During my ten years on the border, I heard politicians utter the "a" word (amnesty) several times. Each time the media broadcast politicians promising amnesty we saw tsunamis of Mexicans trying to fraudulently enter the U.S. at the Port of Entry. They wanted to physically be in the U.S. so they could lie about how long they had been living here when amnesty took effect. It has happened _every_ time. There was an immigration legend that in the first amnesty of the '70s or '80s, thousands of Mexican males were being interviewed by INS adjudication officers claiming to have worked in the fields picking watermelons for years. Other than their hands being perfectly smooth, many claimed to be "experts" at picking the melons from the watermelon trees!

President Clinton's "Citizenship 2000" was an effort to grant citizenship to half a million aliens before the 2000 elections, Al Gore ran the effort to "expedite" the citizenship process. This was another blatant attempt at demographic subterfuge. INS adjudicators are officers who determine each alien's eligibility for citizenship through an interview (in English) of the applicant's knowledge of the United States – particularly of the Constitution. That process was for all intents eliminated due to pressure from the Clinton administration. This process had also included criminal record checks. This "expedited" process resulted in more than five thousand criminals being granted U.S. citizenship. Once this scandal was made public most of those criminals' citizenship were revoked. I'm sure those criminals waited obediently in the U.S. to appear before an immigration judge for deportation.

Special ethnic interest groups routinely exert strenuous efforts to register illegal aliens to vote in elections. Their fraud was so rampant that the FBI quit counting the fraudulent votes after reaching several tens of thousands in the Orange County, California election in which "B-1" Bob Dornan was voted out of *congressional office*. It has happened repeatedly throughout our country.

These same special interest groups are now attempting to gerrymander voting districts prior to the 2012 presidential elections by including in the population count the *total* number of persons of certain ethnicities. This is in violation of state and federal law which requires counting only those *eligible voters* of ethnic groups within a district. This was brought to the attention of Arizona governor Jan Brewer in October 2011. Redistricting committees by law are supposed to be equally represented by both political parties with a "neutral" person chairing the committees as a tie-breaker. The chair of the Arizona redistricting committee posed as a neutral but was in fact a far Left Democrat. Governor Brewer exercised her legal discretion in firing the chairperson so the committee could be reconstituted fairly. The court has not upheld Governor Brewer's decision. Activist courts ignoring the constitution are another discussion.

Special interest group money was key in getting state senator Russell Pearce voted out of office for keeping his promise to address the illegal alien problem in Arizona by helping to write SB 1070 which was overwhelmingly supported by the voters of Arizona.

Sheriff Joe Arpaio, glamorized by some as the "toughest sheriff in America", complained to me and others when we both testified before the Arizona state legislature's Joint Border Security Advisory Committee (http://www.azleg.gov/jbsac/) that he is the only law enforcement officer in Arizona being sued for trying to enforce the laws against illegal immigration. "Why aren't these other sheriff's doing the same thing as I am?" he complained. It's because he is the only one who has a constituency that will support him in doing so. Why aren't other Arizona sheriff's joining him in his routine sweeps for illegals? Fear of offending a voting base and of being sued. Note that Sheriff Babeu's efforts in a largely agricultural county are aimed primarily –and, arguably, justifiably- at the drug routes in a largely unpopulated area of his jurisdiction. He pays as little attention to the illegal population as the other county sheriff's with large Hispanic constituencies. I routinely see illegal aliens selling curios at gas stations along the interstate in his jurisdiction . Sheriff Babeu's claim of preventing thousands of illegal aliens from crossing the border while serving with the National Guard on the Arizona border relies on politically skewed Border Patrol estimates. It was during the Arizona National Guard's time on the border that a National Guard unit was literally pushed off its' observation post by Mexican soldiers escorting a drug load more than ten miles inside the United States. An overlooked statistic by most of the mainstream media is that when the oft-maligned Minutemen lined the border and sat there simply observing and reporting *it reduced illegal entry into the U.S. by 70%*! This despite orders from Department of Homeland Security for Border Patrol agents *not* to respond to reports of illegal aliens entering the U.S. by Minutemen! The Border Patrol initially ordered the Minutemen to leave…..until the private property owners told the Border Patrol the Minutemen had permission by the owners to stay on private property– which the Border Patrol did not. The National Guard is so confined by politically imposed Rules of Engagement as to be superfluous. The National Guard was posted in excessive numbers at the Douglas, AZ Port of Entry after 9/11 and again later. They got in the way there. They had no law enforcement knowledge or authority. They were forbidden to assist us is making arrests even if the suspect resisted or fled. It appeared by most of their comments that their primary reason for being there was to get the coveted government per diem pay for active duty.

Since publishing the first edition of this book I have often been asked about the wisdom of putting federal troops on the border. Many who should know better claim that Posse Comitatus makes it unconstitutional. That is not true. If we remember history (which is becoming rarer and re-written) remember that the U.S. army was not only put on the border in Naco, AZ during the Mexican civil wars but we actually *invaded* Mexico in response to providing national security. More Americans are now being killed by illegal aliens on a regular basis than were killed by Pancho Villa's raid on Columbus, New Mexico which justified sending Pershing and the U.S. army into Mexico. The "Battle of Naco" between Mexican government troops and Villistas occurred just across the border town of Naco, AZ outside the little town of Naco, Mexico. During the battle gun shots were hitting buildings on the U.S. side. When an American woman breast feeding her baby on her front porch was killed by a bullet from the battle across the line, the President ordered the army to take up a skirmish line in a ditch with weapons pointed south. The military commander advised both parties to the battle that if they didn't stop shooting into the U.S. he had orders to cross the border and push them further away. Both sides decided to leave and fight another day and at another place . It is a lack of political will that interprets Posse Comitatus in such a limiting manner. Does anyone remember President Reagan deploying the Marines on the border? Reagan was a president who would have smiled at political correctness, tilted his head …..and done it anyway.

I'm not recommending we invade Mexico by any means. But I think it's way past time we deployed federal troops on the southern land border *with Rules of Engagement that allow them to not only arrest illegals and drug smugglers but to shoot first if threatened.* The persecution - yes, I mean *persecution* - of Border Patrol agents Ramos and Campeon by a U.S. Assistant Attorney General for shooting a career Mexican drug smuggler is a stain on the honor of the United States. Needless to say, the Fast and Furious fiasco and the subsequent deaths of Agent Brian Terry and ICE agent Jaime Zapata only symbolizes how far political correctness has turned into a subversive Leftist agenda.

Many years ago I saw a night vision video by a news agency recording the use of K-9s along the border fence in San Diego. Historical footage by the Border Patrol showed literally hundreds of illegals running rampant across the border every night in that sector. The first night K-9s were loosed to chase illegals it was like the tide going out before a tsunami. It worked. But the Mexican government complained to the State Department and the State Department told INS to cease using them. In my opinion using dogs trained to seek out human beings and detain them the same way bloodhounds are used to track escaped prison inmates is as necessary and life-saving as using unmanned aerial vehicles and tasers.

The subversion of the electoral process has been going on for decades throughout the United States. These attempts to grant citizenship to unqualified aliens so they could vote for a Democrat is just another evolutionary step in the "Long War" of the Left to undermine the will of the majority of the American people. It has only gotten worse and will continue to do so. If this shocks you read "Unlimited Access: An FBI Agent Inside the Clinton White House" by Gary Aldrich. It seems the Clintons didn't like *any* of their pals vetted. The Clinton administration was just a rehearsal for the Obama administration….. as was the "chad" voting during the 2000 elections for those in 2012.

I've fought and studied insurgency for several decades as a Marine in Vietnam, a Green Beret during the Reagan years and a counterintelligence officer in Mogadishu . In some ways, the political subversion of the immigration process by both major parties reminds me of the Iraq War. There are many "sects" within the U.S. intent on destroying our way of life. As Lenin would say "[Immigration] is just one of my scalpels." His favorite "scalpel" was propaganda [the media].

Once aliens' applications are approved for immigrating into the U.S. they are issued immigrant visas by the U.S. embassy or consulate in their native country. Note that I used the term "aliens". "Alien" is a word that has a specific legal definition pertaining to a foreign persons legal status within the United States. It is in no way discriminatory. Despite this, many avoid using the term and the liberals and anarchists substitute the term illegal "alien" for 'immigrant'" to obfuscate the definition and control the language of the debate. Calling illegal aliens "immigrants" subliminally grants them an undeserved legal status that falsely connotes certain legal rights. The term "Alien" has been removed from Resident Alien cards. In furtherance of the PC verbage: the cards now are labeled Permanent "Residents".

The immigrant visa is usually a paper form inserted in a passport. It has their photo and biographical information contained on the visa as well as security measures implanted onto the paper to make production of fake visas difficult. There is a booming market for fraudulent U.S. visas. Sometimes the photo is substituted or biographical information altered but this was significantly eliminated with a new laser process. There are many diverse ways to create or alter U.S. visas. At one time in the '90s a truck containing tens of thousands of blank visa forms was hijacked putting those visas on the black market. The cost of buying such fraudulent visas can go from several hundred dollars to tens of thousands of dollars (China for example).

Once admitted into the United States the immigrant establishes residence and requests a Resident Alien Card. It usually takes about 5-6 years - and a substantial fee- to be processed for U.S. citizenship. During this time the alien is (was) expected to remain economically solvent, obey the laws of the United States…..and maintain residence in the United States.

A major problem I saw on a daily basis in Douglas was many Resident Aliens of the United States living across the line in Agua Prieta, Mexico. Many were on welfare in the United States. Both are illegal for a Resident Alien - and tolerated by every Port Director I worked for.

Another change to the immigration laws we can thank Ted Kennedy for is that, once immigrated, the new Resident Alien/Citizen can immigrate a host of more distant relatives than under the previous immigration law. Not only are the categories of aliens entering the U.S. turned upside down and broadened, the number of new immigrants have multiplied from tens of thousands a year to over a million a year. No society can sustain that kind of growth and maintain its' identity. For a very vividly displayed sense of proportion comparing current with historical immigration quotas see "NumbersUSA" sponsored by Roy Beck. It will astound you. Another book I happened to read while attending the immigration academy was "Alien Nation: Common Sense About America's Immigration Disaster" by Peter Brimelow. I highly recommend it to those concerned with the demographic debacle our politicians have created in the last three decades.

The other kind of entry into the U.S. is as a "non-immigrant". These persons are issued a non-immigrant visa (sometimes called an "NIV") that can be an official page of biographical information and their photo inserted into their passport with a valid length of time - usually six months or, if living in proximity to the American border, can be issued a DSP-150 Laser Visa –a Border Crossing Card. These are issued to millions of Canadian and Mexican citizens for the purpose of allowing them to cross the border on a daily basis to visit family and conduct short term business like shopping. These types of non-immigrant visas are permission to visit only – for no more than 24-48 hours and no further than 25 linear miles from the border. The most critical task of CBP officers' jobs is to determine if these Border Crossing Card holders are visiting or using the document to enter the United States to live and work illegally in the U.S.. This is the most abused document issued by the federal government. To make matters worse, when the State Department issued the new "laser visas" – supposedly more counterfeit-proof- they told those hundreds of thousands (if not millions) of persons holding the of old, Border Crossing Cards they could keep the old ones! Those possessing the old cards confidently present these invalid cards to many interior law enforcement officers – assuming such are still questioning suspected illegals- and are released because the officer doesn't realize this official looking document is now invalid. It also created another lucrative black market for those holding the cards to sell to the unsuspecting aliens from further south.. All inspectors on the line have seen it. Latinos who, by appearance, dress and mannerisms are obviously from further south approach the pedestrian lane and confidently present an invalid Border Crossing Card that they've paid their last pesos to an illegal document vendor at the bus station across the line. I only saw one incident in which a Latino man returned to the bus station to demand his money back from the illegal document vendors in Mexico. He was beaten so badly he needed medical attention. It's truly pathetic.

Although applicants for admission into the United States may be issued entry documents of one sort or another, EVERY person seeking entry into the United States must present themselves at one of several hundred Ports of Entry for inspection by a CBP officer. This is true for land, air and sea ports of entry. There they MUST declare their citizenship ("U.S. or "French" or whatever country) and present legal documentation from a U.S. embassy or consulate allowing them entry into the United States. These documents allow the person to apply for admission into the U.S. Simple possession of a visa or passport does not automatically qualify one for entry into the United States. A Customs & Border Protection Officer (CBPO) must take each individual's oral declaration of citizenship and inspect the person through questioning and reviewing documentation to determine if that individual is admissible into the United States. It's an important job requiring extensive legal training as well as good people skills. At airports for the last several decades, the airlines have pressured immigration officers into perfunctory inspections of aliens with no verification of the aliens residence and economic solvency in their native country. This has to stop. A nominal effort has been instituted after 9/11 called "pre-clearance" in which CBP officers are sent to a few foreign departure ports but they are few and the pressure by management to not "impede" travel to the U.S. is still monumental.

The determination of admissibility of every person requesting entry into the United States usually occurs "on the line" at a land, sea or air Port of Entry (POE). This is where you see long lines of traffic awaiting entry on the southern (U.S./Mexican) land border or U.S./Canada border. Anyone who has taken a luxury cruise outside the territorial waters of the United States has been through both a Customs and Immigration inspection – as have those who have flown. Though many see this inspection as a nuisance it is absolutely critical to determining who is admissible for entry into the United States and who is not. We saw the results of airlines' induced lax admissibility inspections on 9/11.

Prior to 9/11, Customs and Immigration inspectors were specialists in their own areas of expertise. With the establishment of another useless government bureaucracy –Department of Homeland Security (DHS)- Customs inspectors focused on finding contraband –drugs, weapons, money in excess of ten thousand dollars, etc.. They wore solid blue uniforms and could usually be seen walking with curved, aluminum tubes with mirrors attached at the bottom for looking under cars – or with a K-9 drug-sniffing dog. The U.S. Customs Service was under the Treasury Department. They could impose fines for importation violations and make arrests for felony violations. They manned the vehicle inspection lanes intermingled with immigration inspectors and inspected incoming persons for admissibility also but were not required to speak Spanish to perform their duty.

Immigration inspectors wore white shirts and black pants. We are federal law enforcement officers with the powers of arrest as is Customs but our area of expertise was on people and their entry documents. We are required to speak Spanish to perform our duty on the southern land border. We are extensively trained on the myriad categories of immigrant and non-immigrant categories and the documents associated with them.

Hundreds of times a day we (both immigration and customs inspectors) ask every person in every vehicle or on the pedestrian lane "What is your citizenship?" or "De que pais es ud ciudadano?" or –for the regular crossers who know the routine- "Ciudadano?" if they don't offer it automatically or simply show their Border

13

Crossing Cards. The question is intentionally "open-ended" so as not to lead the applicant toward a pre-determined response – like our local Border Patrol checkpoint agents do-"Are you a U.S. citizen?" "Yes". ......Why, SURE I AM! –(since you offered!)" It provides too much wiggle room during the interrogation when yes or no questions are asked. It also avoids foreigners' defense that they are intimidated by the uniform and say yes to everything. Both Customs and Immigration inspectors ask the same questions.

The second question always asked is "Que trae de Mexico?" – "What are you bringing from Mexico?" Those two questions begin the inspection process for everyone requesting entrance into the U.S. - if you don't count the scrutiny conducted on them as they approach for inspection.

I'm amazed we don't do this in our sleep. Most inspectors working the line will inspect approximately _700-800 vehicles_ in an eight-hour shift. I'm guessing the average vehicle contains 2-3 people. This means each inspector determines the admissibility of from 2,100 to 2,400 _persons every day_. Just as state or city police officers take a risk every time they makes a traffic stop, Customs and Immigration inspectors have to assume that every vehicle they "stop"-inspect- is a potential felony stop (management denials to the contrary). All the violations of law we are looking for are federal felonies. State and local police officers make an average of ten (?) stops each shift and have the luxury of time on their side. Inspectors must determine if each "stop" is a felony stop within 20 seconds per vehicle or catch Holy Hell from the supervisor. Most inspectors get pretty good at – and take great personal pride in - maintaining a good traffic rhythm yet picking out the imposters, oral and documented false claims to U.S. citizenship, fraudulent documents, wanted criminals, drug and alien smugglers who try sneaking through our lanes. If we see or hear something that causes our internal "radar" to go to red, we either refer it to secondary where off –line inspectors conduct a more intensive inspection or, if we consider the persons to be flight risks, walk the car ourselves back to secondary while adjacent inspectors keep an eye on our lane until we get back from secondary. It requires maturity, judgment, honed people skills as

well as team work and trust in your fellow inspectors to work. Our
lives literally depend on it. I'm proud to say that the Customs and
Immigration inspectors _–those working the line-_ at the Douglas,
Arizona Port of Entry – the east boundary of the busiest corridor into
the United States for drugs and alien smuggling- were
overwhelmingly a good team. That's not the case at other POEs. At
many POEs Customs and Immigration inspectors don't even talk to
each other.

After a short while most inspectors start remembering local, daily
crossers and it appears they are simply waved through. What the
casual on-looker doesn't see is the inspectors' radar scanning the
person(s) for behavioral anomalies. Is he/she acting different? More
friendly than usual? Eyes staring forward? Fingers with a death grip
on the steering wheel? And many, many more subtle indicators of
deception. If we see the driver or a passenger acting suspicious or a
person's story just doesn't jive, we send the car with the occupants
to secondary –whether he's a "local crosser" or not. If we think it's
a contraband issue we note it on a 3"x5" paper, place the paper under
a plastic, yellow cone on the hood or roof of the car and send them
on. The off-line inspectors in secondary wave the referred vehicle in
to the secondary inspection area, read the noted information on the
referral slip and take another declaration from each person asking the
exact same questions.

The declaration of individuals requesting entry into the United
States is critical for a) determining their status and therefore their
entry into the United States; and b) obtaining a legally binding
statement by the person for use in making –literally- a federal case
for prosecution if they are lying. After taking the declaration from
the driver and each occupant of the vehicle every vehicle occupant is
asked to step out of the car and stand in a specific area. This is
usually on the other side of a table adjacent to their vehicle so they
are safe from doors opening, passing K-9s and are not able to
interfere with the inspection. There will be at least one other
inspector of either service standing by to monitor the occupants
behavior and to back up the inspector conducting the secondary
inspection. If they were referred to secondary for a suspected

15

contraband issue, a Customs inspector will usually be called to check the vehicle out. They are experts at locating hiding spots in vehicles for drugs. If they were referred for suspected fraudulent entry an immigration inspector will conduct the interview if available. The "old salts" who have been around enough and worked shoulder-to-shoulder with the other service can do a pretty good job of conducting both types of inspections. If nothing out of the ordinary is discovered the vehicle and occupants are allowed to continue on their way – "down the road" or "DTR".

However, if either inspector(s) see or hear anything suspicious in or on the vehicle all occupants are immediately and physically controlled and escorted to a holding cell. The driver and occupants are watching the inspector looking for contraband in the vehicle they just drove in. It is real tempting to run or attack the inspector if they see the inspector identify an anomaly –or K-9 "hit"- where they know the drugs are. It's worth the risk to run rather than go to prison – as rarely as that happens. Depending on the type and amount of drugs it's also worth using deadly force to escape – which explains why, depending on the circumstances, some occupants are patted down immediately upon exiting the vehicle.

We used to have runners more often in my early years at Douglas. Since the Assistant U.S. Attorney raised the amount of marijuana above 500lbs before she would prosecute we haven't had as many smugglers trying to escape. They just laugh as we create a file on them and send them back to Mexico. The prosecutable minimum for drug smuggling rose so frequently, the joke for the last years of my time on the border between law enforcement agencies was: Question: "What's the limit now for your agency before the drug smugglers are prosecuted?" Answer: "Whatever you caught plus ten pounds!"

If the referral is an immigration question and the occupants' stories and documents don't check out they are brought into the immigration secondary office. They are placed in an interview room and an inspector begins to examine the applicant(s) in more detail. If direct evidence of fraud or an admission is obtained, the inspector begins creating a file on the Subject. The mandatory first part of this process is reading Subject his/her rights. The Supreme Court, in its' infinite wisdom, has granted the same constitutional rights to illegal aliens who haven't even successfully entered the United States as a U.S. citizen. After a sworn statement consisting of specifically scripted questions pertaining to the offense is obtained from the subject, their fingerprints and photo are taken, a criminal history is conducted for prior arrests, they sign their sworn statement then are given copies of two forms explaining their rights and appeals process. A call is made to the Assistant U.S. Attorney's office where prosecution is overwhelmingly denied on the run-of-the-mill cases and the Subject is escorted back to Mexico. With good team work, each case can take an hour and a half minimum. At some POEs, inspectors (especially senior inspectors) drag out these cases for over four hours doing them alone in order to get paid overtime. In many ports of entry there are now designated case officers who still take an inordinate amount of time to an unnecessary amount of paper work just to escort the illegal back to Mexico.

This is the "Expedited Removal" process. Not much "Expedited" about it when we were doing 200-300 cases a month. When this ER process was first mandated, the Douglas Clique (DC) didn't know what to do. They thought those who prepared the most cases would get promoted first but they weren't literate enough to prepare them correctly enough for presentation to the Assistant U.S. Attorney without them being sent back. My suggestion on the first ER case we had was to obtain a correct and complete file as an example and break down the file sections into subtasks for other inspectors to complete while the lengthy sworn statement was being taken. Management ignored that outright. They didn't want to share the "glory" of "making the case". When the DC realized it wouldn't get them promoted faster – and they *had* to depend on the literate inspectors to get each ER case processed in less than seven or eight hours they started getting organized. It was like watching a Chinese fire drill at first. A good shift of literate, cooperating inspectors was like working on an Indianapolis racing team.

The immigration secondary office is also where "permisos" or permits are obtained. The permit process is where the Douglas Clique "no border" crowd maintained their control over admission into the United States and made it the sieve it has been for who-knows-how-many years.

The entry document for Mexican or Canadian citizens within commuting distance of the U.S. border is a DSP-150 "B1/B2 Border Crossing Card". To obtain one of these the applicant is supposed to show the consular official in their country "comprobantes" or proof of residence and economic solvency in their native country. The amount of documentary fraud in this process at all the embassies and consulates around the world is breathtaking when one includes management's pressure on inspectors to "service" the "publics' right" to travel to the Promised Land. Proof of residence usually takes the form of utility receipts for their residence for the last year, rental receipts, property tax records, etc. in their name. Economic solvency is provided in the form of paycheck stubs, "nominas" (a listing of employees working for a certain employer), bank records showing regular deposits (and withdrawals) in a local bank in Mexico in their name. These Border Crossing Cards allow the entrant to cross into the United States for no more than 48 hours and a distance no further than 25 linear miles from the border to visit and conduct temporary business (shopping). Some linear extensions are made for "economic zones". This is true for the Nogales, Douglas, Tucson triangle. In my opinion, this only facilitated illegal residence and employment in a major city – and easier access to an international airport for the alien smugglers. Shortly before boarding my flight to Atlanta from the Tucson airport, I saw a group of six "UDAs" (undocumented aliens) rush up to the boarding counter to present their tickets. I strode over and informed the boarding representative that these were illegal aliens and requested she call the border patrol. "How do you know they're illegal?" she asked. "Believe me, I've worked on the border for X years and they are illegal" I said. She called airport security and the resident Tucson police officer. I explained the situation to them. Then I asked the group for their papers. They were all from Mexico. Some had illegal Arizona identification but no document authorizing their presence in the United States. A few had DSP-150 Border Crossing Cards but no I-94s allowing them to leave the commercial zone between Douglas, Nogales and Tucson. All were boarding the flight to Atlanta. The airport police radioed the on-site Border Patrol agent. When the BP agent arrived I had to explain the DSP-150/I-94 requirement to him because he had only been out of the academy for three months and had not worked in the field long enough to understand the documentary requirements. All six were taken into custody and "VR'd" (voluntarily returned) to Mexico.

The same documentary requirements are used when Border Crossers wish to travel more than 25 linear miles from the border and stay longer than 48 hours. They are inspected on the line for initial entry then enter immigration secondary offices where CBP officers examine their "comprobantes" prior to issuing I-94 Permits or "Permisos". When I first started working for INS in 1996, it was an I-444 Permit that allowed the alien only the time and location stated on the permit. This way if a law enforcement officer encountered the alien within the interior of the United States he could easily tell by the details on the permit if the alien was abiding by his status or was "out of status" and therefore in the United States illegally. Each permit cost $6.00 for each person regardless of age. This money adds up to significant amounts when one considers how many foreigners enter the U.S. each day at each of 327 Ports of Entry. The money from the permits goes into a congressional "General Fund".

For some unexplained reason in the late 1990s, INS changed the permit process and directed that all I-94 Permits would instead be for a blanket six months regardless of purpose or duration of the trip. No notations on the purpose or location of the aliens' visit would be made. When the Mexicans heard this they were incredulous – as were we inspectors but for totally opposite reasons. This was obviously a government de facto "amnesty" to allow "visitors" time enough during their "visit" to get a job and a home. Mexican border crossers entered our office demanding the "six-month permit" and laughed out loud as they left the office to go live illegally in the United States. When the six months expired on their permit the alien simply crossed over into Mexico, made a U-turn back into the traffic lanes of the U.S. Port of Entry with their Border Crossing Card and demanded another six month permit.

This is where much of the "war" between "enforcement-minded" CBP officers and the "no-border, 'service-minded'" officers and management occurred. The Douglas clique I worked for told me it was the Mexicans' right to have such permits. In fact many of them frequently expressed the opinion there shouldn't even be a border. They also continuously harassed – even persecuted -the "enforcement-minded" officers when we asked for "comprobantes" before issuing permits. Supervisor Ernestina Morris (I eventually gave her the well-deserved title "Mexican Moses") led the offense in this battle. She continually harangued me and other inspectors saying "Nowhere does it say you HAVE to have comprobantes to get a permit!" As mentioned in the introduction, the Immigration & Nationality Act (INA) that we operated under states we are to use the same vetting process as the American consular officials use.

Since "Mexican Moses" was also fond of citing "local policy" for her and others' refusal to enforce the law, I also found a memorandum by her boss, Waync Morris, dated September 12, 1985, SUBJECT: Inspectional Procedures, paragraph 4. "Requests for I-94 or I-444 Permits should be supported by current proof of employment or support. Proof may take the form of a letter and check stubs; nomina de sueldo, property records, tax records, credit cards, bank book, etc. ...."

Another problem with permits based on "comprobantes" was that the required proof of residence and employment could be bought for the right price from any private business or government office in Mexico. The mayor of the little town of Naco, Mexico ten miles east of Douglas routinely sold utility receipts to anyone with a hundred dollars. My radar was going off on a woman who presented legitimate paycheck stubs from the Mexican Federal Department of Transportation. Upon further intensive interviewing, she admitted her girlfriend who worked as a pay clerk for the Mexican DOT printed them out in her name for $50.

CHAPTER 2. GLYNCO, GA

I will never forget my first day at the Immigration Officer Basic Course, Federal Law Enforcement Training Center (FLETC), Glynco, Georgia. Located in the southeastern corner of the state, approximately 80 aspiring immigration inspectors assembled at the appointed area on the former naval air base a few minutes before 8a.m. on July 11, 1996. We were milling around getting to know each other when a short, red-faced, pudgy man in a bellboy's uniform appeared. He was wearing a white uniform shirt with major's rank on each black shoulder board and black pants. Maybe it was a Coast Guard uniform – all I knew was he wasn't doing much credit to that uniform much less the military rank he wore. He didn't know quite how to say it but we gathered he wanted us to get into some type of organized assemblage. Over half of us were veterans. Several were former Marines and of those two were former drill instructors. One of them asked this wimpering brass hat if he wanted us to fall into formation – like the military. He immediately managed to exclaim "NO! NOT like the military!.....but, well, sort of ." While the snickering slowly ebbed one of the former drill instructors took charge and quickly got us in the "non-military" formation.

The roster was called breaking us down into twenty students per class and we filed into our respective classrooms. We were told to write our names and our assigned Ports of Entry on a placard at the front of our desks. For the duration of the academy the first thing each new instructor did upon taking the podium was look at the placards to see where we worked. Every one of them shook their heads and expressed condolences to the three of us assigned to the Douglas, AZ Port of Entry. Each of us wondered why. They told us ominously "You'll find out". None of us knew it was a harbinger of a worsening nightmare.

On the other hand, firearms training at FLETC was excellent. Those instructors were selected from all the federal law enforcement agencies that trained at Glynco. They were not the usual milquetoast immigration cadre by far. Many of us looked forward to it and we weren't disappointed. The first week one of my classmates timidly asked why INS issued such "big" weapons. We were issued Beretta Brigadier Model 96 .40 caliber semi-automatic pistols with fully-jacketed, hollow point ammunition. One instructor immediately replied "Because the first accurate round you fire will penetrate the chest cavity and sever the spine immediately neutralizing any threat to you, your fellow officers or the public". I was amazed at the stunned look on the faces of some of my classmates. When I accepted the job over a phone interview with the Douglas Port Director he informed me we would be required to carry weapons. I just naturally assumed so – being on the border and all. One of our classmates said every time she had the weapon in her hand on the range she felt like throwing it on the ground. Another classmate belonged to a "worldwide" church that didn't believe in international borders. Shortly after arriving at the Port for duty I was amazed to learn that immigration inspectors had the option of carrying weapons on duty until about 1993 and that many at the Douglas POE chose not to. Once I started working there it became clear to me very quickly why they felt they didn't need them. It appeared there was little to no enforcement ergo no threat.

Returning from lunch a week before graduation, someone told me one of our students said he would never use his weapon. Up until then I had liked the fellow. He was from India and had worked for a computer company prior to hiring on. I had eaten dinner with him and his beautiful wife. I asked him directly if that were true. He said "there are no circumstances under which I would use my gun". I told him he should resign immediately as a potential threat to his fellow officers. Instead, he ended up as the honor graduate of our class. That was so symbolic of the immigration service.

A few years later we heard of a shooting at a neighboring Port of Entry. The video showed an elderly man being escorted into secondary. When told to empty his pockets he pulled out a gun and shot the inspector sitting behind the counter. After an exchange of gun fire by the wounded officer and the escorting officer, the elderly man was killed. Instead of rushing to assist his fellow officers, our honor graduate hid under a desk in an adjacent office – with no bullets in his weapon.

During physical training we were taught how to frisk suspects, how to control an escalating confrontation and how to subdue and handcuff suspects. During the defensive techniques portion I was paired with a female who had a master's degree in Criminal Justice – as I did. Comparing notes on graduate school curriculum I was astounded to learn she had never been required to brief a legal case - but even more so when she told me every time she looked up she feinted. She graduated.

Prior to physical training I had to go see the doc. Just before going back down to Arizona to report for the job, I went on a cattle drive up in Rich County, Utah. I had bought a nice home and ten acres next to Bear Lake two years before retiring from the army. It was an idyllic place to live and raise kids – if you didn't mind dressing up like an astronaut much of the year to stay warm outside. I intended on staying there but good jobs were scarce and my kids were still young.

My trusty quarter horse "Tucson" couldn't get shod in time for me to take him on the drive and my friend's horse that I'd used two years before had been sold. McKay called around and said he found me a horse "If I wanted him". Well, I violated my own rule to always follow my gut instincts. I'm no horse expert but this one didn't look trail worthy and acted as if he hadn't been ridden in a while. I knew this would probably be the last cattle drive I would ever go on so I overruled my own good judgment and saddled up the spindly-legged brute. He was a little testy at first but by the time we arrived at the rendezvous point where the other drovers and their cattle were waiting he seemed ok.

As we drove the herd up the mountain, McKay tasked me and a young, local kid to ride up the other side of a ridgeline to make sure no cattle had gone up that side. We didn't find any and arrived at the top of the draw before the main herd. We rode down to meet them. I rode up the side of the draw to allow them to pass. As I did one of the drovers said "Careful. It's loose up there." "I'm just going up a bit and turning around" I said. I should have listened, stayed there and let the cattle go around me. A more experienced rider would probably have done just that. Rather than riding straight back down the hill I angled the horse down. I figured that's how men and wild animals climb and descend hills so horses do too. About halfway down my horse started tumbling. The only right thing I did was to get my downhill foot out of the stirrup and launch myself off the horse on the uphill side. The horse rolled over and over down the hill about fifty feet. I hit the ground so hard it nearly knocked me out. The lights went out and I was consumed with pain. I could hear myself moaning then someone yelling from a long way away (he was kneeling right beside me) "Are you ok?" Once I stopped moaning and groaning I asked through the fog of pain if the horse was alright. I heard the cowboy kneeling next to me sort of laugh and say "Yeah, *he*'s alright! How about *you*?" By that time my vision was clearing and I slowly stood up. My main concern then was finding my cowboy hat. Once I did the only thing left was to get back in the saddle and "cowboy up".

Thankfully we stopped under a grove of sycamores for lunch a few minutes later. After eating I dropped my jeans below my right cheek trying to get a looksee. I wasn't flexible enough to see much but the grins from the other men told me it was a beaut. "You going to be able to ride with that?" one asked. "Well, I guess. It's not like I have a choice! I'll ride it out" I said with less conviction than it sounded. That was one long, cattle drive. We drove the cattle up to their summer pasture in the Uinta Mountains. On the ride back down the mountains McKay told me how the Uinta Indians used to pow-wow at the south end of Bear Lake –below us in one of its' 19 splendorous shades of blue when he was a kid and the first time he saw a man riding a motorcycle through his home town of Laketown. McKay, didn't talk much. He said it was from spending summers alone herding sheep in the mountains as a teenager. I've not allowed myself to wonder how different the next ten years would have been for my children and me if I could have found a good job there.

My right buttock still hurt two months later when I arrived at Glynco. I thought I'd better have it checked out since we were going to be doing some physical contact training like how to subdue resisting suspects. When the doc (from India, of course) came in and I dropped my pants his hands jerked away from my cheek. "How could you receive a bruise this severe and not break something?" he asked. "Well, doc, I'm not too sure I *didn't*! That's kinda why I came in to see you!" I said. The x-rays came back and the newest fracture in that area was mostly healed by that time. He signed a waiver allowing me to "sit" out doing sit ups for a while.

The immigration officer basic course is the longest and most difficult academy in the federal government (google 8 CFR Section 212 for an insomnia cure). It's because we're required to memorize hundreds of immigration laws – and their exceptions. It is no understatement to say it is second only to the federal tax code in complexity. Most students who fail the course (after re-testing ad nauseum depending on who you were related to in the service) did so for failing two exams: Immigration Law and Non-Immigrant Law.

Sunday, July 28, 1996 - <u>EMERGENCY ALERT:</u> Information Sheet, Department of Justice Students: "Due to the recent incident at the Olympic Games, the Attorney General of the United States has requested that all Department of Justice students attending the Federal Law Enforcement Training Center (FLETC), Glynco, Georgia, be temporarily assigned to assist with security in Atlanta. ……Duty assignments: Following the incident Saturday morning (the pipe bomb blast), Attorney General Reno and Treasury Under Secretary for Enforcement Ray Kelly agreed to consider sending students at the Federal Law Enforcement Training Center (FLETC) to assist with security measures. On Sunday, July 28, the FLETC was requested to select 800 students and 80 supervisors to respond to this need, and have them ready for departure –either by bus or air – on Monday, July 29."

After the pipe bomb went off, all the Olympic volunteer security took a hike (or, more accurately, a sprint) from the premises. Returning from church Sunday morning, the gate guards told us to report to our billets for a briefing. There we were told we would be convoying in busses to Atlanta the next morning to provide security at the 1996 Olympics. Border patrol students were told they would be staying with "Delta". They made it very clear to us lowly immigration inspectors they were even more cool than us for being selected to work with the Army's famous counter-terrorism unit. Imagine their chagrin when their busses peeled off from the convoy to be housed in the Delta Airlines hangars! That's as close to counter-terrorism as they got.

Of course the bombing had been on the news. During that same newscast it was reported that a sniping had occurred on the interstate highway allegedly by a member of a Georgia militia group. It was also on the news that eight hundred of us federal officers were going to be convoying up to Atlanta the next day. The route we were taking from Glynco to Atlanta was the same highway where the sniping occurred. At the chow hall that evening word quickly spread that we were not going to be allowed to carry our service weapons with us. I approached a supervisor and asked if that were true. He said it was. I asked if anyone would be carrying weapons. He said the Director felt it was unnecessary. I asked if he was aware that we would be traveling right through the middle of good 'ol boy militia territory, one sniping had already occurred and, thanks to the media, every one of the 'ol boys knew we were coming. I asked if he knew the "esteem" most militias had for "jack-booted" federal officers. As he began rationalizing I told him he could explain to my wife and kids why I was left defenseless when killed by a sniper on the way to Atlanta – or someone else's family. It would take only one shot at any of eighteen busses to kill one of us. Then I realized the Director of the academy was sitting opposite him at the table – along with several other members of the headquarters staff. I concluded with "Well, it's just food for thought".

The immigration academy staff thought a lot like members of the State Department I had encountered overseas. In my opinion State Department staffers delayed making a decision as long as possible and then usually made a bad one. As we boarded the busses the next day we noticed that only the cadre was wearing their sidearms.

That's tantamount to having the Girl Scouts protect us. Most of them – with the exception of the firearms cadre - achieved their coveted academy positions by working at airports which for some reason was perceived as having more clout within the service than us peasants on the land borders. None of them wore weapons at the airports. Years later during post-academy training we could tell who worked at the airports by how new their service weapons looked. Southern land border inspectors wore their weapons every day and the bluing was worn off in several places. Almost none of the airport inspectors had even taken their weapons out of the box they were issued in. Driving up to Atlanta felt like whistling through a graveyard but we made it without incident.

We worked long hours in Atlanta. We checked tens of thousands of people coming through the turnstiles each day. One rich, young Arab paid one of our guys $300 for his pith helmet – a quite campy piece of headgear issued by the Olympic committee. Word of the sale spread like wildfire and we began earnestly searching for other Arabs we could sell our ridiculous headgear to and make some coin. The Russian wrestling team came through my lane and the coach gave me a few of their pins. Pins were the goodwill currency of the international athletes. Non-athlete status was established by how many different countries' sport pins you collected. INS even issued all of us a gold pin after it was over with the Olympic torch and writing on it that was almost impossible to read.

When the crowd was all admitted to the events increments of inspectors were allowed to go watch some as well. Word came back to us the ATF security supervisor (affectionately labeled "Big Badge") was constantly telling INS people "You can't sit here. You can't sit there", etc." - in other words "Big Badge" didn't like us and he was throwing his substantial weight around. All of us had badges with an infinity sign indicating we could go anywhere in the Olympics. It didn't mean a thing to Big Badge. Toward the end of the games the remainder of us finally got a chance to see two events. The first was the baseball game between the Republic of Korea and Australia. It was a close game. An Australian runner to second was called out sliding into second for trying to trip the Korean second baseman. The Australians sitting around us booed loudly and uttered other character assassinations – until the giant TV screen replayed the foul in slow motion. The runner's leg was raised so high toward the leaping second baseman I was surprised he didn't tear a groin muscle. The replay was followed by such thundering silence I laughed out loud.

A group of us walked to the stadium next door to watch the final night of track competition. Michael Johnson was expected to set a world's record for the 440. We walked up a gangway that brought us right behind the media camera crews just above the final turn on the track. We leaned against the walls of the gangway hoping we were in time for the race and could see over the crowd. Sure enough here comes Big Badge telling us we can't stand there. Some of us filtered away but my buddy Bill, me and two others hung around just long enough for the camera crews to take notice of our expulsion and offer us their seats! We had the best seats in the house! Of course no sooner had we made ourselves comfortable and began watching the javelin throwers try to skewer each other than one of the flunkies for Big Badge shows up. A relay was also going on so there was a lot of yelling – particularly by a body of high-spirited, inebriated Australians seated several rows deep around the gangway entrance. They had seen us being expelled from the gangway and were now witnessing his flunky yelling in Bill's ear that we couldn't sit there either. She left when the Aussies began yelling at her to leave us alone. Bill got up a few seconds later and disappeared down the gangway. I thought he had to go to the latrine.

No sooner had Michael Johnson set the world record than suddenly Big Badge is yelling in my face so hard he's spitting. I stood up and yelled back that we worked our bums off for him and I didn't appreciate being treated like scum. The Aussies loved that and chimed right in. Big Badge told me to follow him down the gangway where he wrote down my name and the name of my supervisor. By then it was time for us to rally at the busses to return to Ft. Gillem where we were billeted. En route to the rendezvous point I came upon my supervisor and informed him of the incident.

He knew we had been kicked around by this guy and I was hoping he was going to stand up for us – and me.

While eight hundred Glynco personnel milled around waiting for the busses. I reclined on a wooden porch of a security command post trailer nearby. I saw Big Badge approach my supervisor in front of the mob and saw Bill (the rat) tell them where I was. I felt like Moses parting the Red Sea as the multitude parted to see me get reprimanded. From the comments of those surrounding us I was making more points than Big Badge was explaining the situation to our supervisor. I waited in vain for our supervisor to stand up for us. He didn't. On the bus back to the barracks the rumor started circulating that the supervisor was going to have a formation in the morning where I was expected to apologize for my behavior – and then be fired on the spot. When I was told this at the back of the bus I said aloud *"That ain't gonna happen!"* I wasn't going to apologize for anything in front of anybody. That I knew. Then I crossed my arms on the back of the seat in front of me, put my head down and closed my eyes.

I officially retired from the United States Army on 1 April 1996 – April Fool's Day. It was ironic. Bill Clinton signed my discharge in 1996. Richard Nixon signed my discharge from the United States Marine Corps in 1971. Those signatures symbolized my conflict maintaining personal integrity in the face of a morally bankrupt military environment – the officer corps. Now here I am again in a situation where I stood up for what I thought was right – and wondering, again, if I was going to have a job for "leading the charge" against another fine example of toxic leadership.

The busses arrived back at the Ft. Gillem barracks around 1a.m. as usual. Instead of hitting the sack I waited outside by the barracks porch with Bill and a few others while our supervisor went upstairs to call the academy director and explain the incident. A few of our firearms instructors were sitting on the porch steps and weren't saying much at first. After listening to us talk about the incident with "Big Badge" one of them told me that while we were on "special duty" performing security at the Olympics we weren't students – we were acting as officers and under the protection of the union contract. I asked how he knew this. He was a union steward. He also told me that while the supervisor was convincing the academy director to fire me in front of the entire security element. The senior union steward was waiting to tell the supervisor exactly why that wasn't going to happen.

We waited for over an hour before the senior union steward came downstairs and told me there would be no "public crucifixion" in the morning. HOORAAY FOR THE FIREARMS INSTRUCTORS!! I thanked them profusely for saving my job. I thought how I wouldn't have to call my wife and tell her to sell the house we just bought - and the kids not knowing where they would be going to school.

Within a few months I would wonder if they had done me a favor or not. They did. Being fired from federal employment is a real black mark on a resume'. It's difficult to recover from it and get any kind of decent job afterwards. Despite the next ten years on the line and my war on the border with management at the most corrupt ports of entry in the immigration service, I survived to go on to better things. The incident with Big Badge, my supervisor's spinelessness and the academy director's acquiescence in the attempt to publicly humiliate me only confirmed my first day's impression of the immigration service. I'd seen small-minded people with high rank before.

The day after the "Big Badge Incident", Bill, my "buddy", told me what created the furor. When Big Badge's flunky apologetically told Bill we couldn't sit there, Bill followed her down the gangway and sarcastically asked her "Where were you guys (ATF) when the bomb went off? It's a good thing we came up and pulled your asses out of the fire." I'm sure his comments were liberally sprinkled with profanity. He didn't curb his language for ladies. Realizing how angry Big Badge would be when he heard that, Bill disappeared into the latrine. Big Badge came charging to our seats and thought I was the one who said it. At no time during the entire incident that Bill knew my job was in jeopardy did he step up and tell the supervisor he caused the incident.

Despite nearly being fired, I graduated FLETC in the academic top ten percent and tied for high shooter of the class. I arrived back in Sierra Vista and our new home just before Thanksgiving – November, 1996.

CHAPTER 3. THE DRIVE

It is exactly 51 miles from my driveway to the Douglas POE parking lot. I enjoy the view of the Huachuca Mountains abutting Sierra Vista to the west of my house, the Dragoon Mountains to the north, the Whetstone Mountains around Tombstone to the northeast and the Mule Mountains to the east. The colorful names of the mountains tell the area's colorful history. Leaving for work at 7a.m., I see the sun rise on the mountains giving them all sorts of colors depending on the season – snow on the peaks in winter and the gold, red and green in fall. In the fall the sycamores create a north seeking gold carpet along the San Pedro River half way between Sierra Vista and the Mule Mountains. Often on a moonlit night I would come to a full stop at the intersection of state highways 90 and 80 at the edge of the Mules just to smell the sagebrush and look up at the full moon.....wishing I was going on another cattle drive instead of going to Douglas.

Driving through Bisbee Canyon never got old to me. It was a challenging, twisting two-lane asphalt road with scenery I never tired of regardless of season. In the spring, long stretches of the highway are bordered by wildflowers of various colors. In the winter snow contrasts beautifully with the rocky, scrub brushed mountains. In winter with a lace-like shroud of snow the town of Bisbee looks like a Currier & Ives post card. During the two "monsoon" seasons Bisbee Canyon has several beautiful waterfalls cascading from the heights. More than once I've almost ran off the road (at considerable speed) trying to take it all in.

The "monsoon" rainy seasons can provide some unpleasant surprises as well. During one an elementary school teacher was swept to her death in a wash along Moson Road just east of the city limits. A lot of students later related regret at labeling her in ignominious terms.

I was driving through the twisting canyon after a heavy rain one afternoon when I suddenly arrived at a cloud of dust immediately in front of me. The car in front of me put on his brake lights but continued driving so I did the same. That was a mistake. It was like driving through a thunderstorm of rocks. I was hearing rocks of such size hitting my windshield I couldn't believe it hadn't shattered. I couldn't see anything to my front but figured the best way to get out of this was to keep going. Suddenly a voice in my head yelled "LEAN FORWARD!" I instinctively did so pressing my face almost flat against the windshield. I thought "What am I doing this for?" when my driver's window exploded into pieces. "Oh! THAT'S WHY!" I said looking upward. My window exploded and all the glass and rock went flying past my back – where my head would have been. I continued driving to work where I found my left headlight shattered and some dents on the left side of the truck in addition to the shattered driver's window.

All during that day shift my back was itching like a sunburn. Just before the shift ended I went to the men's room and "popped a squat". Sitting on the throne in the men's room is a minor production because you have to remove your gun belt as well as your pants. As soon as my gun belt was loosened I heard glass hitting the floor and saw what was making my back itch all day. A lot of the glass from the driver's window had settled between my pants and me.

The town of Bisbee is an old copper mining town that eventually evolved into a smaller version of Haight-Ashbury with niche arts and craft shops and restaurants – quite good ones. It is also the county seat where my seemingly interminable divorce hearings were held. But on through Bisbee past the big hole in the ground that was the pit mine itself, around the traffic circle that used to have a white star on the Christmas tree but was replaced with a red star (appropriately considering the political bent), past the Sheriff's Office on the left and out onto the Sulphur Valley floor and highway 80.

The stretch from the east mouth of Bisbee Canyon to the Douglas city limits turns into a quasi-Grand Prix about 7:30 in the morning. Passing multiple cars already exceeding the speed limit – and also running late to the port of entry or the border patrol station- fed the Mario Andretti in me and a few others. The fact that we were taught evasive and pursuit driving at FLETC didn't help. The only thing highway 80 had that the Grand Prix didn't was the Arizona Highway Patrol.

Douglas had been a town where many of the miners working at the Bisbee Copper Mine lived before the mine closed down. It's only claim to fame is the infamous Mexican bandit, Pancho Villa, rode his horse up the ornate, wooden stairway of the Gadsden Hotel. There is an airfield outside of town that the Department of Defense wanted to build but the city leadership didn't want it. Instead, it was moved to Tucson and became Davis-Monthan Air Force Base. The financial impact of having that base in Douglas would have been tremendous. It also would have upset the political apple cart in Douglas.

Speaking of apple carts, I was amazed to read that Douglas, Naco and Nogales' school districts use the *least* amount of government funds allotted for English As A Second Language (ESL) programs. The mystery was solved when another inspector (who had her child in school in Nogales before coming to Douglas) told me it was because they teach all their classes in Spanish.

That explained something else. I took a Hispanic woman I was dating on a shopping trip to Nogales one weekend. We parked at the MacDonald's parking lot and went in for lunch before walking across the line to shop (quart jars of very good pure vanilla are very cheap there). It quickly became obvious I was the only gringo in the restaurant. As I worked my way up the line to the counter the young, Hispanic man closed his register and walked to the rear of the restaurant. I thought he had to use the restroom so I didn't mind waiting. While waiting I noticed that every one of five cash registers had little Mexican flags taped to them. I saw my guy return from the rear of the store but, instead of re-opening the register I was at, he stopped for a rather lengthy, casual conversation with another counter person two over from the one I was standing at. I waited another minute or two until my guy looked over to see me still waiting – and again disappeared to the rear of the place. "Did I just get dissed?" I asked my date. "Looks like it." She said under her breath. *"This is Baloney! I fought for this country and I'll be darned if I'll be treated like a foreigner in my own country!"* I yelled. The restaurant suddenly became very quiet and she pulled me out of the place while I wondered how many in there were carrying guns or knives. It was the first time I was treated like an outcast in my own country – other than on duty at the Douglas, AZ Port of Entry.

One night as I was coming home from the 4 to midnight shift I was approaching the San Pedro River. I've heard it's the only river in the United States that runs from south to north. It has had a narrow two-lane bridge across it for decades. As I was speeding my way home I began negotiating the last curves to the river when I started seeing some kind of debris scattered in the road Slowing down to avoid causing damage to my truck I quickly came upon the reason for the debris. A small truck had rolled over multiple times – and for quite a distance. It was lying upside down on the westbound shoulder. The dust from the rollover was still hanging in the air when I drove up and saw three young people standing in the road waving a flashlight. They told me they witnessed the truck's accident and one of their friends was on the shoulder kneeling beside the driver. I pulled over and approached to see if I could help. The three standing in the road said they had called 911 and an ambulance was on the way. The one kneeling told me the driver was conscious. I placed my hand on his back and spoke to him. I asked if the driver could hear me – hoping he wouldn't move. The driver lifted his face up out of the dirt and was very alert. He wasn't aware of the blood pooled beneath his face that had poured out of his mouth and nose. I put a T-shirt offered by one of the witnesses under his face and tried comforting him until the ambulance arrived. In that flat terrain at night we could see it coming about five miles away. I retrieved his driver's license from his wallet to know what to call him. He could wiggle his fingers but not his toes. And he couldn't feel me touching his legs. The EMTs and the state trooper arrived about the same time. The female EMT didn't have the strength to cut the driver's sleeve open to start an IV. I was holding his head still while the male EMT isolated his head on the body board. I offered to cut his shirt if she would hold his head. While the male EMT was taking the driver's vitals the state trooper ran the driver's name through NCIC. I overheard the dispatcher tell him there was a felony warrant for burglary outstanding on the driver from Green Valley south of Tucson. "Not a good night for this guy is it?" I said. "We'll just let a Higher Power play this one out for a while" the trooper said. About a month later I saw a white cross on the side of the road with the driver's name on it. He had died.

I very nearly became one of those white crosses myself at almost the exact same spot. I probably would have if I hadn't been driving my old '92 Ford truck. It was during the years that I was repeatedly falling asleep on the way home. Driving home at the end of another stressful day at the Douglas POE, I was approaching the same curves near the San Pedro River . When I jolted myself awake I was heading right toward a large, white truck in the on-coming lane. As I jerked the wheel to the left I saw the young male driver and his two companions' jaws open wide in disbelief. As they came to a stop I zipped by them on their right onto their shoulder, over corrected across the middle of the road and ended up skidding to a halt backwards into a dirt berm on my side of the road – not 50 feet from that white cross. My first thought was I was grateful I hadn't hurt the kids in the other truck. Then I had this weird euphoric sinking feeling that I had almost died - and what a relief it would have been from the life I was having at the time if I had. It was as if the real pain could have been over in seconds but, no, here I was still alive. The driver of the other truck and his friends ran up to me and immediately asked if I had fallen asleep. They could see me asleep at the wheel as I approached him head- on in his lane. I felt bad thinking that I could have also killed these young people. They helped me get the back axle out of the dirt rut it had created and went on their way. They were good farm kids. I felt very guilty about endangering them.

It was my daughter who saved both my life and the lives of anyone else on the road with me. She was in nursing college and was visiting me that evening. I told her what happened and how I couldn't help falling asleep coming home from work. I told her I thought it was stress or depression but she insisted I go get a check-up so I did. It was diabetes Type II. Once the doc got the medication right I felt like a human being again and not a zombie.

There are bicyclists who ride the Sierra Vista – Bisbee- Naco-Sierra Vista loop usually early in the mornings. They don't know how much they are risking their lives riding bicycles on state highways driven by tired, overworked, overstressed CBP officers and Border Patrol agents.

On one of those beautiful winter days driving to work through Bisbee Canyon I was zipping along at my usual speed when I came upon one of my fellow inspectors crashed into the rocks eastbound on the westbound shoulder. I immediately pulled over and jumped out to help her but as soon my feet made contact with the pavement I went sliding all over the place. As she was explaining how she had hit the black ice I was asking myself "*I was driving how fast on this ?*" I've heard that angels above protect children and fools .....and I was certainly the latter that day! She was ok but worried her husband would be angry about wrecking the truck. She was a muscular, black female who was also very enforcement-minded. I gave her a ride to work and back home afterwards. When her husband retired from the army he got a job with INS in Texas. She quit her job with INS at Douglas and went with him to keep her family intact. I admired her for that. Many others wouldn't have taken that risk.

During this time INS was refusing to allow married couples to transfer to the same Ports of Entry as their spouses. It was brought to a head when two or three inspectors committed suicide within a few weeks of each other presumably because their requests for joint assignments were repeatedly denied. I didn't understand INS' refusals. They let locals work at the same ports of entry where they lived all their lives but wouldn't let husbands and wives work together?

I bought a huge, white Suburban that was lifted about 8 inches. I called it Moby Dick. It was spacious enough for my four kids and two German Shepherds. I knew it was a gas hog but had to drive it the 102 miles to work and back one evening shift to see how fast the gas gauge fell. Coming back into town at 1245a.m. on a Wednesday night I slowed down approaching Jimbo's Beach Shack. I had previously nearly T-boned drunks pulling out of the bar's parking lot there. A couple of drunks had been killed there staggering out into traffic as well. Another had his leg ripped off. It was an obvious spot for the Cochise County Sheriff's deputies to stake out and make DUI arrests. When I passed the deputy parked on the shoulder a few hundred feet east of Jimbo's he pulled out and started following me. I figured he saw the temporary license plate and didn't recognize the vehicle. I maintained my speed until he started tailgating me. He was following so closely I could only see his left headlight in my side view mirror. I slowed down waiting for him to either back off or turn his overhead lights on telling me to pull over. He just kept tailgating me. When I slowed to five miles an hour and he still didn't back off or pull me over I just pulled onto the shoulder, turned off the engine, turned on the interior lights, opened all the windows and kept my hands on the steering wheel. "Why were you going so slow? Why'd ya pull over?" he asked. "Well, I slowed down so you wouldn't rear end me. I figured I'd pull over so you wouldn't climb into my trunk" I said. "I wasn't tailgating you" the deputy said. "What do you call it when all I can see in my side view is your headlight?" I said. The deputy started tapping his long, black, Maglite flashlight in his other hand menacingly. That really angered me. It was a threatening gesture. I knew he didn't have any probable cause to pull me over and was tailgating me for so long hoping I'd give him a legal reason to pull me over. He insisted again that he wasn't tailgating then had the gall to tell me "Well, you need to maintain the speed limit so you don't *impede traffic!*". That's when I got out of the car. "It's one in the morning in the middle of the week. *What traffic?*" I asked. "Just keep your speed up" he retorted lamely as he walked back toward his car. "Is that the best you can do? *What's your name deputy?*" I asked. Having been a cop myself I hated it when people with attitudes asked for my name. I told some inspectors at work who had been deputies. They knew who he was without telling them his name.

What do most people do when someone tailgates them? Tell me you don't tap on your brake lights to get them to back off! The idiot deputy was too close for that. When I had my Toyota truck I was zooming back down the west side of Bisbee Canyon one night with a fellow inspector. We had just finished a busy midnight shift – which was no excuse because I always drove fast. Some dingaling was tailgating me and flashing his bright lights on and off – like he wanted me to speed up or let him pass! I kept tapping my brake lights until we got down the mountain - where the Arizona state trooper could pass me......and he did! I guess he was in a hurry to get home too. He was one of the troopers who backed us up at the POE on occasion – and we them on the road.

CHAPTER 4. THE LINE

20 December 1996 – While conducting inspections on the pedestrian lane, I discovered U.S. Department of Agriculture Food Coupons in the purse of ***** when she asked for an I-444 permit to go to Tucson. Senior Inspector Joe Perez, a Douglas native, told me I could <u>not</u> cancel her visa *just because she was (illegally) on welfare in the United States.* He was telling me I could not enforce Section 212(a)(4) of the Immigration & Nationality Act (Public Charge) requiring her entry document to be cancelled and her deportation.

The first" shot" in my war on the border was fired......and it was fired at me by someone wearing the same uniform.

18 January 1997 - At approximately 1340hrs. Mario C***** entered the U.S. through vehicular Lane #1 and presented his

38

Arizona driver's license as proof of U.S. citizenship. Mr. C*****
had a wallet in his hand which had an embroidered marijuana leaf on
the outside of the wallet in plain view. I asked Mr. C***** and his
passenger if they smoked marijuana. Mr. C*** said "No! But my
buddy does!" His grinning passenger said enthusiastically "Yeah!
Every once in a while!". I referred Mr. C*** to secondary where
Customs inspectors found approximately 3.5 ounces of marijuana in
Mr. C***'s possession. His audacity got him arrested by the
Douglas Police Department.

**20 January 1997 - Insight Magazine Special Report "Border
Agents in Douglas Have Waved It on Through" by Jamie
Dettmer, p.13**

"To the casual observer, Douglas, Ariz., is just a sleepy,
unremarkable frontier town – a place to hurry through on the way to
or from Mexico. With a population of only 14,000, what could
happen of any importance to the nation in this dusty tank town? A
lot apparently. Despite its' diminutive size Douglas is figuring
prominently in the war against drugs – and not in a way that casts the
town in a good light. The Douglas port of entry fast is gaining a
reputation of being the most corrupt and inefficient of any of the 38
frontier crossings dotting the Southwest's border with Mexico. And
if just a fraction of the stories told by U.S. Customs and Immigration
and Naturalization Service, or INS, inspectors "walking the line" are
true, then the Douglas crossing represents only a minor
inconvenience for Mexican drug traffickers.

"Dysfunctional" is the most charitable description one Customs
internal affairs, or IA, investigator can muster for a port that during
the last four years has seen the successful prosecution of half a dozen
U.S. law enforcement officers for narco-related corruption.

Some Customs and INS inspectors are seething. "There is open
bitterness and disgust being expressed by many of the port staff –
including supervisors- in regards to the widespread corruption they
believe is going on around here," remarks a veteran Customs officer.
Concern is also mounting in Washington about a port that some
federal lawmakers fear has spun out of control. Arizona's

Republican Sens. John Kyl and John McCain have sent a joint letter to INS Commissioner Doris Meissner asking her to comment on the persistent allegations of corruption among INS and Customs inspectors at Douglas. Meissner was guarded in her reply and trotted out the well-worn refrain other top law enforcement officials use whenever concern about border graft is raised: Misconduct on the border won't be tolerated. Dissatisfied, Kyl means to hold discussions with U.S. Attorney General Janet Reno to "find out what's going on there." According to Arizona Assistant U.S. Attorney Daniel Knauss, Douglas represents a "severe corruption problem." Speaking in the aftermath of INSIGHTS disclosure in November of federal border-corruption probes in California (see "Mega-corruption at the Border," Nov.11), Knauss told one newspaper: "The entire operation down there (in Douglas) is under scrutiny."

As with California, so with Arizona: Open talk about border corruption is not appreciated by those in authority and Knauss, say law enforcement sources, was slapped down by his boss, the nation's U.S. Attorney General Janet Reno, who called her subordinate on the carpet after receiving a fierce complaint from Customs Commissioner George Weise. Rebecca Even, Napolitano's spokesperson, now maintains Knauss's comments were taken out of context. She declined an INSIGHT request for an interview with the Tucson, Arizona-based assistant U.S. attorney. ......

"It isn't easy to tell," says a veteran Customs IA investigator who was based in Arizona for several years. "When we look at corruption allegations at the port it was hard to sort out whether the accused were lazy, or dumb-stupid, or whether they were receiving something in payment for their actions," he says. "It is difficult to mount undercover IA investigations there – it's a small port, there are complex family ties among the port personnel and with some traffickers – and outsiders stick out." But as with other well-placed Customs sources he believes there is enough "smoke to suggest the possibility of a raging fire." Several incidents at Douglas since the late eighties have prompted official and undercover IA probes of senior management at the port and of several inspectors. What particularly has disturbed investigators over the years has been the failure of the port management, led by the facility's director Frank Amarillas, to ensure systemic inspection of border crossing trucks belonging to suspected traffickers or hauling firms with known ties to drug-smuggling organizations.

.......And the old boy network persists in Douglas under Amarillas. One Customs inspector talks of a "systematic and long-term pattern of discrimination and retaliation against anyone who doesn't conform to what Amarillas and his management personnel desire." He continues: "They regard the Douglas port of entry as their own private little world or family business, ***and they resent and fear any outsiders, especially non-Hispanics working in the port.***"
......

MY COMMENT: *It's not just Customs!!! It's Immigration as well*!! Ernestina Morris is the immigration version of Frank Amarillas. She rose from secretary to Assistant Port Director with little or no qualifications and having failed repeatedly every management written examination. She is local, she is dating a married Mexican rancher and she intimidates and harasses inspectors who try to enforce the law on a daily basis. She allowed ineligible Mexicans to enter the United States almost on a daily basis. She has made comments expressing her dislike and distrust of the United States government. She is the leader of the Douglas, Arizona clique that has made the Douglas Port of Entry the internationally-known sieve that it is.

This problem can be easily solved by CBP not allowing local hires to work at the POEs in their home town! The Border Patrol doesn't allow this for the obvious reasons. Every "survey" taken by INS revealed massive inspector disgust at INS for allowing this to occur. The surveys were all ignored. INS management can transfer supervisors and higher based on "the needs of the service". The needs of the ***nation*** demand this be done with the Douglas, AZ Port of Entry management. Why hasn't this been done?

The topography surrounding Douglas allows heavy rains to be funneled into the Mexican sewer system. This system feeds into a large ditch separating Douglas and Agua Prieta along the border. U.S. cavalry troops took up positions in the ditch during a pitched battle between Pancho Villas forces and the federalistas in one of the many Mexican revolutions of the early 1900s. The ditch runs east to west along the border and under the road leading to the inspection booths on the U.S. side –where a large metal grate was installed- the ditch then turns north to parallel the southbound lane into Mexico. The ditch at that point is about ten feet deep and fifteen feet wide with concrete walls on each side. It was frequently used by fence jumpers as a concealed entry route into the United States. One inspector rigged up an alarm device in the ditch with simple wire and tin cans. It worked perfectly!

Prior to his retirement, Frank Amarillas arrived at the Port of Entry to supervise flood control of the Port during a deluge. A crane had been summoned to remove the debris blocking the grate causing the Port main office and traffic area to be flooded. It was after dark when Frank spied what he thought was a bundle of marijuana "grass" sticking out of a black, plastic bag mixed in with the debris being lifted out of the ditch. He ran toward it as it was being lowered and grabbed it with his hands….only to discover it was the hair on the head of a drowned Mexican woman. Five Mexicans were dredged up from that logjam – and one diaper bag. No baby or small child was ever found. We all hoped that as they heard the water rushing through the sewer they were walking through to get to the U.S. the mother had been able to give her baby to someone who managed to get out in time.

INS headquarters in D.C. called after the flood and asked if the Rio Grande had subsided. They obviously had neither worked the southern land border nor checked Google maps. Texas did have major flooding of the river at the same time though and one border patrol agent drowned trying to save an illegal's life.

I was surprised to hear there was a sewer system in Agua Prieta large enough for people to walk through in a country where its' citizens have to put their used toilet paper in baskets because the sewers won't handle it.

9 February 1997 - Supervisory Immigration Inspector (SII) Chavez, a Douglas native, rated me "low" in administrative duties despite Morris ("Mexican Moses") telling me my work was "perfect". SII Chavez rated me low for failing a "post-academy" test. I had just graduated from the Immigration academy three months ago in the top ten percent of the class. There was no need for me to take a "post academy" test when I had just passed the most rigorous academic training conducted by the federal government. The test that was administered was an out-dated test and the Hispanic, Douglas native inspectors were given the answers to the test prior to taking it. The non-Douglas inspectors were not. It was an effort to overcome the qualifications of the new incoming inspectors in upcoming promotions. Other non-Douglas inspectors – usually the Caucasian inspectors- were all rated low on performance evaluations. SII Chavez disappointed me a lot when he did this. I respected him because he was a Vietnam veteran who had survived a murderous ambush in the Ia Drang Valley. He had a large scar on the back of his neck behind his right ear where shrapnel had almost paralyzed him. He was a very soft spoken, easy going man – and the best pistol marksman in the District. Despite the fact he spent all his time in his office across the street and never came out to observe operations, I felt he would at least give me a fair shake. He lost my respect when he bowed to the Douglas management clique's agenda to force non-locals from the Port. He's another bureaucratic willow tree.

March 1997 – Area Port Director Wayne Morris told me during my in-brief July 1996 that if a fight occurred he expected me to jump in, back up our fellow inspectors and we'd figure out the details later. Today he called me into his office and informed me that an EEO complaint of racism had been filed against me for not issuing enough permits to Mexican citizens requesting entry into the United States. This was my fourth month working at the Douglas Port of Entry. Federal law allows border inspectors to search anyone and anything at random. While working the permit desk I routinely inspected purses and wallets. Apparently no one had done this before because it caused quite a stir among the local inspectors. I did this if the applicant didn't have the standard "comprobantes" - proof of employment (paycheck stubs, "nominas", etc. and/or proof of residence (utility/rent receipts, etc.). Sometimes it benefited them because I found documents proving they actually did live and work in Mexico- but it was very infrequent. I had been repeatedly told by the "Mexican Moses" supervisor, Ernestina Morris, and other Douglas native senior inspectors that I didn't HAVE to require proof of residence and employment to issue a permit – the unmistakable inference being to STOP ASKING for such proof.

That explained why I found so much proof of illegal residence in the United States in their wallets and purses – U.S. driver's licenses, Arizona ID cards, utility receipts, shopping receipts over a long period in distant states. I also found cocaine in a Colorado teacher's purse and a Tucson man's wallet within two days. The Douglas native inspectors had not been requiring such proof – ever. It was the only documentation proving the alien had a reason to return to Mexico. The embassies and consulates world-wide use that standard in issuing visas. It was stated in the INA that those were the "usual" standards of admittance into the U.S. . Senior inspector Grijalva - a Douglas native- had even snatched an applicant's border crossing card out of my hand when he saw I was going to look in his wallet. Grijalva wrote out a permit for the Mexican without asking him anything. I saw this done to almost every new, non-Douglas inspector for ten years. While inspecting the luggage of a young, Chinese woman I found a letter from her pen pal in San Francisco. Her pen pal wrote telling her to purchase a plane ticket from Beijing, China to Mexico City then take a bus to the Douglas, Arizona Port of Entry because "it was the easiest Port to get through".

Mr. Wayne Morris, to my great relief, then told me that the Inspector General's investigator had checked our records and had found that I had actually issued MORE permits than many inspectors combined. The accusation was found without merit. The reason I was issuing more permits than several other inspectors was because I actually sat at the permit counter where I was supposed to be when not on the line inspecting vehicles. I wasn't standing outside in secondary ogling the passing women. This didn't prevent Mr. Morris' replacement, Charlie Stemple from using that unsubstantiated complaint against me a year later in another trumped up accusation. The original complaint was lodged by one of the Douglas Clique for my success in finding so much evidence of fraud and illegal entry. It was used by Stemple long past the year's duration for such things to be kept in personnel files to continue their efforts to get me fired or make me quit.

16 March 1997 – MEMO TO ALL SOUTHERN LAND PORTS OF ENTRY AND BORDER PATROL STATIONS: The Office of the Assistant Special Agent in Charge, Calexico, California has received information from a source of unknown reliability indicating that a trafficking organization in the Algodones, Mexico area is offering a bounty of $7,000 to anyone who kills a Border Patrol Agent or federal border officer. The threat applies to the international border and Ports of Entry near the border between California and Arizona. ASAC Calexico agents are working to determine the validity of this information. Michael Freeman, Acting Assistant Director, Border Security, Tucson Field Office". This was to become one of several warnings of bounties on federal border agents and officers during my ten years on the line.

28 March 1997 - At approximately 0357hrs., three individuals approached Lane #1 and stated they were U.S. citizens. The tone and content of their responses to my standard questions were sarcastic and profane from the moment I asked their citizenship. I asked to see identification and all three said they didn't have any – nor did they need any. I asked the driver if he had a driver's license. He didn't. I asked the driver to step out of the vehicle and open the trunk of his car. As he did so I heard expletives in Spanish from inside the car and saw the front passenger leaning back in his seat trying to remove something from his left front pocket. The man in the back seat was leaning forward pointing toward the floor in the front seat and whispering something in the front passenger's ear. The front passenger was still moving around and uttering something about being a member of the 18th Street gang in L.A. under his breath. I told both of them to get out of the car and put their hands on the wall. I attempted to continue questioning the driver while inspecting the trunk but the two men on the wall kept interrupting me and crowded around the trunk. They refused to return to the wall and to quit interfering with my inspection. Then the driver joined in the behavior. I ordered all three to assume the position against the wall. This brought all the inspectors hanging out on the pedestrian lane out onto Lane #1. The three men faced the wall but continued calling me names and putting their hands down to their groin areas. I had to physically put each man's hands back up against the wall before patting him down. The third man, Raymond C****, turned around and flipped me the bird. I put C*** over the trunk of the car and handcuffed him. The other two men turned around and started yelling. C*** saw them and stood up and turned toward me. I was concerned I was going to be sandwiched between them. I told the other inspectors "They're all going in" and the three were put in separate cells – screaming, cursing banging and kicking the cell walls the whole time. I called Douglas PD who were treated to the same behavior. I charged them with disorderly conduct and they were taken to jail.

When I received a summons to testify against C**** at his trial in the Douglas Municipal Court, "Mexican Moses" complained that putting up with that behavior was "just part of the job." C.C. Choate said it was just "pouring fuel on the fire". We inspectors were tired of being treated that way by more than a few local characters. We wanted management to make an example-and set a standard- to make others think twice before assaulting us. Inspector M*****, a female officer, had been punched in the chest by an absconding suspect a few days before. Coincidentally, while waiting outside the courtroom I was surprised to see one of our secretaries arrive to file a restraining order against "Mexican Moses". It was granted.

After C**** quit his quibbling before Judge Borane, the judge asked him "Did you flip this officer the bird?" "Yeah, ...so what?" C**** retorted. "I find you guilty and sentence you to six months confinement in the County jail – or 30 days community service" the judge said. "I'd rather do the time than community service!" the idiot proclaimed. "I can arrange that very easily, Mr. C**** - if that's what you really want!" says the judge. "Well,...I guess I'll take the community service" C*** says condescendingly.

April 8, 1997 – Wrote a memo (memos were flying like snowflakes about this incident) to Port Director Wayne Morris complaining of Senior Inspector Dan Lilly releasing a Resident Alien three-time accused child molester H#### G#### F####, DOB: ##/##/##, FBI # S####### and allowing him to enter the United States prior to my obtaining an update from INS higher regarding his status and if any warrants for him were outstanding.

Lilly was a strange bird. He looked like Bert the Muppet – the one with the moustache. The day I reported for duty at the Douglas Port of Entry Lilly was manning the immigration counter in secondary. I walked in, introduced myself as a new inspector and asked for the Port Director. I thought Lilly had a hearing problem because he was always talking loudly – at least to me. He immediately began regaling me with stories of how he tried to clue the CIA in on an impending coup in Chile while on a mission for the Mormon Church. Then he asked me if I was really working for internal affairs sent to Douglas to find out what was going on. "Where in the world is this character coming from? And why would he think I'm from internal affairs?" I wondered. It dawned on me that the Port Director may have shared some of my resume' with the staff. It may have been interesting reading but he wasn't doing me any favors by doing so.

28 April 1997 – Supervisor Ernestine Morris (aka: "Mexican Moses") told me I couldn't relay biographical information on L.A. gang members entering the U.S. from Mexico to the Arizona Gang Task Force (GITEM). For some reason there had been quite a few crossings in a relatively short time. When they crossed I had been preparing a dossier on each one to include biographical information and photographs of their face, profiles, as well as any other info they would offer. Every one of them said they were visiting "abuela" – grandma. Right. This intel was much appreciated by my contact with the Gang Task Force but "Mexican Moses" Morris told me to quit doing it. I kept doing it anyway and word soon spread they were being tracked and they quit coming across at Douglas – at least during my shift.

Soon after I started doing this, Charlie Stemple, the immigration port director, began touting himself as a Subject Matter Expert on gangs and began soliciting appearances at immigration conferences around the country. Two problems with this: he stole the portfolio of gang information from a former fellow Douglas police officer who had laboriously built it, and, having only been a Douglas police officer himself, he hadn't exactly worked in the maelstrom of gang activity in a big city. He was also promoted through the Douglas police department with the good graces of the same Borane who had been busted by the FBI for attempting to sell drugs. I was tipped off to Stemple's megalomania by Stemple himself one day as a few of us Douglas inspectors went to Naco for some training. Stemple was the immigration guy in charge at that two lane Port of Entry (How slow was it at Naco? They never opened the second lane). When he heard us coming down the hallway he came out of his office and immediately began regaling us with cop war stories in which he was invariably the hero. I counted sixteen "I"s in his first five minutes of speaking. He carried himself like the portly politicians I see caricatured in cartoons.

Naco is a sleepy town on the border about ten miles west of Douglas. The immigration inspectors loved being there as opposed to Douglas. As mentioned it was basically a one-lane Port of Entry first supervised by Charlie Stemple then by his cousin Bobby Frias – who was dating a Mexican woman he eventually "immigrated" and married. He was of the same "service-mind" as our "Mexican Moses". Immigration inspectors at Naco could basically hide there for their entire careers without ever making a case or an arrest. I knew some who did just that. They could "get along by going along" and issue everyone permits without asking for proof of residence and economic solvency in Mexico and conducting "Pasale" primary inspections – just waving traffic through. There were a few frustrated inspectors there that were enforcement-minded but the majority of the immigration inspectors understood management's intent and just waved Mexicans through.

The Douglas Port Director is over the Naco POE. For a brief period, Naco inspectors had to rotate through Douglas for a week to get "refresher" training in conducting primary inspections and making cases. The Naco inspectors absolutely hated it. It was a big deal to have one fraud expedited removal case a month in Naco. For several years when amnesty was being discussed in D.C. we at Douglas were making 200-300 fraud cases per month. The Mexican media publicizes our politicians' discussions of amnesty and it always results in a tidal wave of Mexicans trying to enter illegally to benefit from amnesty. Each expedited removal (ER) case –subjects caught attempting to enter by falsely claiming U.S. citizenship, presenting fake or altered entry documents or documents that weren't theirs (imposters) - took an average of 2-3 hours of paper work. That was a lot of man-hours spent on cases the Assistant U.S. Attorney refused to prosecute 99.99% of the time. We invariably ended up walking the subjects back to the line after completing the cases and releasing them back to Mexico.

When Douglas inspectors were sent to Naco to basically decompress, we would invariably upset their peaceful existence by immediately finding fraud. Within ten minutes of my first tour on their only traffic lane I made a case. When I got off the line a few minutes later no one had started the case because the Naco inspectors had difficulty finding the Miranda Rights form that started the expedited removal process.

23 May 1997 - Below is a futile appeal for reconsideration of my first six-month performance appraisal. I should have taken it as a warning that my failure at this job – regardless of my qualifications (or in spite of them) and how well I was really performing - was a foregone conclusion by the Douglas Clique.

> MEMORANDUM FOR: Wayne Morris, Area Port Director

> SUBJECT: Performance Appraisal for period Nov. 18, 1996 through March 31, 1997.

On May 8, 1997, Supervisor Ray Chavez gave me my performance appraisal for the above period. Prior to this performance appraisal, Supervisor Chavez spoke to me once during the six month rating period. On that occasion, supervisor Chavez made a rare appearance from his office in the main building, approached me in secondary and told me to give two Mexican males permits to enter the United States. I had denied their permits and seized their Border Crossing Cards because they had no proof of having lived or worked in Mexico since 1992. Apparently instead of returning to Mexico to get the required documentation, they called supervisor Chavez and asked him to intervene on their behalf. As the two young men waited for me to issue them the demanded permits I asked if Ray Chavez was a friend of theirs. They both smiled, nodded their heads and said "He's our padraste (godfather)!" I left the office for another inspector to give them their permits to live illegally in the U.S.

During supervisor Chavez' verbal appraisal of my performance I repeatedly asked him to give me specific examples of the areas he rated me as "needed improvement." Instead, Chavez simply stared at me in silence a few seconds before going on to the next job element. At the conclusion of my performance appraisal I asked supervisor Chavez if there were provision –or space- for a rebuttal. Supervisor Chavez flatly said "No". This was a lie. Every federal employee in OPM has the right to rebut an appraisal. Until Chavez gave me my appraisal not only did I not ever see him come out of his office but the only time he spoke to me was to tell me to give two malafide permit seekers permits.

"….needs to improve in [sic] his communication skills…." I tested out of two years of English at Brigham Young University. I received a "B" in a speech class at same. I have been published in two magazines and completed a Master's thesis. I received an "A" from a semester of Interpersonal Communication and Organizational Behavior taught by Stephen Covey. I attended the U.S. Air Force Special Operations Cross-Cultural Communications Course and been commended for excellent communication and "tact" on numerous occasions by American and foreign general officers on three continents. During this rating period, Customs Port Director Frank Amarillas told me –in the presence of supervisor Chavez- that a local resident had written District Headquarters in Phoenix informing them of what a polite and courteous inspector I am. The wife and teenaged children of the Mexican Army battalion commander in Agua Prieta presented me with a set of engraved shot glasses (not knowing I didn't drink) in appreciation for helping them with paper work permitting the kids to attend the private Catholic school in Douglas. I taught my stepbrother English and he taught me Japanese. I know how to communicate.

"….and in the area of team work….". I specifically asked supervisor Chavez what he meant by "team work". Supervisor Chavez again failed to provide examples of when I was not working as a team. I reminded supervisor Chavez that I had performed successfully in the United States Marine Corps, as a weapons/commo specialist on a Military Free-Fall operational detachment in 5th Special Forces Group and as a Military Free-Fall Detachment commander in 7th Special Forces Group. I coached three football teams to winning seasons. I know what team work is. I told supervisor Chavez my definition of working as a team meant arriving at work on time, not using sick leave as an excuse to not come to work, attending to secondary duties at the permit counter rather than playing computer games, smoking outside, or ogling passing females in secondary instead of helping out at the counter. I also told supervisor Chavez my definition of team work included helping other inspectors adjudicate permits when flocks of customers came in rather that getting up and leaving an inspector alone to handle the crowd, backing up other inspectors during secondary inspections and sharing my knowledge with others. (All these things I did which a lot of his fellow Douglas Clique were not)

I gave supervisor Chavez eight firearms training booklets from the FBI Academy for everyone to use. When Chavez did not make them available for inspectors' use, I asked for them back and loaned them out. I loaned senior inspector Schwamm my copy of Stephen Covey's book "Seven Habits of Highly Successful People" knowing she was trying to improve her managerial skills. I brought in a pile of military counterintelligence manuals pertinent to INS procedures (interviews & interrogations, taking sworn statements, etc.) and placed them in supervisor Boatwright's book shelf for other inspectors to use. I have shared both my undergraduate and graduate criminal justice books and training materials regarding interviews & interrogations with other inspectors. I gave supervisor Boatwright several White Papers on the Bosnian conflict published by the Strategic Studies Institute of the U.S. Army War College to send to her daughter who is in Bosnia.

I've shared my newspapers and even my lunch with other inspectors. I bought inspectors sodas and large boxes of pastries when I was shift leader. I disseminated a copy of the INS history and mission I obtained from the Federal Register for other inspectors' use in completing resume's and in furtherance of their professional knowledge. I attended the Port picnic and participated in the softball game when many others chose not to go.

The performance standard for this job element states "….resolves incidents disturbances and/or complaints so that no more than ___ is/are improperly handled by the inspector as determined by the inspector (they probably meant "supervisor"). The only incident observed by supervisor Chavez was the one in which I refused to issue permits to his malafide godsons. That was the only time Chavez spoke to me or observed my conduct in six months."

Supervisor Chavez, I came to realize, was a "willow tree" whose branches sway with the direction of the Douglas Clique wind. He was brain dead. He seemed barely literate and avoided being a real supervisor when he could. The responsibility of the position scared him. All immigration supervisors wore the insignia of a major's gold oak leaf on their shoulders. At Douglas that was a monumental miscarriage of rank.

The fix was "in" against outsiders working at the Douglas Port of Entry. I wasn't the only outsider "gringo" slammed on our first appraisal. The DC management used bullets from my first appraisal for the next ten years in their attempts to get me fired.

01 June 1997 - Sierra Vista Herald (Associated Press) "Gunfire by brazen drug smugglers on the rise" "Brazen and trigger-happy drug smugglers in recent months have been unloading their weapons on Border Patrol agents. The latest shooting occurred Thursday night as smugglers driving hear Naco fired upon a U.S. Border Patrol agent's car 20 times or more. No one was injured and the agent didn't return fire. It was the second time in May that drug smugglers fired upon officers near Naco, just south of Bisbee along the U.S.-Mexico border. On May 12, smugglers fired several shots at Cochise County Sheriff's deputies and Border Patrol agents. In March, smugglers fired across the border twice in one day at agents in Nogales. 'We're obviously concerned about the number of border-type violent incidents that are occurring and the use of weapon fire to get away from our agents,' U.S. Border Patrol spokesman Rob Daniels said. ....Daniels said patrol agents have reported 38 assaults and 13 armed encounters this fiscal year. .....Daniels said an AR-15 semi-automatic rifle found confiscated from the vehicle was fully loaded combat-style with twin magazines."

01 June 1997 - At 1620 hrs. Mr. Luis S***** attempted entry into the U.S. via the pedestrian lane. He walked rapidly through the pedestrian inspection line and said "U.S. citizen." I stopped him and asked for some proof of citizenship. He showed me a laminated card containing the "What-A-Burger!" logo and his photo. When I informed Mr. S**** that a "What-A-Burger!" ID card was insufficient proof of U.S. citizenship he told me in a very surly manner "check with Mr. Hurtado because he (Inspector Hurtado) had let him enter the United States twice with his What-A-Burger ID. I called secondary to let them know I was escorting a Subject in. As we walked to secondary Mr. S***** was becoming so argumentative I gently held onto the back of his T-shirt to prevent him from running away or assaulting me. I escorted Mr. S***** into the holding cell and conducted a pat-down. During the pat-down Mr. S**** became more argumentative and non-compliant. This was in the presence of inspectors D****** and J*****. I turned the What-A-Burger ID over to inspector J**** and returned to primary.

I assumed that because I didn't turn Mr. S**** over to inspector Hurtado or another member of the Douglas Clique, Mr. S**** was processed for deportation as an oral False Claim to U.S. citizenship.

04 June 1997 - At approximately 1430hrs., while observing traffic on the primary line, I observed every Customs Inspector in the secondary area run toward the southbound lane. A white, Ford truck was attempting to escape from the pursuing Border Patrol by speeding through the Port of Entry toward Mexico. As the truck arrived at the Port of Entry's southbound lane the Customs inspectors had formed a seven-man, blue line in the lane with me in a white shirted Immigration uniform at the tail end of the line. It momentarily reminded me of a kick-off return play my Northside football team in high school executed successfully to be the first team to score against the state champions in Macon, Georgia that year (1969). Except each of us had our duty weapons drawn and pointed at the vehicle. The driver of the truck maintained his speed and aimed his truck at the inspectors. It looked like a bowling ball knocking blue pins to the sides as they leaped out of the way of the truck. I took one step to the side and, aiming my weapon at the head of the driver, yelled "STOP!" I was close enough to see the whites of his brown eyes over the front site blade of my weapon. For a reason I will never be able to explain he jammed on the brakes. He had a clear lane to the Mexican Port of Entry about fifty yards away. My sights followed him to a complete stop about ten feet past me. I held my aim at the left rear corner of the cab of the truck.

We had heard drug smugglers firing automatic weapons at Border Patrol agents just west of the Port a week or two before and I was not approaching the truck without backup. I was maneuvering to obtain a view into the cab of the truck when Customs inspector Phillips ran toward the truck on my left. As he approached both truck doors flew open. That was the first indication to me there was a passenger in the truck. I was very much target fixated on the driver. The passenger ran between two vehicles that had pulled over to the southbound curb and ran into Mexico – past the Mexican inspectors with impunity. The driver exited the truck and was immediately grabbed by Phillips. Phillips' arms were slipping down the body of the driver and the driver was succeeding in wriggling out of his grasp. I ran up, withdrew my weapon to my waist to prevent him from grabbing it, and put a half-nelson around the driver's neck. Phillips still had his feet so I threw my body weight to the ground and slammed the driver's face and chest into the hot asphalt. My left forearm was burning from the hot pavement as I heard other inspectors rush up and wrestle with the driver's arms and legs. After a few seconds I said, "Let me know when you have him cuffed!" My arm was getting hot! I twisted around and they were all standing back enjoying seeing me proned out with the driver on the road. "Very funny, guys!" The driver was escorted to the cell as Phillips and I inspected the vehicle. Sure enough, five 50-pound bales of marijuana were lying in the bed and cab.

A few of the Customs inspectors told me "Good job, Mike!" But when I entered the Immigration secondary office (the "Head Shed"), I was immediately told by the shift leader, Ernestina Morris that I had violated immigration policy. For what specifically wasn't made clear to me at the moment. I was incredulous. A written reprimand was being prepared by the Douglas-native immigration chain of command. The only thing that stopped it from becoming official was a memorandum for record written by the Customs shift supervisor praising my work in effecting the arrest of the drug smuggler. I was just beginning my year of probation as an inspector and I could have been terminated from employment for violating whatever "policy" prevented me from backing up fellow officers in a felony arrest. Customs management on the other hand recommended I be awarded 8 hours administrative leave – a paid day off- for helping out. Thus began a pattern causing me to wonder if I had picked the wrong service to work for. With my background and skills I still conclude I was in the right job – determining admissibility of persons requesting entry into the United States. I had good people skills and good law enforcement instincts. I was just working in a very small fish bowl for management who thought of themselves more as Mexicans than Americans. That was not a good thing when enforcing the immigration laws of the United States on the southern land border.

Most of the time we didn't receive early warning of the evading drug smugglers and they would zoom right through our southbound lanes. Then we took cover. If the smugglers tried to run the Mexican Port of Entry it was anybody's guess where those inspectors' bullets would go. I always enjoyed the transfiguring miracle that occurred in a surly suspect's demeanor when we told him we were turning him over to the Mexican police. One guy had to be cuffed hand and foot –and defecated his pants- when the Mexican police backed up to our door near the holding cell as we dumped his petrified carcass into the bed of their truck. He had shot a Mexican policeman while shooting his way out of his barricaded house in Agua Prieta.

06 June 1997 Subject presented his Border Crossing Card and an expired I-94 Permit to me in the immigration secondary office. He presented the attached proof of employment but could not provide proof of residence for the last six months. I seized Subject's BCC and deferred his inspection. I observed Subject leave the office and enter a late model Dodge truck parked in secondary driven and occupied by two other Hispanic males. I exited the office and stopped the vehicle's exit from Customs' secondary. I asked to see the two males' documents. I directed Subject to walk back to Mexico but changed my mind and examined the wallets of all three. I discovered an application for a health plan in Subject's wallet citing employment and residence in Tucson for the last seven months. Subject admitted to have both worked and lived illegally in Tucson during that time. Subject admitted to using a fake Social Security number when applying for health benefits in Tucson. He stated he submitted the same Social Security number and a fake I-551 Resident Alien Card to the Arizona Dept. of Motor Vehicles for an Arizona driver's license. Subject said he paid $100 for the fake Resident Alien Card and obtained it by sending a picture to a place in Los Angeles. Subject was Mirandized, fingerprinted and photo'd. Subject was processed for expedited removal, served with originals of Forms I-860 and 296 and returned to Mexico. (I provided the address for the "place in Los Angeles" where he obtained the fake documents but senior inspectors who were members of the Douglas Clique told me take it out of the report.)

June 13, 1997 – Supervisory Inspector Choate overturned my denial of a permit to a Mexican male national who could not provide proof of living or working in Mexico. The applicant told me he lived with a friend, didn't pay taxes, rent or utilities, and had no bank account or employment check stubs. SII Choate issued the man a permit to enter the United States.

June 15, 1997 – SII Choate ignored Hispanic Douglas native senior inspectors S### and Del Rincon's lateness – then berated me for arriving at work *early*! He also made derogatory religious comments about me to acting Port Director Lisa Boatwright who relayed them to me, i.e. "He already has a bishop. He doesn't need a rabbi!" I asked for my first transfer based on a hostile work environment. It was denied. Inspector Del Rincon failed to come in for an entire eight-hour shift because the schedule had been changed at the last minute (a recurring problem with supervisors unable to publish schedules on time). SII Choate took no action against Del Rincon yet docked my pay for two-hours of AWOL for coming in late on the same schedule.

June 19, 1997 - Senior Inspector Joe Perez, a Hispanic Douglas native, yelled at me in front of other inspectors and the public requesting permits for denying his Mexican niece an entry permit. Prior to him yelling at me I heard her complain to him that I had "asked for 'comprobantes'" (proof of residence, employment or –in her case- perhaps schooling in Mexico) . She had none.

24 July 1997- Notes from conversation with Acting Port Director Lisa Boatwright:

Me: "Do you think I'm deferring too many people asking for permits?" ("deferring" is a common practice by inspectors of temporarily seizing applicants Border Crossing cards and giving the applicant two weeks to go back and obtain the required documentation. If the applicant fails to return with the required documentation, his Border Crossing Card is cancelled. My cancellation rate averaged around 60-70%.)

Lisa: "Yes"

Me: "Why? All I'm basing my referrals on is what I've been taught by the senior inspectors here – proof of residence and economic solvency. If they don't have that I defer them to give them a chance to go back and get it."

Lisa: "Why do you feel you *have* to ask *every* person who's requesting a permit for comprobantes?"

Me: "Because that's what the *law* says we're supposed to do! They taught us that at Glynco. How else are we supposed to know if each person is bona fide for entry into the United States – and that they have a reason to return to Mexico?"

Lisa: "You will not find written anywhere that you *have* to ask for or that they *have to* provide proof of economic solvency or residence in Mexico in order for them to obtain a 6-month permit to enter the United States."

Me: That's not true. The Immigration & Naturalization Act states that is *exactly* what the State Department does when issuing visas overseas. If not that then what standard are we to use to determine admissibility?

Lisa: "AHA! *That's your problem*! You can't think you are going to stop *every* illegal from entering the United States! If they want to come here illegally they're going to come one way or another." (she doesn't address the "standard for inspection" question)."

Me: "I would be derelict in my duty if I didn't ask every person for comprobantes who wanted a 6-month permit to enter the U.S. Didn't I see an immigration poster that had the Statue of Liberty with the inscription "Guardian of America's Gates"? –it's on our uniform as well."

Lisa: "There you go again! Can't you see? *You have to quit thinking of yourself as protecting America! You have to get that out of your head!"*

Me: "I'm aware that I personally won't stop all illegal immigration into America. But I feel it's my duty to ensure everyone who enters the United States through me is bona fide. Every inspector here (of the newly hired) asks for comprobantes – except the local inspectors. Are you telling us we don't have to – to quit doing so?"

Lisa: No Answer

Lisa: "You gotta figure 85% of the people coming from Mexico are legitimate – focus on the other 15%. Why do you think it's necessary to ask everyone for comprobantes?" (She kept berating me for this but would not answer when I said it was our job to do so.)

Me: "The economic situation in Mexico is so bad our country is being flooded with people going north. That makes lying to get across the border worth the risk (I was amazed I had to explain this to a GS -12 Immigration Supervisor.) And from what I've seen in the short time I've been here the Douglas POE has become a sieve for Mexicans entering the U.S. to live and work illegally. Based on the complaints of Mexicans we've heard for the last several months, none of them were being asked for it prior to us new inspectors' arrival. The fact that so many don't have it – and so many don't return in two weeks with it should be an indicator of how many are living and working illegally in the U.S. I'm not the only one with a 60-70% cancellation rate."

Lisa walked away.

MORAL: "Do your job but don't do it too well." This was told to me verbatim and repeatedly by every successive acting and permanent Port Director at the Douglas Port of Entry after Wayne Morris retired. It's especially ironic that a supervisor told me I had to quit thinking of myself as protecting America when five years later our new name would become Customs & Border *Protection* (CBP).

07 October 1997 - MEMORANDUM FOR: Lt. Dan xxxxxx, DPD/GITEM - At 1900hrs. Jesus Manuel Gutierrez crossed the border into the U.S. through the Douglas Port of Entry. He claimed to be a United States citizen but spoke and understood very little English. He said his mother was in L.A. but later said she was in

Chihuahua, Mexico. He was in possession of rental car keys given to him by a friend ("Octavio" LNU) in Mexico. Jesus claimed to have been in the "Westside" gang where his gang name is "Chui". Jesus has a scar along his left index finger and his right eyebrow. He has a cross tattooed on the intersection of his left thumb and index finger and 3 dots on his left wrist. Warrant check was negative.

8 November 1997 – Supervisor Ernestina Morris "Mexican Moses" told me it was *my* burden to prove aliens were *not* bona fide to receive permits – versus *federal law placing the burden of proof on the alien requesting admission.* Acting Port Director Lisa Boatwright told her she was wrong. ......but it didn't stop Morris from incessantly harassing inspectors who continued requesting the requisite proof of residence/economic solvency for the entire ten years I worked there.

"MM"s efforts to keep the Port "sieve service" open didn't stop there. Despite H***** M***** Velasquez being deported in 1991 for aggravated assault, domestic violence and two drug charges, "Mexican Moses" issued him a temporary I-551 "Resident Alien Card" and allowed this criminal to enter the United States.

25 November 1997 - MEMORANDUM FOR: Office of Inspector General

ATTN: R.D.M.

"Attached is a copy of Form I-213 referring to the expedited removal of Veronica L****-L****, A70***330. When I brought her into INS secondary all the interview rooms were full. We were standing in front of the holding cell and I asked how old she was. Before she could answer immigration inspector Ernest Arvizu, one of the Douglas clique, yelled at me to bring her into supervisor Boatwright's office where he was. He told me she was a juvenile. I asked Arvizu how he knew she was a juvenile. He didn't answer. Just prior to entering the office she told me she was born in 1997 – making her 20 years old. She sat down in the office and I heard Arvizu asked her if, as she had claimed, she was a U.S. citizen. I saw her shake her head vigorously admitting she had lied. She also admitted to Arvizu she was 20 years old. I knew Arvizu had demanded she be brought into where he was working because she was an attractive female. I told Arvizu "not to screw around with this case. She's *not* going down the road." (meaning being allowed entry into the U.S.). After being relieved on the line and returning to the secondary office a few minutes later, immigration assistant Velasco came up beside me at the counter and wrote "You would not believe what Gene (Arvizu) is doing in there with that girl. He's *really* flirting with her." I went into the office expecting to see Arvizu completing a "Q&A" – the sworn statement required for an expedited removal prepared for deporting adults who entered fraudulently. Instead, Arvizu was preparing an I-213 required in preparing a Notice to Withdraw – the process for allowing juveniles to be released back into Mexico without a felony record.

Arvizu appeared very nervous at my entrance. I told Arvizu I wanted a copy of the I-213 (a basic incident report) when he was finished. I returned to the permit counter. Moments later, IA Velasquez approached me again and whispered "it's really getting bad. It sounds like he is going to let her go!" I went back into the office and told Arvizu I was taking over the case. When Arvizu got up to surrender the chair to me, the female started crying, grabbed Arvizu's arm and pleaded "No! No! I want *you*!" I completed an expedited removal case on the Oral False Claim to U.S. citizenship and walked her back to Mexico. Upon returning to the office IA Velasquez told me Arvizu had bragged to her he was "going out" with L***-L****.

I emailed supervisor Boatwright about what happened. Boatwright verified Arvizu had told her he was going to allow her to withdraw her entry. Arvizu bragged to inspector Del Rincon that he was "going out with her" and allowing her to withdraw rather than do an expedited removal.

Immigration inspectors at this time were rotating inside the main office and processing Mexican citizen's applications for obtaining Border Crossing Cards. Inspector Arvizu always volunteered for what most inspectors considered boring paper work. It soon became obvious to all of us why. He was filling up his "little black book" with names and phone numbers of pretty, young Mexican women whom he processed for Border Crossing Cards. Arvizu's "vetting" of their "comprobantes" (proof of residence and employment in Mexico) consisted of just getting their names and phone numbers. When I heard of this I discussed it with another inspector to find out if it was true. Inspector ***** said, "Mike, it's gone a *long* way past a conflict of interest." He refused to provide details.

This incident occurred during a time when Herlinda "Bonnie" Velasquez, the "Italian –NOT Hispanic!" and I were getting along very well. I don't know what turned her against me. I believe she just wanted to fit into the Douglas clique. Too bad. We used to have some very good conversations about the Mexican language and history. On one evening shift she and I were working the permit counter. An apparently successful Mexican businessman and his wife came in and requested permits. They didn't have any documents showing they were living and working in Mexico. I denied permits to them both. He was aristocratically affronted. I didn't care. I applied the standard to everyone regardless of station in life. If anything I cut less affluent –but honest- applicants some slack if they answered my more in-depth questions correctly. Bonnie agreed with my decision. She was standing at the cash register at the end of the counter when the two slid over to her. I heard both of them ask her how much it would cost them for her to issue them a permit. At first she didn't understand. I did. They offered her some "mordida" (bribe) to get permits from her. She got angry and explained that this wasn't Mexico and we didn't work like that – at least she didn't. The businessman replied that he had done it here before. I seized their Border Crossing Cards and summoned "Mexican Moses" Morris. I informed her of the bribery – a felony. "MM" gave them their cards back and allowed them entry into the United States.

11 December 1997 - Perla O***** - de C***** requested an I-94 to go to Phoenix to visit her sister. She presented nominas and a utility receipt dated June '97 – five months old. Her demeanor was such that I felt the paycheck stubs were fraudulent. When confronted with my suspicion, she admitted that a friend of hers had made them on a computer and had then taken them to the Instituto Federal Electoral for them to be stamped. OC was processed for expedited removal under INS Section 212(a)(6)(c)(i) Fraud at Entry and removed to Mexico.

The issue with the "officially stamped" nominas is that many (local) inspectors are willing to accept a stamp from that Mexican government agency as gospel. This woman paid $1,000.00 to have her fake nominas stamped by a government official. This makes two known locations where government officials are "authenticating" fraudulent documents – Chihuahua and Naco. It is undoubtedly rampant throughout Mexico.

26 December 1997 - Javier D****** - G*****, a Resident Alien, entered the pedestrian lane accompanied by two other male Resident Aliens. He claimed the three suitcases and everything in them as his. I asked if the female clothing in a suitcase was his. He said they belonged to his mother and sister. I found 3 Mexican passports in three females' names in another suitcase. I found a probation card on his person from the Mequite, NV police department. I asked DG if he had ever been arrested. He said he had for "6AA". I asked for an explanation and he said it was for child abuse. "Child abuse or child molestation?" I asked. He admitted it was for child molestation. Inspector C******** called DG's probation officer who said DG did not have permission to leave the United States. The charge he was convicted of was lewd & lascivious conduct with a minor under 14 years of age (a felony). He served 211 days with five years' probation. His conviction for "Moral Turpitude" offenses qualified him for deportation. A record of such was made and forwarded to his file for review by an immigration judge upon DG's request for citizenship. In addition to child molestation, we added alien smuggler.

What our supervisor should have done was set up DG for a deportation hearing before an immigration judge – called a Notice to Appear (NTA).

18 January 1998 -. I wrote a memorandum for record to Area Port Director Charlie Stemple complaining of senior inspector Geronimo Grijalva encouraging Myra Lizette Arias, a Mexican citizen, to file a groundless complaint against me. On two previous occasions suspects who were resisting arrest called out for Grijalva to come to their rescue.

My first encounter with senior inspector Grijalva occurred shortly after my return from the academy. I was manning lane 1. He drove up to my booth in a garishly painted Suburban. His mom and dad were in the car with him. He declared his U.S. citizenship and that he was bringing nothing back from Mexico. I didn't recognize him as a regular crosser so I asked where he lived. "In Douglas" he replied. "Where do you work?" I asked. "I work here!" with a big Cheshire cat grin knowing I'd be confused. I hadn't been working there a long time but it isn't a large Port of Entry and I already knew everyone that worked there – or so I thought.

After enjoying my ignorance for a few seconds Geronimo explained that he was on medical leave. OooooKay. I was satisfied he was a U.S. citizen and not bringing in any contraband so "DTR" – down the road. He returned to work a few months later because the only decent immigration port director they ever had was pushing to either get him removed from the payroll or get him back to earning a paycheck. Grijalva was on medical leave for a year due to "stress". He was being investigated for leaving a subject in a holding cell in the back of the main office over the weekend without ensuring the follow-on supervisor was aware of his custody. The first day I saw Geronimo at work he was wearing his black uniform pants so tight I was embarrassed. His white uniform shirt was also fitted very tightly with puffy sleeves like Harry Belafonte. Geronimo Grijalva was the ugliest gay man I had ever seen. I've seen some very pretty gay men and some very handsome gay men. Geronimo was just plain ugly. His face looked like it caught fire and the track team tried stomping it out. His hair was styled better than any of the female inspectors'. None of that made any difference to me if he did his job. He didn't. He was the protégé'of Mexican Moses Ernestina Morris– ignorant, virulently pro-Mexican and a Gringo-hater. He would wear "Daisy Duke" blue jean short-shorts to Port social functions. One Christmas party he tried hitting on one of the married, former Marine, Customs inspectors. That didn't go well for him but it provided a lot of laughs for quite a while.   On the other hand there was a lesbian/bi (?), Hispanic, immigration inspector who was very enforcement minded and outstanding in detecting fraudulent documents.   She had also been my best student in Criminology class at Cochise Community College in 1994. She was a sergeant in the army then and earned one of two As in my class. It was also she who asked me why I was being harassed by management for doing things "others" do on a routine basis - trying to enforce the law.

13 February 1998 - Ramon V**** - L**** and his male friend entered INS secondary and requested a renewal of his I-94 Permit. He had no comprobantes for either residence or employment. He stated he writes books and wants to go to L.A.. I queried him for any proof of residence or employment in Mexico. He said he doesn't pay utilities, rent, or taxes, and has no bank account or pay check stubs. He said he has land but "can't afford to build on it". I called supervisor Ray Chavez and related the story to him. Ray told me to make my own decision. I took the man's Border Crossing Card as either a Public Charge (receiving welfare in the U.S. or living illegally in the U.S. I told him to return within two weeks with the necessary proof that he is living and working in Mexico. VL and his male friend walked across the street to the main office and complained to Ray. Apparently supervisor C.C. Choate was in Ray's office. Choate came over and took the man's card from me. He took it to Ray who gave the man his permit.

It was interesting that management dragged out the "Inspector's Guide to Professional Conduct" when reprimanding inspectors for - in reality trying to enforce the law but masked as the smallest of - infractions that were ignored when committed by their sycophants. Two paragraphs in the Guide always brought us inspectors great laughs. On page 14:

"No organization can expect its' employees to act in a professional manner unless those employees view themselves as professionals. That view is molded to an enormous extent by the manner in which they are treated by their supervisors. Inspectors treated by SII's with little respect for their positions as officers of the Immigration Service are unlikely to see or conduct themselves as professionals.

The supervisor must be very sensitive to the tremendous impact his or her comments and criticisms can have on a subordinate's morale. Accordingly, criticisms and reprimands are to be expressed tactfully and with sensitivity to the employer's feelings and should always be in private. On the other hand, SIIs also have a responsibility to take every opportunity to commend and praise employees for their contributions to the program. Immigration Inspectors are officers of the United States government and as such are entitled to respect from the public, their colleagues, and their supervisors."

When supervisors would counter our decisions regarding issuing permits, let aliens enter the U.S. who were obviously ineligible, and even take documents out of our hands to allow people in that we knew shouldn't be admitted, that is not the respect and professionalism demanded by the Inspector's Guide to Professional Conduct. We all wondered if there was a similar Guide for Supervisor's that ours didn't – or couldn't – read. The Douglas Clique countered our decisions so frequently we brought it out and read it aloud on the pedestrian lane during the midnight shift. We laughed so hard at the irony of the situation it brought tears to our eyes.

INS' belief regarding the professionalism of inspectors was way off mark. When it became clear that, of course, the Administration was going to throw money at the 9/11 "problem" and establish a new bureaucracy, we inspectors all agreed that congress could fire every INS supervisor and above and subsume us inspectors under Customs and most of the problem would be solved. The "professionalism problem" was with INS management not the inspectors. The majority of inspectors –except for the "Douglas Cliques" at every Port of Entry- brought professionalism with them when they were hired, graduated from the academy and started work wanting to enforce the law. Our professionalism didn't depend on –or come from- management. It was innate. Management tried their damnedest to snuff it out.

04 March 1998 - Alma Delia C****-L****** entered secondary requesting an I-94 Permit. She presented residential receipts in the name of the man whom she said is paying her rent. I asked for proof of employment and she presented nominas (a list of employees working at a business with the applicant's name included) in the company name of North Vernon Forge Mexcana [sic] S.A.. There was no official seal or stamp on the nominas. She was unsure when she started working at that business. [This meant she couldn't remember the date on the fake nomina] I suspected they were false and advised inspector A*** of my suspicion. He accompanied me into the interview room where CL was sitting. I advised CL that lying to a federal officer was a criminal offense. I asked her who gave her the nominas. She gave me the name of Manuel Molina. She also gave me the phone number of the business. I left the office and returned a few minutes later. I informed CL that no one by that name worked there and the phone number was not that to the business. [***This was a ruse***. I had not called] Then she said in Spanish "Listen, I don't work there. I knew I had to have nominas in order to get a permit. I have to get a permit to go to Utah to talk to a judge to prevent my husband from marrying another woman." Her Border Crossing Card was cancelled and she was returned to Mexico. Presumably Mexicans whose cards are cancelled have to wait a "whole year" to get them back.

05 March 1998 MEMO TO Lt. Dan xxxxxx: DPD/GITEM - Antonio Gonzales Lopez (aka: "Daddo" or "Daddy" tattooed on right arm) giving residence at xxxxxxxx, Phoenix, AZ entered the U.S. from Agua Prieta through the pedestrian lane at 1415hrs. He had no identification. IDENT was negative. I recognized him from a previous crossing at which time he said he had crossed here nine months ago with his girlfriend who had been referred to secondary then. His stated purpose in going to Mexico was to see his grandmother. The "ASUR 13 714" tattoo on his left bicep and shoulder stands for "A___ Southern United Raza, 13th Street, 714 is the area code for Orange County, California. He said that's how they identify their turf – by zip code. He has an approximately 5-7" vertical scar near his left kidney. At the bottom of the scar is what appears to be a puncture scar. He said he jumped in then jumped out of the gang in CA when he moved to Phoenix about three years ago. He said one of his seven brothers shot himself in the head in CA about three weeks ago. His brother was in the same gang. Subject says he doesn't belong in the gang anymore because he found religion. Found in his pocket was a folded piece of paper with the Lord's Prayer completely colored in red crayon and another piece of paper inserted with a prayer beginning with "Padre Cholo…..". It was the gang members' prayer.

05 May 1998 - Mayra Adanira L*****-V******* entered secondary requesting an I-94 Permit to Phoenix. She presented typewritten paycheck receipts from a company called "La Critica"- supposedly a newspaper in Agua Prieta – and a laminated card identifying her as a reporter for La Critica. She was dressed in a provocative manner. The paycheck receipts appeared to be copies with her name typed in. There was no employment start date on the laminated ID card. I told LV that I had called the newspaper and they said she didn't work there (*another ruse*). LV then admitted the paycheck receipts were fake. She was processed for deportation and her Border Crossing Card was cancelled.

16 May 1998 - Jose Isaac V***** - B****** entered INS secondary requesting an I-94 Permit. He presented documents claiming to work for Cruz Garcia Bustamante. His behavior was such that I believed his documents were fraudulent. Further interviewing (I told him I called his boss –and hadn't ….*another ruse*) resulted in his admission that he paid $20.00 for the paycheck stubs and had lived in the U.S. illegally for three months last year in the State of Washington. He also admitted that his purpose in obtaining an I-94 Permit was to return to the U.S. with the intention of working illegally. His card was cancelled and he was deported.

15 June 1998 - At this time, every senior inspector at the Port of Entry was from Douglas. During this morning's staff meeting, every senior immigration inspector (a GS-11 position) complained of having to be shift leaders. Apparently they hadn't read their job description in a while that required them to be team leaders.

A couple of years after I began working at the Douglas Port of Entry, INS came out with another survey. One of the last questions asked on the survey was what could be done to improve the immigration service. This same survey actually went out twice within a few years. The nation- wide response from most inspectors hired in the big hiring push of 1996 was "STOP ALLOWING PEOPLE FROM THE SAME TOWN AS THE PORT OF ENTRY TO WORK AT THAT PORT OF ENTRY." The border patrol has never allowed that and it has reduced to the opportunity for corruption – the kind rampant among immigration inspectors at hundreds of southern border ports of entry.

In another inept, INS attempt to "professionalize" the service, they sent out a form requiring all inspectors to provide qualifying experience. The categories of experience covered many types of assignments veterans had occupied through a normal military career pattern. Points were given for qualifying experience. These points and a written test were to be used in determining who was going to be promoted to senior inspector and supervisor. Such wailing and gnashing of teeth among the Douglas clique! Almost every one of them had never left the small town of Douglas and had been hired because they either were related to someone already working there or had gone to high school with them. Few if any had any advanced education or qualifying experience leading people. They immediately told us that any "experience" gained prior to immigration employment did not count. That was a lie. It did.

The promotion exam was written by someone on cheap street drugs. There were so many double negative questions that it became quite confusing. There were two parts to the test. If you passed the first part you could take the second part. I managed to score fairly well on both parts. Not so for most of the Douglas clique -

including our infamous Mexican Moses. After seeing her dazed and confused trying to read the Supreme Court cases I showed her regarding ruses I would have bet a paycheck she couldn't read well enough to pass the supervisor's test. She didn't.

I doubt many Hispanic inspectors hired under the "Special Emphasis Program (SEP)" could pass the management promotion test much less claim much professional experience and education points. INS threw out the test. And "MM" was promoted to supervisor – a GS-12 position – without it….. and the nepotism/"good 'ol boy"/clique continued.

15 June 1998 - Memorandum for Dan Nelson, Douglas Police Department, Gang Intelligence Tactical Enforcement (GITEM): At approximately 2100hrs subject attempted entry into the United States claiming to be a U.S. citizen. He gave me and Customs Inspector Jesse Arrellano his name and claimed to have been born and raised in Douglas. Inspector Arrellano was born in Douglas and didn't recognize subject. A subsequent records check revealed, if subject is who he claims to be, he has an extensive criminal record for armed robbery, burglary, assault with a deadly weapon, and several aliases in Idaho and California. Our information lists him as being born in Mexico. I know he is not a Resident Alien. Under the name and date of birth he gave me there are no warrants for him. Unable to determine subject's true identity, I sent subject back to "grandma's house" in Agua Prieta, Mexico. Identifying marks: "CONE" tattooed across his back stands for "Conehead" – his gang name. "13" corner of right eye. "Trinidad" in cursive left side of neck; Chinese writing ("girlfriend's name" vertically right side of neck; numerous tattoos on both arms. He said he had been in "Surentos 13" gang saying it was a local Douglas gang that didn't exist anymore. He wasn't going to "break" under interrogation and if he insisted he was a U.S. citizen in front of a supervisor he knew –at this port of entry- he would be allowed to enter the United States.

19 June 1998 – "MM" took the side of a known alien smuggler who had complained about me asking him if he had ever been arrested. Morris reprimanded me in writing telling me *I can't ask "law* *enforcement questions."* Morris and supervisor C.C. Choat accused me of being a "trained intimidator." I feigned offense but took no small degree of perverse in that. With Morris' permission I tape recorded her formal reprimand of me for asking "law enforcement questions". During this reprimand Morris referred to "fags" and "when I (Morris) see blacks I automatically think they are guilty" and, "I mean I don't trust the U.S. government!" I still have the tape.

On the other hand, Customs Port Director Tong knew the man as a constant trouble maker who owned a theater in Douglas. Mr. Tong backed me up but he couldn't prevent the written reprimand for "asking law enforcement questions" from being put in my local file – the one MM refused to let me see because "there are things in your file we don't want you to see".

I don't think every black person is "guilty" any more than I think anyone of any other color is guilty. I base my suspicions on their conduct and attitude not the color of their skin. Several years later I began receiving threatening phone calls. I was arriving close to home returning from a day shift when I noticed an older black man pull up to a stop sign where I was passing. I don't know why my radar went on but when he pulled out behind me, instead of turning toward my house I conducted a counter-surveillance route. He followed me through every turn of the eight blocks. We ended up at the same place where we began before he broke contact. He was wearing a tan, flat, '20s era hat. The very next day he showed up at the Port of Entry 51 miles away. He came up to the pedestrian lane which I was manning claiming to have gone to Agua Prieta to buy some cigarettes. He was wearing the same distinctive hat. He claimed he hadn't been anywhere near where I lived the previous day. I watched him walk down the pedestrian lane and get into the same car he had been driving the day before. I kept his driver's license information in case something happened to me later.

02 July 1998 - MEMORANDUM FOR: Lt. Dan XXXXX, DPD/GITEM- On this date Juan C. A**** (DOB: 10/**/**), a Resident Alien (A#xxxxxxx), entered the United States through the pedestrian lane of the Douglas, AZ Port of Entry twice between the hours of 1600 and 2400. He states he is a former member of the 18th Street gang in Los Angeles, California but is not active now. He gave his current address as 10** S. C*****, #6, Santa Ana, California, 92203. The address on his driver's license lists xxxxx, xxxxx. Santa Ana, CA. 92707. Aside from his markedly oriental-shaped eyes, other distinguishing marks are some very ornate tattoos on his chest: i.e. a woman with the name "Amalia" written in cursive on his right pectoralis; on his sternum a very ornate tattoo of two angels kissing; on the left clavicle a tattoo of a gecko which is probably his gang name.

He stated he gets "hassled" every time he comes here for vacation. From his statements he comes to this area annually to cross into Mexico to visit his grandmother in Agua Prieta.

He admitted to having served time for armed robbery. I smuggled this information to my gang enforcement contact.

25 July 1998 - At 1750 hrs inspector C***** phoned from primary and said he was sending in a white Toyota truck with a male, US citizen driver and his female, Mexican, I-586 Border Crossing Card holder wife. Inspector C***** related to me that he asked them where they lived and they said "We live in Sierra Vista". Senior inspector Grijalva was holding the referral slip in his hand as I approached the vehicle in secondary and was speaking very familiarly with the female. I saw the notation on the referral slip regarding the female living illegally in Sierra Vista. I asked the driver whose clothes they were bringing from Mexico. "They're my wife's. We're moving her stuff to Sierra Vista." I informed Grijalva of his statement and took both driver and wife into the interview rooms in preparation for cancellation of her entry document as an intended immigrant out of status. As I was interviewing the driver, Customs inspector L**** told me the female Border Crosser was employed by a well-known company in the area and was "well known" to everyone at the port. I went to primary to verify inspector C**** receipt of their incriminating statements. Upon returning to secondary to resume cancellation of her document, I saw the driver and his wife driving north into the United States.

I asked senior inspector Grijalva to explain his rationale for allowing an I-586 Border Crossing Card holder to enter the United States when she admitted to living in the U.S. illegally. Grijalva said "Oh, I know her. I warned her about living here. They are just on their honeymoon."

This is another example of why INS should not allow locals to work at the same Port of Entry they are from. CBP should immediately transfer any supervisor who is from the area they are working. CBP can transfer supervisors who have 'grown up' at the same POE they work at using "the needs of the service" as justification to reduce corruption. Their hands are not tied. They just allow the corruption to continue by ignoring it.

29 July 1998 - Email from Supervisor C.C. Choate; SUBJECT: ER Cases -

"I just received a call from Frank Siciliano/DADDE (Deputy Asst. Director, District Enforcement) who has been reading some of our Expedited Removal cases. He asked me to relay to everyone here that when he reads our Q&As (sworn statements) he becomes a very unhappy camper when he sees incomplete work. Here is what he is referring to: We are not following through on places of illegal residence and employment. He sends all good investigative cases to the Agents.

Therefore, when doing Q&As, lets pay particular to things [sic] like "where a person has been working (name of business/address of business/name of owner and who actually gave the job to the illegal). If the alien has evidence of employment, make copies for the files. If the Alien has evidence of residence, make copies for the files.

Frank's contention is they are not going to give up a good job or residence in the U.S. . They will probably show up again and even if they don't, the agents can contact the place of employment with evidence in hand. Most of these folks rent apartments and the landlords are more than willing to cooperate with investigators. I will not belabor the point – you get it!

Like Frank says the worst we can do is put too much info in a file. We will be looking for these points. Thanks."

This message really chapped my butt. I had been doing what Siciliano was requesting as a routine part of the Sworn Statement. I usually found the mentioned proof of illegal residence and employment in subjects' wallets, purses and "pocket trash". Supervisor Ernestina Morris "Mexican Moses" and senior inspector Dan Lilly told me to quit putting that information in the statement. They not only told me to stop including that information but not to call businesses to determine if the alien was working there in order to make a case. "Mexican Moses" continued harassing and berating me for continuing to do so after the phone call from the senior INS enforcement officer directing us to do just that! When they started deleting that information from sworn statements I had taken, I gave up.

I had taken investigative report writing while attending the Middle Georgia Police Academy, as an undergraduate criminal justice major at BYU, during the L.A. Sheriff's Academy, and both advanced interrogation techniques and report writing at the Rio Hondo Basic Police Academy & Regional Training Center. I knew what should be in an investigative report. I felt like I was having to work against the Mexican lobby at the Port of Entry to make a case. The Douglas Clique led by "Mexican Moses" took every opportunity to thwart inspectors' enforcement of the law.
10 September 1998 -

MEMORANDUM FOR: Doris Meisner, Commissioner, INS

THRU: Channels

SUBJECT: INS Policy Regarding the Use of Ruses During Fraud Interrogations

1. I am requesting official INS policy on two investigatory procedures that I believe are commonly used by immigration inspectors throughout INS yet are being proscribed at the Douglas, AZ Port of Entry. They are: a) the use of ruses by inspectors during fraud interrogations, and, b) asking subjects for any prior problems/arrests by law enforcement. I had been successful enough in determining fraudulent documents and identifying subjects with outstanding warrants using both these approaches to have been recommended for a special detail to Ireland by my immediate supervisors. Now I have been formally counseled to discontinue both these practices or face disciplinary action and possible termination.

2. Job Element number 3 of the Immigration Inspector's Performance Work Plan requires inspectors to "interview, interrogate and take sworn statements.... ." Successful performance of this job performance is rated "Critical". The use of ruses, trickery or inducements during interrogations has been ruled by the U.S. Supreme Court as not illegal as long as neither the "voluntary rule" is violated nor the circumstances are construed as to make an innocent person confess falsely. (see 394 U.S. 731, Martin Rene Frazier v. H.C. Cupp, Warden, 22 L Ed 2d 684, pgs. 688, 692; NC Court of Appeals, State v Robert Lee Chambers, p. 233; NC Supreme Court, State v James Wallace Jackson, 304 South Eastern Reporter, 2d Series, p. 134; Inbau, Fundamentals of Criminal Investigations, 2d Ed.)

3. Job Element #2 of the Immigration Inspector's Performance Work Plan requires the inspector to "intercept malafide applicants, including those with false documents, those who are status violators *and those who are wanted by other Federal, State, and Local Agencies*...." Successful performance of the job element is also rated "Critical". When other indicators arise during an inspection, I feel being able to ask some of those seeking admission into the United States if they have any previous arrests or problems with law enforcement agencies is critical to successfully performing my job.

4. Local Port of Entry prohibitions on these common, effective and legal investigative practices has placed the burden of proof of admissibility on the inspector rather than on the person requesting admission – as required by statute. Indeed, I have been counseled by a supervisor that applicants do NOT have to prove eligibility for admission. Due to the chilling effect these sanctions have had on my – and every inspectors' – ability to successfully performs out jobs, I am asking for the official INS policy on these practices.

Enclosures (2); cc: Senator Kolbe, Congressman Reyes, Respectfully, Mike Ligon

There was no response – other than thundering silence.

4 November 1998 – A young Mexican woman entered the secondary office and asked to see Supervisory Immigration Inspector Ernestina Morris "Mexican Moses". She wanted an I-94 permit. I told her I could help and asked for her comprobantes (proof of residence and employment). She presented a letter of employment with a rainbow logo letterhead. We had received an alert from District about that letterhead being a fraudulent letter of employment. "MM" was reminded of the fraud alert but simply said "She has what she needs. Give her a permit." I refused and went outside. Another inspector gave the woman a permit.

These permits authorize Mexican citizens to travel further than the 25 linear miles from the border allowed by their Border Crossing Cards (BCCs). BCCs are issued to Mexican nationals (presumably) living within commuting distance of the border to avail themselves of shopping opportunities and visiting relatives just across the border. In reality U.S. consulates issue them to just about everyone. In order to travel further than 25 linear miles from the border, a Mexican citizen in possession of a Border Crossing Card would apply for admission into the U.S. on either primary vehicular or pedestrian lanes, be inspected by either an immigration or customs inspector (prior to establishment of CBP), and, when stating the purpose of their visit to the U.S. being to travel to the interior, would have a plastic, yellow cone placed on the hood or roof of their car and sent to secondary. In the immigration secondary office the applicant would present "comprobantes" – proof of economic solvency (pay check stubs, "nominas" – a list of employees working for a particular business in which their name would be listed; or proof of business ownership) and residence: (utility receipts, rental receipts, etc.). For decades the extended visit form was a simple square piece of paper with the rules governing the visit printed on it – Form I-444. Once the applicant was adjudicated as eligible for travel, the inspector stamped the permit with his stamp containing the initials of the Port of Entry, the date of issue and the inspector's number. This made it possible to trace the origin of the permit if the user violated the terms of the permit or there was a question about the applicants' bona fides. Form I-444 cost $6.00 for each individual (regardless of age) and was stamped with an expiration date – usually the duration of the stated length of stay of the applicant. Just prior to 9/11, in its inimitable wisdom, the Immigration and Naturalization Service replaced the I-444 with the Form I-94 and allowed a blanket SIX MONTH "visit" for the same price. This was quickly perceived by Mexican citizens as a de facto permit to enter the United States on a "visitor's permit", obtain employment and residence illegally and only have to return to Mexico for a few minutes to re-apply for another 6-month permit. Mexicans were literally laughing in our faces while demanding the 6-month permits. And the Mexican Moses was continuing her campaign of harassment to prevent us from requiring proof of residence and employment in Mexico. Multiply six dollars times the number of persons obtaining these permits to enter the United States each day and one can see the amount of money going into the General Fund for Congress. It's substantial. Asking for proof a person lives and works in another country and has a reason to return to his own country can seriously affect the amount of money going into Congress's money pot. That is only one reason INS management harasses inspectors who require proof of residence and employment in Mexico.

Strengthening the statute requiring proof of residence and economic solvency prior to obtaining a permit to travel in the U.S. would significantly reduce the number of illegal aliens living here.

Restoring the line inspectors' authority to deny permits to those without such proof would also drastically reduce the number of illegals living and working here illegally.

Supervisors should have to submit an official memo to District Headquarters justifying overriding inspectors' decisions to deny applicants' requests for entry into the United States.

There should also be severe penalties for inspectors and supervisors issuing permits and entry documents without verifying the applicants' comprobantes. That would have a monumental impact on the number of illegals in the United States.

Would that create an even larger black market for fraudulent documents? Yes, but we have ways of determining if the documents are valid.

6 November 1998 - Immigration Inspector Xxxxx conducted a records check on an El Paso County birth certificate presented to a line inspector by an applicant for admission. The El Paso County Clerk's office told Xxxxx the birth certificate was fictitious. Inspector Xxxxx informed shift leader F. Morris "Mexican Moses" who, without any further inquiry, told Xxxxx the subject was a U.S. citizen and released the man who presented the stolen birth certificate into the United States.

Birth certificates are a vastly abused document used by aliens entering the U.S. illegally. The document has no photo and no fingerprint like the Border Crossing Cards. The number of U.S. birth certificates that have been rented out, loaned or sold to non-U.S. citizens must be in the hundreds of thousands. And they can be rented out innumerable times for big bucks each time. The only time they are taken out of circulation is when an alert inspector detects anomalies in the applicants' behavior and conducts an intensive interview that results in a confession by the holder of the document. In that case, the birth certificate is confiscated and, presumably, logged into the seized document log and eventually forwarded to "someone" higher for entry into a fraudulent document data base. In our case, if we could not contact the county clerk's office we called the 24-hour office of the El Paso Intelligence Center (EPIC) to see if the certificate had come up in previous cases.

Shortly after returning from the immigration academy in November 1996, Immigration Port Director Wayne Morris asked to hitch a ride with me to work. We both lived in Sierra Vista and he had to drop his car off at the dealership for some maintenance. On the 51 mile drive to Douglas, I asked Wayne why supervisor C.C. Choate always sided with the Douglas clique when it came to not enforcing the law. C.C. was a tall, white, male from Texas with a great mane of gray hair. He didn't seem to have native roots in Douglas that would admit him into the inner sanctum of the Douglas clique. Wayne told me he had advised C.C. to quit dating a Mexican woman suspected of storing drugs for one of the cartels on her ranch. Wayne said C.C. told him he had quit seeing her two years ago.

Two years later Wayne had retired. I mentioned to another inspector what Wayne had told me about C.C. having dated a Mexican woman and her drug connections. This inspector laughed and said "He's still dating her! The Mexican army has had her ranch under surveillance (or protection) for years now!" My fellow inspector also told me how C.C. met her. Senior inspector Alma Luna often invited him to a female-only, Victoria Secret "home demonstration". These "home demonstrations" usually turned into quasi-lap dances for C.C. The well-to-do Mexican woman who owned a ranch in Mexico regularly attended these "fashion shows". She and C.C. began dating.

23 November 1998 - I sent a letter to the INS Office of the Inspector General complaining of C.C.'s six year relationship with Josefina Lopez, a Mexican citizen, who was just caught smuggling 200+ pounds of cocaine through the Douglas Port of Entry. In my letter I explained that a few nights prior to Lopez' arrest, I happened to walk by C.C.'s office in the main building. Josefina Lopez was sitting in C.C.'s office with a blank I-94 Permit lying on C.C.'s desk in front of her. It was very unusual for an applicant for a permit to be seated in a supervisor's office late at night. Even though I knew what was going on I stopped and asked if I could help her. She smiled demurely and said "No, I'm being *very* well taken care of, thank you." Her brown hair was tinted red. I said she looked familiar and asked what her name was. She said "Josefina Lopez". That's what I wanted. Two days later during the morning staff meeting she would be the topic of the most recent drug bust. During staff meetings recent drug busts were discussed so other inspectors would be aware of recent trends in smuggling techniques i.e. where the smugglers were hiding their drugs in the vehicles, type of vehicle, etc. . In this case Josefina Lopez was driving through one of the pedestrian lanes in a van and was acting noticeably nervous. Inspector Eloisa Schwamm observed her behavior and referred Lopez to secondary for a more intensive inspection. That's when the 200lbs. of cocaine was found in the floor of her van. I thought it curious that such a large load was only casually mentioned by none other than supervisor C.C. who was conducting the staff meeting. As we took the line after the meeting I was asking for more details of the seizure from a Customs inspector. He said it was C.C's girlfriend who was arrested bringing the cocaine in the floor of a van. When I got off the line I searched for the file on the arrest. It wasn't where those files were usually kept. I found it on top of a file cabinet in the back of the office. I verified that the same woman who had obtained a 6-month I-94 permit "on the side" by C.C. two nights previous was the same woman arrested for smuggling cocaine – Josefina Lopez.

A week later, presumably after my letter to the Inspector General, C.C. again conducted a staff meeting. This time he had a deathly gray palor on his face. He was stuttering constantly and kept the meeting short. He was "allowed" to retire a week later. Instead of being allowed to retire, he should have been fired years ago for violating immigration policy prohibiting fraternization with Mexican citizens - or sent to prison for collusion in drug smuggling. At a minimum he should have been fired for malicious impersonation of an immigration supervisor. If history at that port of entry is any indication, Josefina Lopez probably has her Border Crossing Card back by now – if she isn't a Resident Alien or citizen of the United States.

10 December 1998 - I was assisting a rookie inspector at the secondary counter. She was trying to determine if the Mexican citizen had sufficient "comprobantes" to qualify for a six month permit. She had doubts about the validity of the documents and the applicant's answers to her questions. I suggested we take the applicant into an interview room for a more intensive inspection. Immigration Assistant Herlinda "Bonnie" Velasco began criticizing us for being "too suspicious". She followed us into the interview room and continued haranguing us. I told her politely I didn't want to argue with her about inspectors' responsibilities – particularly in front of a potential suspect. She yelled at me to "Go to hell" and stomped out of the room. I followed her out of the interview room as she went to complain to a Douglas supervisor. I told her to kiss my ass and to stay out of inspectors' business. I got two days off without pay. Nothing happened to her for interfering with an inspection.

Immigration Assistant Herlinda "Bonnie" Velasco's job description required her to ring up the $6.00 fee for the permits on the cash register, to assist inspectors in completing the inspector - approved permit forms and translate when needed. Under inspector guidance she was allowed to look at applicant's "comprobantes" and recommend issuance or denial of permits. She thought she ran the port of entry. The sad truth was – she practically did - with her gossiping, backbiting, and membership in the Douglas Clique. She routinely told Mexican citizens she was an immigration supervisor. She had a soap-opera mentality of pretending to befriend new inspectors to acquire personal information to use against the inspector later – particularly if they didn't fit into the Douglas clique. She and senior inspector Luna were partners in this. I actually overheard Luna telling Velasco "Get to know everything about him so we can use it against him later" referring to a new, male inspector going through a divorce. They didn't have lives of their own so they made it their mission to weed out enforcement-minded inspectors prior to completion of their probation. They usually failed but that didn't stop them from being snitches for the Douglas-clique supervisors. Bonnie claimed to be very educated but never went to college. She did know more about the Spanish language than most of the Hispanic instructors and supervisors. But she adamantly denied being Hispanic! She claimed to be Jewish and Italian. She was a small woman in many ways who did as much to lower the morale of inspectors as the Mexican Moses. Herlinda "Bonnie" Velasco was just one of Mexican Moses' (MM) snitches. She told MM which inspectors kept asking Mexican citizens for proof of employment and residence in Mexico. It drove inspectors crazy having to defend themselves – even against written counseling statements- for trying to enforce the law.

As an example of Velasco's hypocrisy, a Customs assistant I thought was Bonnie's best friend set up a farewell pot luck dinner for a departing and well-liked Customs Supervisor. We immigration staff were invited to join in the feast on the cargo loading dock. Great food, good company. When I returned to the immigration secondary office, Bonnie asked if I had eaten any of her "best friend's" food. I said I had and enjoyed it. Bonnie dripped acid in her criticism of her "best friend's" cooking. Bonnie's food was untouched. I often wondered how such a person lived with herself. After eight years of unsuccessful "snitch patrol" and many inspectors written complaints about her interference, Bonnie quit. She said she retired. Maybe she did. The first day Herlinda "Bonnie" Velasco wasn't in the INS secondary office, the sun started shining again over immigration inspectors at the Port of Entry. We started smiling again.

Chapter 5.

"Controlled Deliveries"

If "Fast and Furious" isn't infuriating enough, I was occasionally informed by other inspectors – not management- that a "controlled delivery" was being conducted through our inspection line. This type of operation was supposed to have been under the guidance of ICE agents who had been informed that an attempted drug shipment was being smuggled through our inspection line but that we were _**not**_ to act on the information provided us regarding the description of the vehicle. I and many other officers assumed this was in order for the ICE agents to monitor the drug shipment all the way to its' final destination where more comprehensive arrests could be made. I know a few ICE agents personally. I do not believe they would be involved in illegal activities. They would, however, be compelled –just as I was- to obey orders from higher. But consider the sworn testimony of two drug smugglers being tried in a Chicago federal court:

"Mexican Media Source Reporting that the U.S. Made a Pact with the Sinaloa Cartel – 06 September 2011:

> According the Mexican media source, Mundonarco, protected witnesses Jesus Manuel Fierro Mendez and Vicente Zambada Niebla of the Sinaloa Cartel have declared before courts in the U.S. that ICE representatives made a pact with Sinaloa Cartel leaders Joaquin Guzman Loera, aka El Chapo, and Ismael Zambada Garcia, aka El Mayo. In their declaration, both stated that the pact offered immunity to El Chapo Guzman in exchange for information he and his counterparts would be willing to provide regarding other cartels. Zambada's sworn statement was made on 29 July 2010 before the North District Court in Chicago, Illinois. Fierro's sworn statement was made on 04 March 2011 before Judge David Briones from the West District Court in El Paso, Texas, where he served as witnesses in the case against drug traffickers Manuel Chavez Betancourt and Fernando Ontiveros Arambula (both sentenced to life in prison). Statements provided by Fierro and Zambada regarding the pact between ICE and the Sinaloa Cartel were similar. Part of the statement made by Fierro was reported in this article as follows:

Interrogator: Did you know that there were other protected witnesses (Sinaloa Cartel operators) besides you that were providing information to ICE?

Fierro: Yes

Interrogator: Was Mr. Arambula one of them?

Fierro: Yes, there were two of us acting working as collaborators. We would pass on the information that came from the top to ICE.

Interrogator: Was El Chapo authorizing that?

Fierro: Yes, that is correct.

Interrogator: What type of information did El Chapo authorize you and others to give to ICE?

Fierro: Unlimited information as long as it would not affect El Chapo.

Interrogator: Were you allowed to give information about El Chapo?

Fierro: No, that was not permitted and I was never asked.

Interrogator: Why were members of the Sinaloa Cartel in agreement in providing information to ICE?

Fierro: Once again, for the third or fourth time, our objective was to take over the plaza from La Linea legally or illegally, via the Mexican government or via ICE.

Interrogator: Was the Sinaloa Cartel using ICE to eliminate La Linea rivals?

Fierro: That's right.

Interrogator: Did you only provide information to ICE regarding La Linea?

Fierro: Yes

Interrogator: Did you speak to Mr. Arambula about providing such information?

Fierro: Yes

Interrogator: Did other people that provided such information to ICE speak to you about it?

Fierro: Yes

Interrogator: Were there other reasons why you would go to ICE?

Fierro: Protection

Interrogator: Did you try to enter the U.S. at that time?

Fierro: No, I was a legal resident of the U.S.

Interrogator: Did anyone else that we have spoken about try to enter the U.S.?

Fierro: Yes

Interrogator: Did Mr. Arambula try to enter the U.S.?

Fierro: Yes

Interrogator: Did providing information to ICE regarding rival cartels, like you just said, allow him to do that?

Fierro: Yes

Interrogator: When key drug traffickers are arrested, is it easy for them to be released?

Fierro: Very easy

Interrogator: Are there times when U.S. agencies can prevent the Sinaloa Cartel's enemies from being released?

Fierro: Yes

Interrogator: Was there a time when key La Linea members were arrested as a direct result of information that you or others gave to ICE?

Fierro: Yes

Interrogator: During the time that you, Arambula, Mayito, and others were providing information to ICE, were you still trafficking drugs into the U.S.?

Fierro: Yes

Additional information provided by Fierro in his sworn statement was reported as follows in this article:

- He discussed the fight between the Sinaloa and the Juarez Cartel and their split in 2008.

- Before his arrest, he worked as Municipal Police Captain in Ciudad Juarez for two years. He also worked for the municipal police for 10 years.

  - In November 2007, he was contacted by Sinaloa Cartel Lieutenants Mario Gomez, aka Mayito, Chavez Betancourt and Ontiveros Arambula to assist them in taking over the Ciudad Juarez Plaza.

  - He had between 10 to 15 meetings with Sinaloa Cartel operators during which time they talked about how to take over the Ciudad Juarez Plaza and how to transport drugs from Sinaloa, Durango, and Chihuahua into the U.S.

  - He said that El Chapo is also known as El Tio (The Uncle) and El Senor

  - He provided information regarding the location of drug warehouses near Ciudad Juarez.

- ***He said that the Sinaloa Cartel [the one he swears is enjoying immunity by the DEA] was transporting between 15 to 20 metric tons of drugs per shipment.***

- He left his position as a municipal police officer and began working full-time for the Sinaloa Cartel as their principal goal was to eliminate La Linea operators working for the Juarez Cartel.

- At the time he was working for the Sinaloa Cartel, Vicente Carrillo was the leader of La Linea in Ciudad Juarez, and Juan Pablo Ledesma, aka El JL, was the leader of La Linea in the rest of the State of Chihuahua.

Information provided in Zambada's sworn statement was reported as follows in this article:

- He said that Humberto Loya, aka El Licenciado Perez, and he were the principal contacts between the Sinaloa Cartel and the DEA.

- He said (as well as Fierro) that El Chapo and his father, Ismael Zambada Garcia authorized Sinaloa Cartel operators to provide information to ICE.

- He said that the DEA was protecting the Sinaloa Cartel and providing them with information regarding DEA operations.

Information regarding protected witness Jesus Manuel Fierro Mendez was reported as follows in this article:

* He was arrested in 2008 in El Paso, TX.

* He plead guilty before a court in Indiana in January 2010

* His case was linked to the Manuel Chavez Betancourt and Fernando Ontiveros Arambula case.

*   He was sentenced to 27 years in prison with the possibility of his sentence being reduced considerably if he declared against Chavez Betancourt and Ontiveros Arambula.

*   U.S. authorities offered a residence and economic benefits to his wife and his three stepchildren.

Comment: To date, U.S. agencies have neither corroborated nor denied the statements made by Vicente Zambada Niebla or Jesus Manuel Fierro Mendez."

(Spanish Source:h ttp://www.mundonarco.com/2011/09/confirmado-pacta-eu-con-el-chapo.html)

Well, a U.S. agency did respond….and not very convincingly in my opinion:

"Mexican Media Source Reporting that the U.S. Denies any Pacts Made with the Sinaloa Cartel – 12 September 2011: According the Mexican media source Mundonarco, protected witness Vicente Zambada Niebla of the Sinaloa Cartel has declared before a court in the U.S. that ICE and DEA representatives made a pact with Sinaloa Cartel leaders Joaquin Guzman Loera, aka El Chapo, and Ismael Zambada Garcia, aka El Mayo. In his declaration, he stated that the pact included immunity to El Chapo Guzman in exchange for information he and his counterparts would be willing to provide regarding other cartels.

On 12 September 2011, a second article released by by Mundonarco reported that Prosecutor J. Fitzgerald from the North District Court of Illinois denied the allegations made by Vicente Zambada Niebla. In his response, Prosecutor Fitzgerald allegedly stated the following:

·   That on several occasions, Vicente Zambada Niebla, asked DEA agents if he could become a protected witness, but that his request was always denied.

·   That the defense is founding their hopes of immunity based on the fact that all charges filed against Humberto Loya Castro (a lawyer and confidant for Sinaloa Cartel operators) were dropped in 2008 in exchange for his collaboration with DEA agents in San Diego. This same individual was originally arrested in 1995.

· That it is a mistake to believe that an agreement made with Humberto Loya Castro would also guarantee immunity to all cartel operators and their leaders.

· That even if Zambada Niebla did receive promises regarding immunity by DEA agents during a meeting on 17 March 2009, as stated in the defense, that those DEA agents were not authorized to make them. (Spanish Source: http://www.mundonarco.com/2011/09/niega-eu-colaboracion-de-el-vicentillo.html)

When does a tried-and true tactic of offering immunity to a well-placed insider of a criminal enterprise become collusion with that criminal enterprise? In my opinion when we allow 15-20 tons of drugs to enter the United States with no consequences and allow the leader of that enterprise to operate with impunity. I find it hard to believe that with all the collection assets available within the U.S. government's intelligence community we are reduced to protecting an entire drug enterprise in order to eliminate their competition. I'm also curious to know if there is a connection between this allegation and the weapons allowed to go into Mexico. Were the weapons provided to just the Sinaloa cartel – which abuts the U.S. border along the Arizona border. To my knowledge no mention of any specific cartel has arisen in the "Fast & Furious" scandal. But it would interesting to find out if those weapons were targeted to just the Sinaloa cartel. That would seem to add credence to the sworn statements of Fierro and Zambada regarding DEA immunity to "El Chapo".

If I hadn't been aware of the "Fast & Furious" debacle by the ATF and the Justice Department I wouldn't have given the above sworn statements a second thought. I would have assumed they were simply self-serving attempts to avoid long prison sentences. As a tie-breaker I decided to conduct a statement analysis of the DEA's response to the allegation.

Indicators of deception are universally cross-cultural whether biometric, oral or written. It was an interesting thing to see as I conducted over 5,000 interviews and interrogations of illegal aliens, false claims to U.S. citizenship, alien or drug smugglers and fugitive criminals. The same indicators also exhibit regardless of rank, class or position....as I found in the DEA's response.

The prosecutor's response would normally be accepted at face value due simply to his "position of trust"....except for a few glaring omissions:

1. The prosecutor never flatly denies immunity was given to Joaquin Guzman Loera, aka El Chapo, and Ismael Zambada Garcia, aka El Mayo. In fact he never even mentions their name in his rebuttal. Instead he uses a deception technique known as attacking the source by focusing on Niebla . He also used "diversion" by introducing Humberto Loya Castro, a lawyer and confidant of the Cartel leaders whom neither defendant ever mentions in their testimony.

2. Whether Niebla received promises regarding immunity by DEA agents was not the issue in Niebla's statement. The prosecutor is introducing a moot issue. Why? Distraction from the accusation.

3. The defendant, Niebla, adamantly. unequivocally, repeatedly and specifically insists he was told directly by primary sources: "El Chapo" the cartel leader himself, and, a "Mr. Arambula" -whom the prosecutor also never refers to (avoidance) - that such a deal was made. His statement rings true as an unqualified statement.

4. Even understanding that where every word is important exact translation may have diluted the exact response by the prosecutor, "it is a mistake to believe" is much different than "*NO*, there is *NO* immunity offered to Joaquin Guzman Loera, aka "El Chapo" or to Ismael Zambada Garcia, aka "El Mayo" or the Sinaloa Cartel in general".

5. The "even if Zambada Niebla did receive promises regarding immunity by DEA agents during a meeting on 17 March 2009, as stated in the defense, that those DEA agents were not authorized to make them" is an interesting statement. This can be compared to a youngster being accused of something by a peer and responding "What if I *did?*" In effect this part of the response is

saying "So what?" The prosecutor then throws the DEA agents who may have offered the defendant under the bus by *post facto* saying they didn't have the authority to do so. That's the same CYA we first saw in Fast & Furious.

The hardest thing for human beings to do is flatly deny guilt - especially if their statements are a matter of public record and can be recalled as evidence in a trial or committee hearing. It's called perjury. I also believe humans are genetically coded to know that the truth is "out there" somewhere and someone always knows the truth – and they fear being caught in a lie. There's too much "wiggle" room – too many "qualifications" in the prosecutor's response. Lenin and Che' Guevarra called it the "art of dissembling"- denying the actual truth (or political agenda) by obfuscation. Our politicians and the Left have become masters of that art.

The fact that a federal counter-narcotic agency (or their chain of command) would offer such a blanket immunity to a major drug cartel would have been inconceivable years ago. And yet, here we are with "Fast & Furious" as a precedent. Who has the most motive for deception? I would like to believe the little twerps do. But my faith in institutions was lost with the Pentagon Papers and Nixon. As the Cheshire cat told Alice in Wonderland "Things just get curiouser and curiouser"... in the archaic sense. It would be interesting to put former ICE agents under oath about "controlled deliveries".

I believe someone in ICE or DEA made as egregious a deal with the Sinaloa drug cartel as the ATF made with southbound weapons.

21 December 1998 - A Mexican male approached me at the pedestrian lane and asked to see senior inspector Joe Perez. I asked why. He said "Joe is waiting to give us permits to go to Phoenix." I told him if that is all he needed than I could help them – if they had sufficient "comprobantes". He returned to the carload of people waiting at the corner opposite the line. Once he explained to the other passengers what I said he entered the car and they drove away – to reschedule their "appointment".

Incidents like this occurred on almost a daily basis. Once the "new" batch of inspectors hired in 1996 arrived, word soon spread that non-hispanic, non-Douglas inspectors were actually asking for proof of residence and employment in Mexico before issuing permits to enter the United States. When I denied a permit to a young Mexican woman for not having such proof, she cried out to her uncle, senior inspector Joe Perez, standing behind me "HE ASKED FOR COMPROBANTES!" He then yelled at me in front of the other inspectors and the public "SHE WAS JUST GOING TO GO BUY A DRESS!" Well, if she lived and either worked or attended school in Mexico she would have the necessary proof of such. More than likely she had been living illegally in the U.S. on six-month permits issued by her uncle or other relatives/friends working at the Port of Entry. I'm sure she returned a few hours later and obtained her permit from a "service-minded" (uncle, godfather) inspector.

It was also not uncommon for the Douglas clique to take their permit stamps and blank I-94 Permit forms home with them and issue the permits from their homes – away from us "non-locals". How much money those inspectors made from bootlegging permits will never be known. That private enterprise declined after 9/11 when the permit numbers actually began to be tracked. I wonder if that's how Grijalva paid for his Jaguar.

The vehicular inspection lanes on the line are numbered 1-7 with Lane 1 being closest to the pedestrian lane. It's interesting that there are seven constantly congested vehicle lanes coming into the United States but only two going from the U.S. into Mexico – and those are rarely congested. One day I was inspecting entering vehicles and their occupants on Lane 5. Between inspections I looked over at the open doorway to the pedestrian lane. It was always kept open except on extremely cold days so either pedestrian or vehicular inspectors could respond immediately to a fight or other emergency at the others' location. I saw a relatively new Customs inspector standing in the doorway of the pedestrian lane area keeping an eye on us while inspecting the passing pedestrians. Good enforcement-minded inspectors of both Customs and Immigration maintain a constant 360 degree situational awareness for others safety as well as our own. One never knew when a drug smuggler would bolt from secondary and try to escape south through the vehicular lanes. Or a suspicious person at the pedestrian or vehicular inspection booths would feel compromised and start fighting the inspector to run back to Mexico. I'm amazed that more smugglers didn't use weapons in their attempts to escape at Douglas because it happened fairly often at other Ports of Entry. Whereas Customs inspectors know vehicles immigration inspectors know documents. We both worked the line so the spotters across the line would try to channel the drugs through an immigration inspector and the fraud cases through a Customs inspector. His attention was divided between concern for backing up fellow officers in his familiar vehicular environment and his position on the pedestrian lane mostly requiring examination of entry documents.

The biometrics of suspicious persons are cross-cultural. The human indicators of deception are the same regardless of what country you are from. I saw a lone male walking toward the rookie inspector a little too nonchalantly and present an entry document. My buddy looked at it and waved him past. I watched the guy continue walking north on the sidewalk. He seemed relieved to have evaded a closer inspection so I called secondary over the radio and asked someone to intercept the man and re-examine his document. The red ink on the counterfeit document was still so wet from being made in Mexico that it smeared when they took it out of his hands. It seems like a small thing but it was always emphasized at the academy to take the document out of the applicant's hand and REALLY look at it.

20 January 1999 -   Gabriel Altamirano, a Hispanic male approached the pedestrian lane. I took his declaration and expected him to continue walking. Inspector Cromwell and I had resumed our conversation when instead he stopped a few feet away and started cursing at me and gesturing wildly with clenched fists. Although I hadn't smelled any alcohol on his breath during the inspection, I thought he might be drunk. I suggested he keep moving but he didn't. I told him he was going to speak with a supervisor in secondary and escorted him down the pedestrian lane in that direction by slightly grasping his right elbow. When we reached the gate to cross over to secondary he balked and began resisting. I pressed my body against his back to pin him against the guardrail. I quickly turned his right arm behind his back and into a department approved arm lock to handcuff him. Every time I handcuff a subject I wiggle the cuffs to ensure they aren't too tight. If the cuffs are too tight it will only make people fight more. He was cuffed for a total of about 20 seconds. Inspector Cromwell assisted me. When we entered INS secondary office, senior inspector Mora greeted the man "How's it going, Gabe?" I turned the man over to Mora and returned to the pedestrian lane to complete my rotation on the line. I asked a visiting Douglas police officer to give Altamirano a lecture on resisting arrest.

About ten o'clock that night Altamirano returned and wanted to speak with a supervisor. He showed supervisor Jose Lopez his swollen right hand and said I had abused him. It was obvious by the abrasion on the back of his right hand that - probably at the suggestion of his drinking buddy, inspector Mora- he had gone home and banged his hand against a wall until it became swollen. There were no bruises around his wrists where the handcuffs were. Several Customs inspectors told me this man has a long record with the Douglas Police department for drunk and disorderly. They told me Altamirano and inspector Mora had been arrested together for those charges. They had asked me before how Mora could keep his job with a record including driving while intoxicated, in uniform, and causing a traffic accident that almost killed an elderly couple – including losing his driver's license for a year. I had no answer for that. All I know is that when Area Port Director Charlie Stemple called me into his office and served me with a notice to suspend, he closed the door and yelled *"If you think your level of ethics is going to determine the way things are done around here you are mistaken! I'm the driver of this bus not you!"* I had no idea how that was related to the situation but I answered that the only level of ethics I expected was for everyone with a gun and a badge on the border to earn their pay by enforcing the law. He told me to get out. He was so mad spittle was running down the side of his chin. And he was sweating – but he seemed to be always sweating…… I was suspended. Case #98X03647. Not long after this, our "bus driver" Charlie Stemple screwed (sexually) Mexican Moses Ernestina Morris and was discovered by his wife, a Customs supervisor at our Port of Entry. We were all mystified at this as his wife was a very attractive woman – even in uniform- while Mexican Moses dressed out at about 5'6" and 300 pounds!

For years afterward my fellow inspectors would joke about me being "the bus driver."

Senior inspector Mora not only had a drinking-in-uniform problem he was seen going into the back room of a local bar where it was common knowledge drugs were being sold and used. He also drove through Lane 1 during a midnight shift and when asked to open his trunk sped away from the inspector so fast he burned rubber from his Camaro's tires. The Custom inspector doing the inspection asked Mora to open his trunk because Mora's female passenger was a convicted drug smuggler. Her father was a local cartel leader. Mora bragged incessantly about possessing the "world's largest" collection of pornographic movies, his drinking capacity, and his sexual prowess. His philosophy was "as long as I can see their toes wiggle they aren't too fat." He may have played a large role in getting them fat. He was an excellent cook. If an inspector was processing a pretty female subject, Mora would rotate nervously in his chair at the secondary counter, fingers fidgeting, knees swinging open and shut. He would only volunteer to help process a case if the subject was a pretty female. Then he would breathe heavily while fingerprinting her and shower her with suggestive compliments. He sometimes, however, amazed me with his knowledge of immigration law. He was my first field training officer – such as immigration had such a thing. He always talked in a low mutter that sounded like mumbling.

Management had difficulty not only preparing proper disciplinary paperwork but understanding our rebuttals. Most disciplinary action by management didn't stand up well at District headquarters – if the rebuttals were received. Disciplinary paper work on me was always accepted despite the obvious distortion by management. I often wondered if my rebuttals even made it to the District Director. The few times I went around the local management I came out pretty well. When Mexican Moses became a supervisor I walked into her office and asked to immediately see my local file. She flatly said no, "There are things in there we don't want you to see." She was amazingly honest in her malicious ignorance.

23 January 1999 - Francisca V*****- N***** entered the United States by presenting her and her daughter's I-586 Border Crossing Cards. She entered immigration secondary requesting I-94 permits for herself and her daughter to go to Phoenix. She presented pay check stubs from Seguro Social – the Mexican Social Security agency that provided various social services. I suspected they were fraudulent and took her into the interview room for a more intensive inspection. She admitted she didn't really work there but had paid a secretary $50 to issue them to her. She also admitted to having lived in Mesa, AZ for the last two years where she had been illegally working cleaning the Mesa Police Department. She also admitted her husband and two other daughters were still in Mesa illegally and that they were all receiving ACCCHS funds (welfare) illegally. She was deported under Section 212(a)(6)(C)(ii) of the INA. "Mexican Moses" was not on duty.

5 February 1999 - Conversation with Hispanic inspector Sxxxx on the pedestrian lane. I told her about another inspector ignoring fraudulent documents and issuing a permit. She said the shift leader did the same thing yesterday – obviously fraudulent documents! She also noticed yesterday that Anglo non-Douglas inspectors were getting "picked on" more than "others".

9 February 1999 - Memorandum for Record to District Director, Roseanne Sonchik requesting a transfer to the Naco, AZ Port of Entry due to a hostile work environment by the Douglas, POE management and a few Douglas-native inspectors. I also complained of a Douglas-native, Hispanic inspector returning an I-

586 Border Crossing Card to a Mexican citizen who presented obviously altered comprobantes. No action taken by District. It was ignored.

14 February 1999 - Supervisory Inspector Mexican Moses (MM) Ernestina Morris refused to place a copy of her recommendation that I be selected for a special detail to Ireland in my personnel file. Mexican Moses told me verbally during my evaluation that I was one of the top three inspectors at the Port of Entry for making cases but she didn't include that comment in my written appraisal. I asked if she would start including "attaboys" in everyone's local files. She said she would but she hasn't. None of my "dope buster" or high marksman certificates – not even a lifesaving recognition- have been placed in my local file nor ever mentioned in any of my appraisals. Counseling statements and letters of reprimand are supposed to be removed from our files after a year. APD Stemple and his girlfriend, Mexican Moses, have kept mine in my file in perpetuity. Mexican Moses and Supervisor Ray Chavez routinely rate their Douglas clique inspectors higher than non-hispanic, non-Douglas native inspectors despite our superior ability to correctly process criminal cases with minimum errors and without being returned by District. We have been rated low in language ability despite speaking better Spanish than the Douglas clique. I quit signing the appraisals and encouraged the other inspectors to do the same.

28 February 1999 - Memorandum for Record to Special Agent Jacobsen re:

1)   On 21 February 1999, Customs Inspector xxxxx and I saw senior inspector Mora cross into the United States in a car driven by Christina Monique Villaescusa. CI xxxxx informed me she had been arrested twice on heroin charges and her father Francisco Villaescusa was a known heroin dealer. Customs inspector J***** told me at that time also that an informant had told him Mora had been seen with a known cocaine user entering the back room of a bar in which four other persons were using cocaine.

Customs Inspector B**** also told me he had discussed senior inspector Grijalva taking money for issuing permits off-duty with a female employee at the Office of Internal Affairs. Customs inspector B**** also told me the female internal affairs employee was directed or "influenced" by someone higher in INS to not investigate Grijalva.

2)   22 February 1999, Lizeth Quintero and Jose Munoz were caught with 30 packages of marijuana weighing 30.5lbs in the tires of their vehicles. Supervisor C.C. Choate gave them their Border Crossing Cards back – instead of cancelling them as drug smugglers.

3)   26 February 1999, supervisor Mexican Moses told me she went to Hermosillo, Mexico with her married Mexican rancher boyfriend. She complained of being left alone in a hotel room for hours while he conducted "business". She later introduced him to me as they entered my lane for entry into the United States. He was wearing a wedding ring. MM is not married. She later told an immigration secretary "What does it matter if no one knows about it?"

Seeing MM's vulnerability I decided to conduct an experiment. I started complimenting MM every day. I told her she had Sophia Loren's smile and eyes – which she did. I started making casual social conversation with her but always including comments on how nice her hair looked – and "was she losing weight?" The results were immediate and dramatic. MM no longer stood almost literally behind my back watching my every move. I told some other male inspectors the secret to getting Mexican Moses off our backs. It didn't last long because we still continue trying to enforce the immigration laws and she continued to override us and let illegals and criminals into the United States.

6 March 1999 - Memorandum for Record to Area Port Director Stemple: I complained of senior inspector Mora interfering with my inspections when pretty women are the subjects – yet leaving the office or ignoring inspectors who need help processing cases.

"Something *has* to be done about those senior inspectors not helping junior inspectors just because they don't like them." It was ignored.

08 March 1999 - SUBJECT: Hostile Work Environment by Senior Inspector Mora.

On March 4, 1999 you issued an I-94 Permit to a female Mexican I-586 Border Crossing Card holder who could not give you the name of the employer who signed her pay check nor any other question about her alleged employment.

On March 6, 1999, you angrily and falsely accused me of "abusing customers" – again female Mexicans- because they were waiting a few minutes in the permit office while we were busy preparing ER cases. Mora made this accusation in the presence of the public and fellow inspectors.

On March 7, 1999 you again interfered in my inspection and allowed a subject I had deferred and told to return to Mexico to enter the United States. Senior inspector T***** and I both felt he was an oral false claim to U.S. citizenship yet you injected yourself into our inspection for suspicious reasons to allow this man to enter the United States.

This interference in my inspections is creating a hostile work environment. This unwarranted interference is intolerable and cannot be allowed to continue. Your willingness to accept obvious fraud on March 4th and 7th brings into question your ability to conduct unbiased inspections.

Nothing was done by management about this. Mora is another "rat" for the Douglas Clique. Well, I said "nothing" was done. That's not exactly true. Mora was selected for the "Special Enforcement Team (SET) by Charlie Stemple. Stemple was determined to get his own "SWAT" team. Something he only fantasized about as a local police officer in Douglas.

10 March 1999 - Memorandum for Record: Release of felony fugitive Carmelo Balderra, on 9 March '99 by senior inspector Alma

Luna. Another female senior inspector had referred Balderra to immigration secondary for a warrant check that came up positive. The NCIC information matched the biographical information on Balderra. Even the coded fingerprint patterns matched all ten of his fingers. The New York City felony warrant requested extradition. Despite this evidence, Luna, with supervisor Chavez' permission released Balderra to return to Mexico –with an "order to return the next morning." I bet supervisor Chavez dinner Balderra wouldn't be back. He wasn't. Luna let a convicted felon escape despite solid, confirmed NCIC information. She told supervisor Chavez she let him go because Balderra told her "he had never been to New York City."

As long as outside investigators (like the "politically pure" FBI) continue labeling the corruption camouflaged as "service" –aka "Pasale" attitudes by disloyal, fifth columnist Hispanics at the Ports of Entry that, and many, many other Ports of Entry will continue to be the sieves they have been for decades. In effect, there is no border control at the Ports of Entry.

16 March 1999 - Letter to Roseanne Sonchik, District Director, expressing concern for the safety of my family and me. I had been receiving anonymous phone calls and had been followed home twice. The person calling said "Don't catch too much! I know where you live!"

More thundering silence.

18 March 1999 - At approximately 1415hrs. Pedro M****- A***** entered the pedestrian lane of the Douglas, Port of Entry and presented his Resident Alien Card (#*******). I asked him what he was bringing from Mexico. He claimed to be bringing nothing but clothes from Mexico. His demeanor aroused my suspicion. I searched his bag and found a wad of Mexican money rolled into a sports shirt. I called for back-up due to another suspicious person being present in the pedestrian lane and a line of pedestrians forming. Upon arrival of back-up I found three more bundles of

Mexican money in MA's clothing. Senior Customs Inspector M**** found several more bundles of Mexican money on Subject's person. SCI M*** took a monetary declaration several times from MA who continued to deny bringing more than the allowable limit. SCI M**** seized the money after determining the amount to be $12,581.06 US.

Immigration Inspector E****** conducted an NCIC check and found subject had prior arrests for alien smuggling and assorted other offenses.

This reminded me of two other incidents involving cash. Within a week or two after returning from the academy, a woman and her small child were referred to immigration secondary. I don't remember what the woman was referred for but her little girl was bundled up nice and warm in a thick winter coat. It was November so that wasn't extraordinary. Something was out of the ordinary with the mother but the inspectors interviewing her couldn't pin it down. I was working the counter and said "Don't forget to check the kid!" Immigration Assistant "The Italian" Herlinda Velasco snorted at that and said I should leave the four year-old alone. No one was checking the kid because "The Italian" had scoffed at the idea. I got up from the counter and opened up the little girl's jacket. The woman had hidden over 15 thousand American dollars in the girl's coat.

A few years later senior inspector M***** was conducting a sworn statement on a woman who had attempted entry as an oral false claim to U.S. citizenship. M**** left the office for a minute or two and when she came back the woman wanted to know where her money was. No one had found any money during the initial pat-down. This was an attack on an inspector's integrity and no one took that lightly – at least regarding theft. Supervisor Boatwright was summoned and without hesitation took the woman into a cell and spoke to her. When she came out the woman had the roll of money in her hand. Boatwright had told her she knew where the woman had hidden the money and if she didn't get it herself the female inspector who would have to go in and get it wouldn't be so gentle. The woman immediately retrieved the gooey, smelly, wad of money from her vagina. Boatwright asked aloud "OK, who's going to count it to make sure it's all there?" Every inspector immediately found another place to be or something else to do. Boatwright got the woman to sign a statement agreeing all the money was there.

21 March 1999 -   Inspector Sxxxx directed a man to open the trunk of his vehicle during an inspection on the line. She suspected the man of being an imposter – not the person on the document he presented to her for entry into the United States. When she asked to see his wallet he claimed he had none. As he walked to the rear of his vehicle, Sxxxx saw a wallet in his back pocket. He still refused to give it to her until a male Customs inspector ordered him to give it to her. All the documents in the wallet were in another man's name. She referred the man to immigration where senior inspector Grijalva, without further inspection, allowed the man to continue north into the United States. Although Sxxxx is Hispanic, she is not from Douglas and not one of the clique. She's a very enforcement-minded inspector with excellent instincts. This was another incident of a Douglas Clique inspector failing to support – even thwarting – a non-Douglas inspector attempting to enforce the immigration laws. We not only had to be alert for illegal entry and drug smuggling by Mexican aliens but we had to watch our backs from the Douglas clique. This included management up to the Port Director level who felt there shouldn't even be a border. One Douglas inspector told me that very thing to my face. I overheard two others say so in the break room – as well as "we've gotten rid of one Gringo, we only have three left."

28 March 1999 -   Management was continually publishing the work schedule late and making changes in the work schedule at the last minute. This drove the inspectors crazy and several of us missed whole shifts because we weren't made aware of changes made during our days off. This violated union agreement to publish the work schedule no later than a week prior to the new schedule going into effect. Today inspector Matheson missed his entire evening shift. I asked our union representative what management did to Matheson. "Nothing". I was charged "AWOL" hours for missing a

few hours of a shift for likewise being unaware of a schedule
change. Management was very selective in who they called when
inspectors failed to show up for duty at their scheduled times.

28 March 1999 - Mario L**** entered the United States as a
passenger in a vehicle. His demeanor was such as to arouse my
suspicion that he was under the influence of drugs. I asked if he had
ever been arrested (Yeah, I was STILL asking that question in spite
of MM writing me up for it). He hesitated, then said "Just for
juvenile stuff". I asked him what "juvenile stuff". He finally
admitted he had served time for Grand Theft Auto. I referred him to
secondary where it was determined there was an outstanding felony
warrant for him and that he had absconded from the Adobe Hills
Juvenile Detention Facility in Phoenix. Douglas PD was notified
and, upon verification of the warrant, took L**** into custody.
Supervisor Jose Lopez was not on duty.

29 March 1999 - At approximately 1620hrs, Jorge Humberto
R****- G**** approached me as I was conducting inspections on
the pedestrian lane. He said "Excuse me, sir. There is a warrant out
for me and I want to turn myself in." I asked him what the warrant
was for. "Murder" he said. "I shot my girlfriend's boyfriend three
times with a 357 Magnum". I asked him where the warrant was
from. He said Safford – a small community northwest of Douglas. I
asked him to turn around and handcuffed him. I escorted RG to
secondary and turned him over to Customs inspectors H*** and
B***. This murder suspect was almost released by a less-than-
conscientious supervisor who said there wasn't a warrant out for this
man. That's why I turned him over to the Customs inspectors I did.
I knew they would exhaust all resources to confirm the warrant.
Sure enough, Stafford PD had entered the 2nd degree felony-murder
warrant on the Arizona data base not the National one.

This "kid" had run to Mexico after doing the deed to his
"girlfriend's boyfriend". It shows how miserable things are in
Mexico for a gringo kid when he prefers to surrender himself to a
murder charge rather than continue living across the border.

4 May 1999 - A Mexican man approached me on the pedestrian lane and asked in Spanish what was required to obtain an I-94 permit. I informed him he needed proof of employment and residence in Mexico – and an I-586 Border Crossing Card. He showed me his I-586. I noticed it was issued three years ago and the computer showed he had only crossed the border once in those three years at the El Paso Port of Entry. Suspecting he had been living and working illegally in the U.S., I asked where he lived and worked. He responded in Spanish "No, trabajo. Vivo con mis padres." In Spanish he was telling me he doesn't work. He lives with his parents. Inspector Joe Acuna, a Douglas native interrupted my interview and told me the man was working and supporting his family. I asked Acuna if he knew this man. Acuna said he didn't know the man he was "just translating for me." Now, I'm not a native Spanish speaker. But I did take six months of intensive Spanish language training at the U.S. Army John F. Kennedy Special Warfare Center, Ft. Bragg, N.C.. My instructor, Sra. Pena, taught Spanish to high school students in Puerto Rico. She was invited to Spain to update the Spanish dictionary. She was an excellent Spanish teacher. After her course I taught tactics and operations to Central American soldiers in Spanish. As an immigration inspector I had taken several hundred sworn statements of subjects in Spanish while preparing cases for the Assistant U.S. Attorney.

I was stunned that Acuna would think me so inept at the Spanish language to have not understood that this man was telling me he didn't work and was living with his parents – the standard lie when they didn't have the required comprobantes and were living illegally in the United States. To ensure Acuna heard the man clearly I asked again where he worked and lived. The man was becoming angry and shouted "NO! Vivo con mis padres!" Again he told me he didn't work and was living with his parents. Acuna was mistranslating the man's responses to me so I wouldn't seize the man's document and require him to return to Mexico to obtain the required proof of employment (for the past twelve months in cases where we suspected them of living illegally in the U.S.). This was the same inspector who tried to dissuade us from inspecting the vehicle containing marijuana and who complained to supervisor C.C. Choate that I "needed to keep my mouth shut".

12 June 1999 - Inspector Sanchez caught a wanted felon. During her initial interview she asked if the man had ever been arrested. She laughed incredulously when I told her I had been counseled in writing for asking a subject (Mora's drinking buddy) the same thing. Senior inspector Lilly overheard my comment and said "Asking them that is a legitimate way of determining their admissibility." So why was I counseled? And why was it still in my local file over two years later?

Determining a criminal record is not only a basis for assessing admissibility but it is a very direct way of determining if the subject is a threat to the officer.

10 July 1999 - Inspector G**** told me he had an argument with immigration assistant Velasco similar to mine. His memo responding to Velasco's complaint wasn't included in his local file. Nothing he wrote about the incident with her was in his file – except the counseling statement they gave him for arguing with her. Port Director Stemple and Mexican Moses are violating federal Office of Personnel Management regulations by omitting statements in disciplinary incidents – but only those of the non-Douglas inspectors.

13 July 1999 - At approximately 1715hrs. I was providing information to a woman on the pedestrian lane regarding obtaining entry stamps for her children's passports. Daniel V***** C***** was standing two people back in the line and shouted "U.S. CITIZEN!" Mr. C***** presented his Arizona driver's license. While comparing his face with the DL photo I noticed his cap was askew and bulging. Upon removal of his cap I found a clear, plastic bag containing a moldy, brownish-green leafy substance that later tested positive as marijuana. I turned Mr. C**** over to the custody of Customs inspector C****.

This old man's eyeglasses were so thick he could see into the future. His brain wasn't operating with all the oars in the water –

105

possibly from all the pot he smoked in his life. He went across the line to score some "medical" marijuana and, of course, the Mexicans ripped him off. He's lucky they didn't just beat him up and rob him.

2 August 1999 - Supervisor Choate tells senior inspector Schwam in front of the English speaking subject "she (the Subject) is just being as asshole". I get suspended for two days without pay for speaking like that to an immigration assistant for interfering in a case. In fact, Choate was the one who suspended me. Schwam, a Hispanic, Douglas inspector attended the Victoria Secret parties Choate is invited to. Schwam's husband, a Customs supervisor, found an email between her and Acting Port Director Jesus Jerez discussing their rendezvous on the Douglas golf course one night. We all felt bad for her husband because he was a decent guy. More than one Customs inspector told me her marriage to the supervisor saved her from drinking herself into a ditch. Her lover, Jerez, was the one who told me about his father keeping two sets of books in Mexico – and "there are laws ...then there are laws". Apparently so!

13 August 1999 - At approximately 1540hrs I was driving to work at the Douglas, POE when I observed two or three vehicles in front of me slam on their brakes. They began swerving to avoid a string of illegal aliens crossing Highway 80 from west to east approximately a half mile north of mile marker 353. The vehicles in front of me managed to maneuver through the crowd without hitting any of the aliens. I had to come to a complete stop to avoid hitting those walking casually across the road. A white van (Mexican plate 237SWA4) and a blue van (Mexican plate: ZVW 2965) were parked on the east side of the highway where the aliens were crossing. I drove approximately twenty yards further down the highway to distance myself from the group and to obtain license plate numbers to report to the Border Patrol. Some illegal aliens were still crossing the highway with oncoming traffic so I pulled over to the shoulder and exited my vehicle. As I approached, the last of the group finished crossing. Upon seeing me in uniform most of the group seemed undecided as to whether to run or give up. The coyote gave himself away when he walked over to the driver's window of the white van and placed both hands and arms inside the vehicle. He appeared to be telling the others to continue getting in the van. I thought if he saw me in uniform and he was telling the others to continue getting in the van he was probably getting a gun. I drew my weapon and told him in Spanish to put his hands up and walk toward me. I could see the muscles in his forearms flexing as he hesitated. While he was making up his mind he looked up and down the highway several times. It was just him and me on the road. He slowly brought his hands into view. Ignoring me, he walked to the rear of the van and began to open the rear door. I again ordered him to stop and walk toward me. He walked to almost arm's length of me, stopped, again looked up and down the highway and began to grin. Expecting an assault, I pulled the hammer back on my service weapon and told him to stop. He did. I asked him for a driver's license and he told me he didn't have one. I told him to go sit down by the fence and told the others to exit the van and join the driver at the fence. I counted 12 men, 1 female and the driver. I called the Port of Entry and informed a secretary of the situation and to call Border Patrol. At 1602hrs., BPA Banks and others arrived and took control of the situation. I also informed BPA Banks of the possibility of a weapon in the vehicle and continued on to work.

This reminds me of two other incidents that occurred on the way home from work: I was heading west inside Bisbee Canyon not far from the Sheriff Department when I came upon a lone, Border Patrol Agent (BPA) with an M-4 rifle standing on the shoulder of the road with about eight UDAs (undocumented aliens). Seeing him alone I pulled over and asked if he wanted me to hang around until back up arrived. He thanked me for doing so and said, "I tracked this group from the other side of the mountain. I think the smuggler is just around that dirt mound but I didn't want to go after him until someone else was here to cover me." The smuggler was in a dead end and couldn't run without being seen so we both waited for another BPA to arrive. While we were waiting a cell phone started ringing in the grass between the legs of one of the UDAs. Well, that identified the other smuggler. He had straddled a small, grass covered drainage pipe and thrown four cell phones inside. The BPA answered the phone and told the smuggler's contact he wasn't going to be at the rendezvous. Instead of another BPA, a thirty-ish man in civilian clothes pulled over and offered his assistance. While we both believe you can never have too much back up we were both leery of this guy's "enthusiasm". Neither of us said yea or nay about him staying. He started telling us – in a somewhat pre-orgasmic manner - how he had customized his rifle and "would show it to us if we wanted". We exchanged glances (and poorly concealed grins) and declined. Luckily, by that time another BPA arrived and "John Wayne" took the hint to leave when I did.

Another time I was returning home late from working a little overtime on the day shift. Just a few hundred yards east of that location, a SUV was parked on the side of the road. Two young females were trying to change a tire. I pulled over and offered assistance. The driver kept emphasizing she HAD to be in Phoenix at a certain time or her boyfriend would be furious. Her reason for being in this part of Arizona didn't seem valid. Her friend wasn't saying a word. I called the Port of Entry to send out a K-9 but the handler on duty was out on another call. I called the Naco BP station and they sent an agent out. I left them in the care of the BPA and never heard if they were carrying a load of drugs.

2 September 1999 0440hrs - Inspector W***, a non-local hired the same time I was, told me inspector Axxx, a Douglas native, asked him to "cut her some slack" when W**** told a Mexican woman she could not bring her baby into the United States without a visa. In effect, A**** was encouraging Witte to allow an alien to enter the U.S. without documentation. The baby probably didn't have a visa because the woman had been living in the U.S. illegally and did not have the required Mexican documents to qualify the baby for a visa issued by a U.S. consulate in Mexico.

Just then inspector Noriega came in and told us senior inspector Mora had come through Customs inspector Madrigal's vehicle lane driving a vehicle that was a TECS hit. The vehicle had been used to transport drugs across the border. Area Port Director Stemple is promoting Mora to a career enhancing position on a special traffic enforcement team. I'm glad Stemple's level of ethics is "driving this bus"!

10 September 1999, Friday, Sierra Vista Herald: "Douglas judge indicted" by Herald/Review staff and Associated Press. *Douglas – A Cochise County justice of the peace who built a real estate empire while a police officer faces charges of conspiracy, attempted money laundering and fraud. Ronald Joseph Borane was arrested Thursday but was released later on his own recognizance pending a Sept. 20 arraignment. He was taken into custody by officers of the Department of Public Safety and agents of the Federal Bureau of Investigation in Tucson where he was attending the League of Arizona Cities and Towns annual conference. Besides filing criminal charges, investigators seized one building and filed a $350,000 civil racketeering lien against all of Borane's 126 properties in Cochise County. ......He is also the brother of Douglas Mayor Ray Borane, who has attracted widespread attention by accusing President Clinton of failing to address the continued problem of illegal immigrants crossing the Arizona-Mexico border. ....The indictment alleges that Joe Borane dismissed traffic tickets and suspended parking fines between March 1998 and July 1999 for someone he believed to be a drug dealer but was actually an undercover FBI agent. Joe Borane is also accused of giving the undercover agent money on several occasions to purchase drugs."*

This wasn't the first time Judge Borane was investigated and indicted. In 1990 a drug tunnel was found under a warehouse located along International Avenue (the line) owned by him. A local Mexican singing group in Agua Prieta wrote a song called "Cocaine Borane" that was popular for a long time. George Magazine listed Douglas, Arizona as the sixth most corrupt city in the United States. Quite a distinction considering its' size and competition.

"One-Eyed Jack" - There was a real tall, white guy who showed up as a regular late-night crosser "buying cigarettes" every night. This guy showed up from nowhere and was very friendly to every inspector he met. He also had a black eyepatch over his left eye. He was a little vague about how he lost that eye the first time I met him. I told him to lift up his eye patch so I could verify he wasn't smuggling drugs in it. That wasn't as bad as checking dead bodies for drugs that came across in hearses fairly frequently. I'm sure more than one of those were later dug up in the Douglas cemetery. One night he came in really wasted and uncooperative to the point that we put him the holding cell. While summoning a supervisor we could hear him yelling at the invisible devils with him in the cell. He was so scared of them it scared us and we didn't really want to go back in the cell with him and his "companions". In fact, we did wait until he calmed down – and the devils left- before we went back into his cell.

Another good source of information on potential drug locations in Douglas were the FedEX and UPS delivery persons. They often commented on picking up boxes from "stores" that had no furniture or business equipment inside. I don't know if the agents ever talked with them – or if they were even allowed to. Under Attorney Janet Napolitano, agents were told they were prohibited from acting on information provided them. In other words they couldn't initiate their own investigations to bust drug or alien smugglers. That prohibition lasted the rest of the time I was there. They could only respond to cases we had already made at the Port of Entry. Their morale was at the bottom of the Mariana Trench.

We received this huge X-ray machine on the pedestrian lane one day and, rather than having to hand check everyone's hand-carried items, some inspectors began running the articles through the machine. None of us were trained on what to look for – what contraband or improvised explosive devices looked like. I and many others didn't use it. Well, one night "One-Eyed Jack" showed up after a fairly long absence - wasted as usual. He again vociferously insisted he wasn't carrying anything illegal. We avoided patting him down for the germ farm he was. He insisted strenuously that he was "clean" - to the point of volunteering to lie down and be rolled through the X-ray machine. Boy were we tempted! He had been down in Houston trying to fraudulently obtain some federal recovery money from Hurricane Katrina. He bragged and laughed about receiving several thousands of dollars from FEMA. Well, my partner on the pedestrian lane that night was a new black officer whose mom's home had been flooded by that hurricane. "One-Eyed Jack" was soon reported to FEMA but the response was very tepid.

110

Speaking of being scared, of all the close calls with guns drawn or near head-on collisions going home exhausted I remember being really scared twice. Once was on a quiet midnight shift and I was manning lane 1. This guy appears out of the darkness from across the line walking down lane 1. I first thought he was drunk and disoriented – missing the entrance to the pedestrian lane. As he nears I see he's wearing a dark gray hoodie with the hood low over his face and both hands in his pockets. I couldn't see his face in the shadow of his hoodie nor his hands in his pockets. He was walking very slowly. After failing to respond to my order to stop and go around to the pedestrian lane I ordered him to take his hands out of his pockets – "Manos Arriba!" He just kept slowly approaching without looking up and keeping both hands in his pockets. I drew my weapon – as did the other inspectors spilling out the pedestrian lane door. I was only momentarily hesitant to approach him because I expected him to be a high, down-and-outer wanting to collect on some of the cartel bounty on a border officer. Or a suicide wanting "death by cop." Well, I was the primary officer so I ran up to him and planted his body against the wall of the pedestrian lane. He still didn't respond either physically or verbally. I looked in his eyes and there was no one at home. He didn't have one item of identification on him or anything else in his pockets so I pointed him south and got him walking back into Mexico.

The other time I was scared was in the middle of a hot, monotonous day shift. One of those days when you check your watch often and the shift never seems to end. Traffic was heavy and I was manning lane 2. A sedan packed with Mexican men drove up to my inspection booth and I knew in a milli-second these guys were enforcers for a cartel. They were all hefty Mexicans but it was the way they looked at me that made my blood run cold. With no other "proof" than that I got on the radio and called for back-up. When some fellow officers arrived on the run I pulled them off to the side a little and explained the situation. No one laughed or ridiculed my decision. They escorted the vehicle and its' occupants back to secondary for an intensive inspection. They were "clean" and had the appropriate entry documents. The only unusual thing about the group was they were from Tijuana and their stated purpose for coming into the U.S. was shakey. A week later cartel hit men burst into a popular Agua Prieta restaurant and machine-gunned to death the owner and some employees.

For the last few decades of my life I've begun to suspect that a higher power puts things in front of me that I will make use of in some form or fashion in the future. I felt that way the two years I worked the midnight shift to stay away from management. I would sit on the pedestrian lane when not on the line and read books on counterinsurgency, revolutionary and guerrilla warfare. I had worked in that arena for most of my army career and taught it my last two years in the army. For some reason felt compelled to continue my study of the subject. Somehow, I didn't know how, I knew I was going to teach it again. Several inspectors made fun of me for reading instead of watching porno movies on the midnight shift.

While attending FLETC at Glynco, Georgia I hung out at the academy's library quite a bit the last month of training. Perusing their video library one day I saw an interesting title – which I don't remember- that dealt with Satan worshipping. Now, I am a Christian. I believe there is a God and there is a devil just like the Bible says. So, on Sun Tzu's premise of "know thy enemy…" I watched the video. Years before I had seen the effect the movie "The Exorcist" had on my sister. I never saw the movie but it scared her so much she couldn't sleep in her own house for several months. That's because she thought it could be true. I know the devil can't do anything to us we don't allow him to do. This video was different – and more ominous. Most of the film showed a social worker in southern California explaining how common it is for her to come in contact with children who have been victimized by Satan worshippers. She would take teenagers in her car and drive through their neighborhoods asking them to point out the houses of those they knew to be part of the cult. The teenagers would often point out churches, fire stations, schools and police departments where cult members worked. "Most Americans don't realize how pervasive this problem of Satan worshipping is" she said. She related an incident in which she was interviewing a young woman who wanted to break free of the "circle". The social worker learned from this woman that members of these cults symbolize their dedication by wearing a rope or belt of some kind tied around their waist. It must be in contact with their skin. If the rope, string or belt was removed the member was loosed from their vow not to talk about the cult. As the video films, the social worker asked this woman what the unusual necklace was draped around her neck – puka shells? "No," she answered "they are the bones from a little's girl's hand that we sacrificed to Satan."

Shortly after arriving for work at the Douglas Port of Entry a young, white, blond-haired girl had been kidnapped in the area. I never heard if they found her. A few years later I was manning the pedestrian lane when a tall, dark-haired young man approached the inspection counter. He had dark eyes, was sweaty, and a dark demeanor about him. The thing that attracted my attention was his coveralls. The strap on his right shoulder was knotted up in an unusual way. I stepped around the counter to feel it for drugs. Nothing. I had him step into the holding cell for a pat down, took the Bible out of his hands and gave it to my back up. His forearms were bare and I asked how he got the three, small, diagonal razor slits on his right forearm. There was a tiny, fresh droplet of blood at the end of each slit so he must have cut himself just before crossing the line – and it looked intentional. He mumbled something about a razor cut. When I got to his waist I felt a rope tied around his mid-section inside his shirt. I turned to my backup – who showed me the Lord's Prayer in the Bible heavily covered in red ink. Inserted onto that page was another piece of paper with the Lord's Prayer written backwards. He wouldn't tell me what his purpose was in entering the United States through the Douglas, POE or even where he was from. So, unable to determine if he was a U.S. citizen, I sent him back to Mexico – and went to wash my hands.

The guy was on a mission to snatch a young person for sacrifice - across the line or locally in a safe house. In a culture where "Santa Muerta" is worshipped, nothing is impossible.

About an hour later the inspector who had been my backup called me back onto the pedestrian lane. "Recognize your friend?" he asked. "No. Who is he?" " He's your Satan worshipper." I couldn't believe it. The guy had showered and shaved, combed his hair and was wearing a suit. He looked like a preacher. He had all the necessary identification and a good story on where he lived, etc. (and no warrants) so the primary inspector released him to go north.

One good story leads to another: I was working the counter one evening and a late '40s to early '50s, well dressed, Hispanic gentleman entered the office. He wanted a permit for his Mexican daughter –a beautiful young woman- to enter the United States. He made much ado about being down in Mexico "on business" and acted as if granting his daughter a permit to travel to Salt Lake City to visit him awhile was just perfunctory. Not with me it isn't. When I asked for the usual comprobantes from her the dad became somewhat testy. He asked why I was asking her "all these questions." That is another indicator something isn't right in "River City." Before I could explain that the law requires all applicants for permits to have comprobantes, he accused me of harassing them "because we're Mormons!" He also looked to the inspector beside me and said "You are obviously more educated than this inspector so I'll talk to you!" Our supervisor that night, Lisa Boatwright, was still cool at that stage and arrived at my request. I walked out to secondary to let her deal with his attitude – and to keep from smacking him upside the head. On a hunch I went back in and got his car keys. I took their suitcases out of the trunk and put them on the metal inspection table. The first thing I saw when I opened the first suitcase was a manila envelope with a marriage license containing the names of his daughter and her new husband (the "boyfriend" inside) – filed in Las Vegas two weeks ago – as well as her visa which had expired while in Salt Lake City.

So I waited until Lisa came out to tell me she enjoyed telling the jerk that not only was I Mormon but that I graduated from Brigham Young University with a B.S. in Criminal Justice and that I had a Master's Degree in Public Administration. Whereas the "better educated" inspector – as fine an inspector as he is- does has a two-year degree. Lisa also told him that if his college-aged daughter didn't have the required comprobantes she wasn't going to get a permit. When I told her what I found Lisa guffawed loudly. Lisa is a tough red-head. She not only had the pleasure of informing the jerk his daughter was not only NOT getting a permit but she was also being set up for expedited Removal as a Visa overstay – her visa was being cancelled and she would not be eligible to request another one for five years.

So the jerk dad's attitude during his attempt to just come down from Salt Lake City and get a 6-month permit (remember the "de facto" permit to live in the U.S.?) resulted in getting his daughter deported.

His pomposity reminded me of another man who demanded a permit without comprobantes. When I denied it he angrily said "I've lived in "this" town (he didn't say which as a Mexican citizen – Agua Prieta or Douglas) for forty years and I've NEVER had to show comprobantes!" It was late on an evening shift and we had no supervisor to overrule me so I sent him back to Mexico. I was out on the line when one of my buddies came out twenty minutes later and said the shift leader had taken a call from Washington, D.C. – a congressman from New Mexico – complaining about me harassing "one of his constituents". When the shift leader, a senior inspector, inquired as to how a Mexican citizen – prohibited by federal law from voting in United States elections – could be one of his "constituents" the congressman abruptly hung up the phone.

While conducting another sworn statement of an "intended illegal immigrant" I asked where subject had been the two years prior to his attempt to fraudulently obtain entry into the United States. "On a mission for the Mormon church. I worked a year in Salt Lake City to earn the money to go on a mission" he said. "So you broke the law by living illegally in the United States so you could go on a mission? Doesn't that seem a little contradictory in view of the question on the temple recommend interview asking if you obey the laws of the nation in which you reside? Did you lie on your temple interview prior to going to the temple?" I asked. His jaw hit the floor.

11 September 1999 - Inspector Bxxx Exxxxx, a fine law-enforcement officer who also is not from Douglas, wrote a memorandum for record requesting assault charges against the man who attacked him on the pedestrian lane. One would think this wouldn't require a formal request but be standard procedure. Not so. Supervisor C.C. Choate responded by saying "Why pour fuel on the fire?" If Choate would think with something above his belt he would realize the deterrent a prosecution would be to others. As it exists now, Mexican males know they can attack us with impunity. Choate's response – and lack of support from Port Director Stemple were devastating on our morale. Customs inspectors were astounded. I was ashamed to be an immigration inspector for the first time (but not the last).

13 September 1999 - I was the shift leader. I made out the rotation schedule and ensured everyone was where they were supposed to be on time. I also assigned inspectors to do the paperwork for the cases that were made. The shift leader is the acting supervisor. I asked inspector Arvizu to go to the secondary office and adjudicate permits (rather than his usual 'T&A' inspections in secondary). He refused. Not once but several times. Arvizu is another Douglas native inspector who hates Gringos. When I noted this in a memo to supervisor Choate he asked that I sit down and "discuss" the issue with Arvizu. I refused. I insisted on being supported by the chain of command in trying to maintain smooth shift operations. Instead I received a written counseling statement from Choate that was put in my file.

On 23 September 1999 I wrote a memorandum to the Office of the Inspector General Mr. Pedro White complaining of the harassment by APD Stemple and supervisor Choate. Shortly after several white, non-Douglas inspectors transferred from the Port. I walked by the lunch room and heard Arvizu gloating loudly "Only three more white guys to go!" I received no response from the IG's office – again.

29 September 1999 - Inspectors S*** and Bailey told me of an argument Bailey had with senior inspector Grijalva. Grijalva was refusing to authorize a deferred inspection of an I-586 holder. Bailey had interviewed the man and felt he was living and working illegally in the U.S. due to a lack of comprobantes. Grijalva – being one of Mexican Moses' sycophants – was refusing to support inspector Bailey's decision. It apparently became a heated argument as Bailey told Grijalva it was a "chicken shit" decision. This indicates the frustration level many inspectors felt at not being supported in the exercise of our discretion and authority to determine admissibility into the United States. A relatively few but strategically placed persons were refusing to enforce the immigration laws. The level of stress and frustration were palpable. Customs inspectors would try to direct suspected cases to those of us who would conduct a thorough investigation - only to be overruled by the Douglas clique.

Inspector Harry Bailey is as honest as the day is long. He is a faithful husband and father. He's a gentleman, a former Marine and a patriot in every sense of the word. He walked and talked like a Kansas farmer and I'm proud to call him my friend. He reminded me of the characters Jimmy Stewart used to play in movies – like "Mr. Smith Goes To Washington". He and a few others were stellar examples that being Hispanic and a Douglas native immigration inspector didn't necessarily mean one was corrupt or unpatriotic. For him to get irate enough to tell Grijalva he was "chicken shit" must have been the straw that broke the camel's back.

30 September 1999 - Supervisor "Mexican Moses" came through my vehicular lane on the line at 2400hrs. She was sitting in the front passenger seat of her own car. She introduced the short, mousey man driving her car as her boyfriend. He had the face of an owl with big round glasses. He was an I-586 Border Crossing Card holder which meant he lived in Mexico – or was supposed to. I noticed a wedding ring on his finger. MM was violating INS policy by fraternizing with a Mexican citizen as well as compromising her position as a supervisor by violating ethics guidelines. Yes - INS really did have ethics guidelines. The Port Director who hired me,

Wayne Morris, told me he had told her to stop the relationship with the man about five years ago. This was the first direct evidence I had that she hadn't.

1735hrs: Eleazar Lopez-Mendivil, entered INS secondary and requested an I-94. He was referred to secondary by inspector Del Rincon. Inspectors Cxxxx and Rxxx conducted an IDENT check and found Mendivil had a record for having entered without inspection. Mendivil admitted to having done so. This meant he was picked up by the border patrol and registered in our data base as an EWI (Entry Without Inspection) as most are who jump the line. Coyotes –alien smugglers- often have legal entry documents while smuggling aliens. They don't carry their documents with them while smuggling the people across the line so, once the Border Patrol "VRs" (voluntarily returns) them to Mexico they can continue to cross into the U.S. legally "off-duty" or to recon the Border Patrol checkpoints. Or he had been living in the U.S. and feared compromise coming through the Port of Entry. Senior inspector Joe Perez, one of the Douglas clique, talked supervisor Choate into NOT canceling Mendivil's I-586 Border Crossing Card – and issued the six-month I-94 permit to Mendivil and his family.

Later the same evening Jose Ignacio Cariaga-Vasquez requested an I-94. Again inspector Cxxxx found an IDENT hit for Vasquez having crossed the border illegally. And again, senior inspector Perez gave him his border crossing card back and allowed him entry into the U.S. I started to raise hell about this with Perez but inspector Del Rincon said "Forget it Mike. Don't even try" and threw Vasquez' IDENT printout in the trash. How symbolic. He might as well have thrown the whole Immigration & Nationality Act in the trash as little as we were enforcing it.

26 October 1999 - emailed Area Port Director Stemple pointing out page 12 of the Inspector's Guide to Professional Conduct requiring management to support the inspector when "confronted by physically, verbally and/or profane customers. I asked Stemple to remove the reprimand regarding the fabricated complaint by Mora's drinking buddy. He refused to discuss this with me or to remove the reprimand. Perhaps if I had interfered with an inspection resulting in a drug seizure he would have personally reassured me "not to worry about it" as he did with inspector Acuna.

The enforcement-minded inspectors were catching Border Crossers with records of having crossed illegally and being arrested by the Border Patrol with increasing frequency. Word had spread in Mexico that Douglas wasn't the "freeway" into the United States it had been – despite the strenuous efforts of a select few in immigration uniform to keep the floodgates open.

. If a border crosser with an I-586 was found to have committed a felony by crossing illegally into the U.S., the law (212(a)(6)(A) required the document be cancelled for violation of the conditions for qualifying for it. This became so frequent that the Tucson District Director sent an email –or local management – we never were shown too many written changes in "policy" – that said if the subject had not crossed illegally more than "so-many-times" that we were not to cancel his entry document. The count got up to fifteen times crossing illegally before we were allowed to cancel their cards. Again, just as the permits were changed from "duration of stay" at a specific location on the I-444 to an automatic six months anywhere in the U.S. on the I-94s, the Mexicans were laughing in our faces.

I saw Doris Meissner, former Commissioner of INS, testify before the 9/11 congressional investigative committee on C-Span "it's always been up to the inspector whether to make I-94s for 6 months or duration of stay". I instinctively shouted "bullshit!" from my recliner. Meissner was a Clinton appointee and either had no clue what was going on within the agency she was responsible for or she intentionally lied. I took three legal-sized pages of notes on things she said to the 9/11 committee that weren't true about how the immigration laws were being enforced. I viewed with pleased surprise when she was followed by a younger woman who contradicted everything Ms. Meissner said – particularly the part where INS management was supporting an "enforcement" approach versus a "service" approach. All we ever heard from management was we were a "service" to "guests" coming into the United States.

30 October 1999 - Senior inspector Schwam, of golf course tryst fame, saw me starting an expedited removal file on a subject. Without any further inquiry, she told me I "had to have an admission" before I could start a case. In other words, this Douglas Clique member was telling me I couldn't make a case against an alien unless he admitted his crime. I asked if she had ever heard of 'prima facie' evidence. Like her mentor Mexican Moses, she got that "hog staring at a watch" look on her face. I've found that the one thing that guaranteed angering the Douglas clique is being smarter than they are – which wasn't difficult. They REALLY hate that! At Douglas the pyramid of people who were qualified to be supervisors and management who – well, I was going to say who should've been working the line- was upside down. But Douglas management should have just been fired or jailed for their gross subversion much less for their gross ignorance. Keeping our nation's security in their hands is a national crime.

In this case I was processing an obvious imposter. An inspector on the line had escorted the subject into secondary and I verified that the person presenting the card matched neither the photo nor the fingerprint. The fingerprint on entry documents is always the right index finger. The more they try to change their print the more obvious it is that the document is not theirs. There are only five basic fingerprint patterns. The chances of an alien buying or renting a stolen or "lost" entry document with an identical basic pattern as the alien's if pretty small. The best document catch by an inspector I ever saw was Sanchez' catching a young woman using her twin sisters border crossing card. THAT's good inspection work! That's when finely tuned instincts and interviewing techniques really come into play. You can't imitate that with technology no matter how many hundreds of millions of dollars you spend on thousands of computers that sit in empty rooms in Phoenix.

Inspector Eloisa Schwamm has continued to rise to high levels of management thanks in no small part to her romantic liaison with our temporary Acting Port Director Jesus Jerez.

Speaking of technology and wasted millions, a tech rep from a company contracted with Immigration visited us at the Port of Entry to help us understand an identification verification system that had been in use for a couple of months. It was installed on the pedestrian lane and required a comparably long and confusing sequence of keys to determine if the subject's whose card was run through the card reader was actually him/her. The process took time and resulted in pedestrian lines being backed up unnecessarily for almost a block. Most of us quit using it because it was taking too much time to inspect the pedestrians. During the tech reps demonstration at the morning staff meeting, he ran a woman's border crossing card through the card reader and placed his right index finger on the laser fingerprint reader. It showed a match even though, obviously, he was a he and she was a she – and his finger print was a loop and hers was a whorl. There was a prolonged, uncomfortable silence in the room until I asked "Have you ever received any fingerprint identification training?" He said he had received some. I asked "Do you realize your machine is showing a MATCH when your print is a LOOP and hers is a WHORL? A stunned murmur rippled through the audience of inspectors when he replied "this process arrives at false positives about 40% of the time"! I couldn't resist twisting the knife in his gut by saying "Do you realize that any inspector in this room can identify an imposter 99.9% of the time simply by using our calibrated eyeballs?" Approximately 27 million dollars of taxpayer money was spent developing this system. The meeting was adjourned.

The system was so long ignored by inspectors that when a fact-finding team from D.C. arrived to ….well, I don't know why they were there but I happened to be on the pedestrian lane when they asked to be shown how it works. I said "Well, I would show you but it was so useless I quit using it and I don't remember how to log onto it anymore. Do you Joe?" Joe didn't either. I told them about the tech rep demonstration. They walked away without saying anything.

Not long after this, I also happened to be on the pedestrian lane when Janet Reno and her entourage arrived. Her in-brief was almost over and she was going to exit the office right onto the pedestrian lane where I was conducting inspections. Someone in management saw me there as primary inspector and immediately replaced me with a Hispanic female inspector from Douglas with tight pants and a Julia Roberts' smile. They sent me to the farthest part of the Port of Entry. Guess they couldn't "handle the truth".

9 November 1999 - 0959hrs. We are all stunned to read an email from Tucson District Director Roseanne Sonchik. In paragraph nine of her email she wrote she is on the verge of ordering inspectors to ask for nothing more than a border crossing card when Mexicans ask for six month I-94 permits. No more requiring proof of working and living in Mexico – and proof of a reason to return to Mexico. Her reasoning? "Inspectors are catching too many aliens living in the United States illegally". She didn't really write exactly that but that is what she meant. The Mexican consulate complained that we were "too harsh" in our inspection process.

Reducing the number of Mexicans living and illegally in the U.S. negatively affected the amount of American dollars being sent back to Mexico. It is an astounding amount. Some economists believe it to be in the area of $40 billion a year. Some of these same economists believe those dollars are the only thing keeping Mexico from erupting in revolution. That's $40 billion that's not being spent in the United States – but also potentially providing a relief valve for a worse illegal alien problem in the U.S. So, being the lap dogs of the Mexican government, INS again bowed to their wishes. It wouldn't be long before that accommodating "service" mentality would have disastrous consequences for our nation.

1046hrs. – Area Port Director Stemple sent out an email to all inspectors for immediate implementation: "District Director Roseanne Sonchik is abolishing the requirement that Mexican citizens have six months proof of residence and economic solvency. Only one month is sufficient. Nowhere does the INA or AM (administrative manual) require such proof." That was a lie. First she was only considering it in her email. Secondly the Immigration & Nationality Act (INA) regulation pertaining to issuance of permits states the common standard for being eligible for a permit IS proof of residence and economic solvency (employment) in their country. The District Director was using her position to allow more aliens to live and work illegally in the U.S. The de facto "open border" policy by the "No Border" Douglas clique of immigration officers sworn to uphold the Constitution and the laws within it was receiving some heavy duty support - and probably pressure from the Mexican consulate. I can't help thinking that if only the rest of America were aware of this they would be OUTRAGED!!!!

23 November 1999 - Inspector S***** told a Mexican male the person listed on the birth certificate he presented as proof of U.S. citizenship was supposed to be in prison and, if he was in fact that person, then he was going to prison himself. The man fell for the ruse and quickly admitted the birth certificate wasn't his and he was processed as a Documented False Claim to U.S. citizenship. The problem with birth certificates has already been discussed. Because there is no photo or fingerprint inspector instinct and interviewing expertise is critical to catching this type of illegal entry into the United States. S**** used a ruse to determine if the man presenting the certificate was actually the person on the birth certificate. And, again, it worked. The only difference between his ruse and mine? I was written up for doing exactly the same thing – and I'm not from Douglas.

It was getting cold in Arizona around this time so we were wearing our uniform jackets to work. When we weren't on the line we'd be in the secondary office issuing permits. Our jackets would be on the backs of our chairs. I grabbed what I thought was my jacket to go take the line. As I put it on I noticed it felt just a little snugger than normal. I thought maybe I was gaining weight. On the line I put my cold hands in my jacket pockets and felt something strange in the left pocket. I pulled out a small breath spray canister. The label read "Oral Sexual Stimulant. Just spray directly on the tongue to obtain arousal"! Well, I didn't know such things existed so it wasn't mine and I quickly realized I had grabbed the wrong jacket. Seconds later S***** meandered up to my inspection booth and told me I had his jacket. I asked him how he knew I had his jacket. None of us wore – nor were required to wear- name tags on our jackets and I figured like everyone else he hadn't written his name inside his jacket. I was going to have fun with this! He demanded I give it to him. Traffic was slow so inspectors on the other lanes had sauntered over to see what was up. I had already told them what I found and we were waiting to see who would claim it. I told S***** I would gladly give him his jacket if he could somehow describe how it was his and, since they all looked alike, maybe he could describe anything of his in the pockets? Unfortunately for him, that sexual arousal spray was the only thing in either pocket! S***** kept insisting I give him his jacket and I kept insisting he describe something to convince me it was his. I certainly wouldn't want to give someone else's jacket to him. He finally retreated back into the secondary office while we had a good laugh on the line. We all wondered why anyone would bring something like that to work? One inspector advised handling it with latex gloves because we didn't know what that crusty yellow stuff was stuck around the spray nozzle! Forty minutes later I got off the line and went back into the office – but kept the jacket on. S***** was getting pretty testy about getting his jacket back especially as I asked everyone in the office if the oral sexual stimulant spray was theirs. Right at the point he was getting really angry I gave it back to him. But he wouldn't answer our questions on why he brought it to work. He deserved the hard time I gave him. He claimed to have been a Navy corpsman assigned to the Marines in Vietnam. He called himself a "medic". A Marine _corpsman_ would never make that mistake.

S****** was in good company though. We inherited a Customs supervisor from Nogales Port of Entry nicknamed "Pistol" Pete. His brother, by all reports, was a well-respected, high ranker in the Customs service. "Pistol" Pete on the other hand was a different character. In law enforcement the one partner you didn't want was the one with a "heavy badge" syndrome. A "heavy badge" was almost as bad as someone who wouldn't back you up in a fight or a shootout. Everyone's encountered them on one side of the badge or other. They think because they wear the badge they ARE the law. This type usually gets you into a lot of unnecessary fights and trouble with the chief. Apparently there are those who sexually fantasize about wearing a uniform, badge and carrying a gun. I'm not saying "Pistol" Pete was one of these but he not only "accidently" fired a shotgun into the air while guarding a seized drug load but his duty sidearm went off while he was sitting on the toilet in the men's restroom at the Nogales Port of Entry. Just about every military veteran has heard the refrain "This is my weapon. This is my gun. This is for fighting. This is for fun." Pistol Pete took it to a whole new level.

It also took me a few years to catch on to the reason a few of the same inspectors were disappearing for hours on the midnight shift. I would sit on the pedestrian lane most of the night to back up whoever was manning vehicle lane 1. At our port of entry, INS had at one point 12 different work schedules. Each schedule was two weeks long. It takes the human body about thirty days to adjust to a new sleeping schedule. Changing schedules twelve times every two weeks takes a toll on a person physically and mentally. I figured they were off in a dark office catching a nap. They were watching porno movies. Guys watching porno movies isn't exactly new but the work place isn't the place to do it. In fact watching movies of any kind at work is inappropriate. This was prior to obtaining contracted security guards and illegal Mexicans were climbing the fence and running through the main office at all hours of the night. Young Mexican males were frequently trying to sneak up the south bound vehicle lane at night as well as through the drainage ditch next to the southbound lane. One alert inspector caught a Mexican stealing one of the inspector's cars out of our secured parking lot. And we never knew when a fight would break out with someone trying to enter illegally or smuggling drugs. So even if we weren't scheduled to be on the line every inspector should be there anyway when secondary slowed down. Besides, it was just plain unprofessional and we were getting paid a pretty good salary to be "border security". It seemed juvenile to me.

Speaking of juvenile sexual activity at work, early one evening shift I walked in the side door of secondary and saw inspector Del Rincon on a computer at the customer counter. It took me a second to realize that what he was showing the other male inspectors was an enlarged picture of a woman's vagina he had gotten off the internet. The whole monitor was filled with a woman's vagina – at the customer counter where people entered to request permits. Inspector Del Rincon was a very polished, intelligent local boy who had never left Douglas except for a stint at New Mexico Military Institute. During one of my first encounters with him he told me he had approached Port Director Wayne Morris and said "I want to be just like you." That reeked of kissing butt but other than that and the fact he didn't serve in the military because "my grandmother didn't want me to" he was a good inspector. I nicknamed him the "Perfumed Prince" after those described in Machiavelli's writings. Good family connections – big fish in a small pond. And an outstanding golfer.

I wrote a memo to supervisor Chavez about the stuff going on and the next thing I knew I was being blamed for the internet being cancelled. Port Director Stemple, instead of taking any disciplinary administrative action against Del Rincon, tried covering it up by cancelling access to the internet for everyone. I think this had more to do with a female inspector complaining to the Office of Equal Opportunity. Getting rid of the internet was the only way they couldn't track Del Rincon's activity – or so they thought.

Inspector C***** prepared a pie chart showing who had received training opportunities and special assignments. Del Rincon received 80% of them. Stemple had given these to Del Rincon without even announcing to the other inspectors that they were available.

10 December 1999 - I received an email from James Dayhoff, intelligence inspector from Nogales Port of Entry. He was thanking me for sending him copies of entry documents for some Algerians who had entered through our port. I sent him their documents because they could not explain why they were entering the United States through a little Podunk port of entry on the Mexican border rather than a major airline hub. Dayhoff complained that he has repeatedly asked management at Douglas to send him copies of Russian, eastern European, and all Middle Eastern travelers entering through Douglas. They never sent him anything. This was ten months before 9/11.

2 February 2000 - Wrote another letter to Office of the Inspector General Pedro White regarding another ethics violation by Stemple. Customs had found two illegals in the trunk of a vehicle. Stemple took the vehicle and the illegals and told K-9 inspector Edwards to put them back in the trunk and take a photo of them in the trunk. Stemple lied and took credit for the bust. K-9 officer Edwards was furious about this.

Stemple also started hiring "traffic" cops for the port of entry. Stemple had been a sergeant on the small Douglas police department –and was a protégé' of the municipal judge Ronald "Joe" "Borane" whose brother Ray Borane was the mayor. All seven vehicle lanes coming into the United States at the Douglas Port of Entry had to file into one single lane to exit the port alongside the secondary inspection area. This was done within about 50 feet from the inspection booths to the choke point. This had the additional benefit of allowing the officers in secondary to give each car another visual inspection prior to leaving the port. Despite the volume of traffic within an eight hour day shift, drivers were almost universally cooperative in getting through the one lane. Why this required an off-duty Douglas police officer (and buddy of Stemple) was beyond our understanding. We noticed it did give the police officers plenty of opportunity to flirt with the better looking Mexican females crossing the line – and that it irritated more than a few other male and female drivers because it slowed down traffic.

Someone I respected told me a long time ago that you can judge a man's character to a large degree by listening to how many times he says "I" in his conversation. It took me about twenty minutes of listening to Stemple the first time I met him to realize he was the ugliest megalomaniac I had ever met. Pocked marked face, bulging green eyes, plump cheeks, Liberace lips and sweating – he always seemed to me to be sweating and a little hyper.

3 February 2000, 0730hrs. - Subject and his brother were denied entry into Mexico by Mexican customs inspectors. Upon re-applying for admission into the United States, Senior Customs Inspector L***** found luggage in the trunk of their car. Suspecting the two of living illegally in the U.S. and possibly carrying contraband, she referred them to secondary. Customs inspectors conducted an intensive search of their vehicle. Upon arriving at work at 0755hrs I observed the two individuals standing in customs secondary. I asked immigration inspector Arvizu the status of both men. "The driver has one entry without inspection (EWI – jumping the line) - but that was before his laser visa was issued (another "Port policy" with no basis in law) so they are both "good to go," he said as he handed their documents to me. I escorted them to their vehicle as customs inspector completed his inspection and told him of their status. Customs Inspector R**** told me he thought they were living illegally in Phoenix because of the amount of luggage in their trunk. They repeated that they lived and worked in Mexico. Neither one had proof of residency or employment in Mexico so I asked to see their wallets. On their person I found a fake Resident Alien Card (I-551), a fake Social Security card and nine business and assorted cards with Phoenix and Las Vegas addresses. I asked how long they had lived illegally in the U.S. and they both confessed to having worked in Phoenix as mechanics for several years. Both men's entry documents were cancelled and they were deported to Mexico.

I got off work at 4pm and began the long trip back to Sierra Vista. I was in the middle of a divorce and wasn't looking forward to returning to the house. Management was continuously harassing me for basically "looking too hard". I had lost count of how many times I had been put under oath and threatened with termination or written up for contrived offenses. Highway 80 out of Douglas heads due west for a few miles before turning northwest towards Bisbee. I passed one car, then another. I saw a cement truck in the on-coming lane and still passed the car in front of me. They weren't going slow. I was going fast. I stayed in the on-coming lane looking at the approaching cement truck and just pressed the gas pedal more. I wasn't thinking anything specific except for wondering how quick it would be to get this pain over with – literally and figuratively. I wasn't the only inspector trying to enforce the law at the Douglas POE and being harassed by management for doing so. I wasn't the only one who felt pain in my chest exiting Bisbee Canyon and seeing

Douglas in the distance knowing what I was going to have to go through for the next eight hours.

I chickened out from ramming the oncoming cement truck just as the driver was jamming on his brakes and flipping me the bird. As soon as I returned to my lane an Arizona state trooper pulled me over. It was one of the officers who had visited the POE. He said he knew I had to have seen the truck approaching – "what's up?" he asked. I admitted I saw the truck and told him I just flat didn't give a damn. We talked awhile and, after being assured I wasn't going to try again, he took off. The Arizona Department of Public Safety officers were all good guys – as you'll probably find in every state. They would come to the port of entry occasionally to ensure drivers were buckling theirs kids in their car seats or check for warrants on some of our referred drivers in secondary. We got to know several of them there and backing them up on the highway.

On one occasion I was approaching the Douglas city limits when I saw a trooper pull onto the median. I realized I was speeding and immediately pulled over. "Do you realize how fast you were going?" he asked. "I not only do not know, I wasn't really even in the car! I was back in marriage counseling where I was paying a marriage councilor over a hundred dollars an hour just for her to tell my soon-to-be ex-wife exactly what I've been telling her for ten years!" I said. When he told me how insanely fast I was exceeding the speed limit I thrust both hands out the window and said "Take me to jail! I won't have to go to work at the POE and I won't have to go back to the house! Maybe I'll get some reading done in jail!" As he walked back to his car with my license and registration I thought "Great! This is going to cost a fortune *and* I'm still paying for useless marriage counseling." He returned and handed me my license, registration and the ticket – $40 for wasting natural resources! "Don't ever say the Arizona Department of Public Safety never did you favor!" he said. "Never have and never will!" I exclaimed. What could have been a visit to the jailhouse at worst or a very heavy fine at best was a forty dollar ticket for wasting gas. I can't say I kept my foot off the gas from then on. I was angry for a long time – working at the Douglas Port for another six years.

On another occasion I had just exited Bisbee Canyon on 80 heading south toward Douglas. I was later than usual so I wasn't in on the usual Grand Prix of other law enforcement drivers racing towards Douglas. Up ahead I saw a DPS patrol car with lights flashing on my side of the road. As I approached I saw the trooper in a good defensive stance a good distance from a large Hispanic man. The suspect began waving his arms in an aggravated manner. The difference in sizes between the two gave the advantage to the Hispanic driver. I looked in my rear view mirror and saw it was just us three on the long stretch of road. I figured it was better to back up the DPS officer and make sure the situation didn't get out of hand than be on time to work. I slowed down, turned around and pulled up behind the trooper. The suspect was bigger up close. I got out and approached the left side of the trooper. "You can say good bye to your mom and your son but *you are* coming with me," he said. Again the man started waving his arms and arguing. I asked the trooper if he wanted me to stick around. "Yeah, if you don't mind. This guy has a warrant and he's not really eager to go," he said. I freaked the trooper out when I turned around and walked back to my car. I should have put my gun belt on when I exited my car the *first* time! I returned to the trooper's side wearing my gun belt and he allowed the man to say goodbye to his son and mother under close watch by us so he couldn't retrieve anything from the car. To my surprise the trooper asked me to pat down the guy and cuff him. The state troopers had just recently been authorized the use of tasers so while I was cuffing the man, the trooper shined the red laser on the top of the car next to his head and asked "You know what this is don't you?" "Yeah, you won't have any trouble out of me." We were both relieved to hear that. His mom drove off without a word and he walked over and sat in the patrol car without incident. If he had chosen to he could have made it a lot more dangerous for both of us –much less the trooper alone.

That stretch of road had all kinds of weird things happening. During a day shift I was carpooling with another inspector while my car was in the shop. Going home one day I was wishing the driver would have the nerve to pass the slower cars instead of slowly tailgating them. When he finally did we saw a yellow, department of transportation maintenance truck off to our side up ahead with his yellow overhead light flashing. As we approached we saw the driver running like he'd seen a ghost out from in front of his truck and jump into the cab. Right behind him came the biggest bull I ever saw. He didn't catch the driver so he just stood in the middle of the highway. An approaching van skidded into our lane and down the shoulder striking the bulldozer blade of the DOT truck. The whole right side of the van was peeled off the vehicle. As we pulled over I could see toys and a diaper bag lying on the ground. I approached the passenger side of the truck keeping it between me and the bull. If it charged I wasn't sure a .40 caliber, fully jacketed, hollow point –or two -or three -or four- would do this job! This boy was gigantic! His shoulders were as high as my head (I'm right at six feet) and he was snorting fire! He had saliva drooling from his mouth and crazy wild eyes. He just stood there in the road while cars in both lanes swerved to screeching halts. Once all the traffic stopped he pawed the ground once or twice and nonchalantly trotted south on the shoulder of the highway. I walked over to the van dreading what I was probably going to see. Miraculously the van was empty except for the buckled-in driver and he had only scratched his knee! He and his wife had just bought the van a week or so ago. I recognized him from church. Now *that* was a *lot* of bull! (No, really. It actually happened!)

Getting off at midnight in Douglas one shift I had just driven around the bend in 80 from due west to north toward the canyon when I nearly ran into a cowboy on horseback in the middle of the road. I saw him in time to swerve and didn't hit his jittery horse. He had dropped his lariat in the middle of the road and the horse was doing a jig over it thinking it was a snake in the dark. I didn't know what he was doing in the middle of a state highway in a pitch black midnight until I related the incident to a Border Patrol agent I knew. The cowboy was earning some extra money working "nights" for the smugglers.

On almost that same stretch of highway a few years before, shortly after starting work at the POE, I was again the only car on the road. This time I was driving the family van – a 1990 Plymouth

Voyager Grand Voyager. Suddenly a Ford truck burst through the cattle fence on the opposite side of the road and skidded onto the highway right in front of me heading south toward Douglas. At the time I didn't know that was standard procedure for drug smugglers but I knew the three men in the cab of the truck were up to no good. I put the pedal to the metal in my trusty van and she rose to the challenge! That van had some really good acceleration! I got up on his tail to get his license plate number. After taking a swig of water from a gallon milk jug he spit it out his window splattering my windshield with water and spit – and speeded up. As we approached ninety miles per hour I called the port of entry and asked them to call DPS and/or the Border Patrol. We got up to ninety-seven miles per hour and my blue, 1990 Plymouth Grand Voyager LE with the wood paneling stayed right with that Ford truck As we approached the city limits of Douglas I saw several unmarked cars on the median. They executed a perfect rolling stop of the truck. We all exited our "unmarked" cars with weapons drawn. The three men inside weren't responding to orders to get out of the truck with their hands in the air. I approached the passenger side next to an agent and the three guys were pulled from the truck, proned out on the ground and cuffed. While they were being cuffed, one of the agents told a female Border Patrol agent who had arrived to search the truck. She said she didn't find anything. "Did you check under the hood?" I asked. When she did there it was – two bales of marijuana. I hurried on to work. The agents called the POE later that day and asked if I would write up the incident. In my report I lauded them for the professional and safe manner they executed a rolling stop and prevented a serious mishap during busy get-to-work Douglas traffic. The agents called back and asked me to delete that part because their policy prohibited them from doing rolling stops!

5 April 2000 <u>Sierra Vista Herald</u> "U.S., Mexican Forces Square Off" Nogales, Arizona (AP): "The plan was to repair metal grates in a transborder storm tunnel to prevent its use by illegal immigrants. But for a tense moment, U.S. and Mexican forces reportedly faced off at gunpoint. Mexican officials confirmed the confrontation but told a less harrowing story.

The faceoff occurred Tuesday after members of a special Nogales, AZ police unit entered the tunnel in advance of a city repair crew, Sgt. Eduardo Rosas said. As the officers – dressed in protective uniforms and armed with submachine guns – opened a heavy iron door, they heard noises and saw movement, Rosas said. "As we opened the door, we had our weapons drawn and all of a sudden we see weapons pointed at our faces anywhere from 1 foot to 5 feet away," said Rosas. "We were in a showdown and were yelling to these people (in Spanish) 'Police, put down your weapons," and they were telling us to put our weapons down." Rosas said the initial confrontation lasted 10 to 15 seconds. "A sneeze or someone dropping a weapon down there could have set it off. We were standing there with guns pointed at each other's heads. If there had been a shootout at that range, I don't think there would have been many of us left," he said. Rosas said some of the weapons used by the police officers are equipped with a light allowing the officers to see that the men across from them were wearing green fatigues. When they asked the men to identify themselves the men said they were members of the Mexican army. They told the officers that they were in the tunnel searching for illegal immigrants, and beyond them the officers could see about 30 people, including one woman, sitting down the against the wall of the tunnel.

Mexican Consul spokesman Roberto Burgos confirmed the incident, said the confrontation occurred on U.S. territory, and praised both groups. Colonel Arturo Martinez of the Nogales, Mexico garrison commander, acknowledged that his soldiers ran into police officers in the tunnels but said the meeting wasn't tense."

MY COMMENTS: The garrison commander is obviously lying. Mexican troops don't act without orders from their commander – and he was supplementing his income by hiring his soldiers out as "security" for the alien smugglers. The price for "about 30 illegals" would have been substantial. This is basically an invasion of U.S. soil by a foreign military.

2 May 2000 - Wrote another memorandum for record to supervisor Mexican Moses – as if it would do any good. Faustina Garcia was brought into secondary as an imposter referral. While conducting the interview for her expedited removal case I became convinced she was legally mentally incapable of undergoing a sworn statement. Probably due to the average level of education of most if not all of the Douglas immigration management, mental incompetence as a legal fact was a foreign concept to them. More of the "hog staring at the watch" syndrome. After informing supervisor Chavez that Garcia was mentally incapable of providing a sworn statement –and therefore probably not competent to consciously commit the felony (i.e. no case), he told me to stop questioning her. Ten minutes later he told me to continue questioning her and to complete the expedited removal. After a few more minutes of interviewing her I protested so he told me to stop questioning her again. Again ten minutes later he told me to again continue the sworn statement. Supervisor Chavez, unable to make a decision, was being given bad advice by both Mexican Moses and Stemple by phone. They weren't there and didn't see the shape this woman was in. A family member had probably given her a relative's birth certificate and told her to claim "U.S. Citizen" at the pedestrian lane in order to get her assisted living benefits (Social Security) in the United States. This was a time early in the Expedited Removal proceedings where port directors thought making a lot of cases would get them promoted. I eventually walked Garcia back to the line and released her into Mexico – without the birth certificate. Stemple told Chavez I should have "put more effort into interviewing her."

9 June 2000 - Memorandum for Record: I was escorting a Mexican male to secondary for suspicion of fraudulent documents and an outstanding warrant when he began to fight. I had to grab his shirt and wrestle him to the ground in vehicle lane one to subdue him. I gave him to one of the inspectors in the office and started walking back to the pedestrian lane. One of the line inspectors told me to look behind me. I saw the subject walking north on the pedestrian lane into the United States. Inspector Joe Acuna had released him before I walked twenty yards out of the office. When I confronted Acuna about releasing a suspect so quickly, Acuna said "He told me he just wanted to go back and get a suit case when you tackled him". Right. I've got a bridge in Brooklyn for sale too.

134

Guess I didn't conduct a check of the family tree first. Or maybe even that was too much for someone who was raised in Mexico as Acuna was.

14 October 2000 - A Customs inspector referred two subjects to INS secondary for a more intensive inspection. I interviewed the male driver and his girlfriend passenger. When the driver exited the vehicle he appeared to be under the influence of marijuana. He said he was a Mexican citizen. As his girlfriend exited the vehicle I noticed a bulge in her right front jeans pocket. When I asked what she had in her pocket she glared at her boyfriend. At first she removed just lipstick and a lighter. After insisting she remove the rest of it, she slowly took out what was later measured as 5.5 grams of marijuana. She later admitted she was holding it for her boyfriend. His border crossing card was cancelled, they were both cited by Douglas, P.D., and he was deported to Mexico.

15 October 2000 On primary, Inspector N****** asked a male, Mexican Border Crosser if he had proof of ownership for the vehicle. He didn't. Another red flag for possible smuggling. When the subject was referred to secondary, rather than waiting for instructions from one of several inspectors in secondary, he exited his vehicle, entered the immigration office and asked what the requirements were for obtaining a permit. I told him and he started to leave. When I noticed the referral slip in his clenched hand I told him to give it to me – and to let me look in his wallet. I found two business cards in his wallet: one for Eurofresh Company and the other for a labor contractor – both with Wilcox, Arizona addresses and phone numbers. He was also carrying a letter addressed to a man in Wilcox. He said he lived in Nacozari and worked at the copper mine there. The only proof he had of that was the mine's ID card. There were no other items in his wallet indicating he lived in Mexico. Most mine workers know what the requirements are for obtaining permits. I also knew the mine workers were currently on one of their frequent and prolonged strikes. They also know to stay in their vehicles when referred to secondary. I wanted to defer the man's inspection, have him return to Mexico to obtain paycheck and utility receipts but I was overruled by Ernestina Morris again.

135

23 October 2000 – RAVE, Willem Christaan entered the secondary office and told me the inspector on the line told him he needed to obtain a "green card". He presented his Netherlands passport and stated he was coming from Cancun. He said his flight from Cancun to the Netherlands was cancelled due to weather and that he had a flight out of Phoenix to the Netherlands. "OK. Why ride a bus all the way from the other side of Mexico for twelve hours or so when you could have caught the next flight when the weather cleared?" I thought to myself staring at him. "Do you have an airline ticket?" "No, but I do have a confirmation number." I asked to see his. His hands were trembling as he handed me his wallet. He apparently hadn't heard through the grapevine that Douglas had new inspectors. It looks tiny on a map so we're obviously hick inspectors who don't know nuthin'. After telling him to take his money out of his wallet I immediately found an Arizona ACCCHS (welfare) insurance card and an insurance card for his vehicle – which had been driven across the line by his girlfriend. "Do you have a vehicle registered in Arizona?" "Yes." "Why? If you are just going to Phoenix to fly to the Netherlands?" I asked. I knew the answer but I liked making the ones who think they are smarter than us squirm a little. No answer just more stuttering and trembling. "Where do you live?" "Mesa" he replied then caught himself and said "Netherlands".

In the interview room he admitted to having lived and worked illegally (while committing welfare fraud) in Phoenix for the last five years. He admitted to having used the Visa Waver Pilot Program (VWPP) ruse twice before when crossing the border. He had flown from Phoenix thirty days ago to the Netherlands and "vacationed" in Cancun before returning to resume residence and employment –(and welfare fraud) in Mesa. Apparently he was on the same internet web that told everyone the Douglas Port of Entry was the easiest to get through. Apparently he didn't get the latest memo.

I do know that there is some kind of communication through some media (newspapers, internet, etc.) between some inspectors and contacts to the south. One of the Douglas Clique inspectors made the mistake of mentioning within earshot how inspector Luna was praised in an Agua Prieta media forum for "being the inspector to go to if you want to enter the United States". I'm sure she wasn't the only one. Coincidently I heard from a source that "someone" had tapped our phone lines and heard a familiar female inspector telling someone across the line "Come right now or within the next 20 minutes while I'm on the line". She came into work one Halloween midnight and was very angry that the local Safeway had not allowed her to buy a grocery cart full of toilet paper. Her kids were well known to the local police.

Sunday, 19 November 2000 - Sierra Vista Herald article by K.G. Donahue: "INS apologizes for safety bulletin". Douglas- The head of the U.S. Immigration and Naturalization Service issued a public apology for last month's official safety bulletin to U.S. Border Patrol agents. "The INS apologizes for any misunderstanding this bulletin may have created," Doris Meissner declared in a statement issued in her last hours of office. The statement was read by David Aguilar, chief patrol agent of the Tucson sector, during groundbreaking ceremonies Friday morning for the agency's new facility here. Aguilar had criticized the bulletin Thursday, saying he did not believe there was a threat to agents or border crossers. The original bulletin issued in October, stated "anti-immigration hate crime organizations" were to meet here and their presence "may be a threat to illegal aliens and U.S. Border Patrol agents." The safety bulletin was issued by the INS Intelligence Analysis Branch in Washington, D.C..

Named in the memo were Cochise County Concerned Citizens, Ranch Rescue, Federation for American Immigration Reform, and several others.

The "known racial supremacy hate groups" mentioned in the briefing were to meet near here and help residents repair property allegedly caused by border crossers (*my note: that is incorrect. The ones causing the litter and damage are "ILLEGAL ALIENS"- "border crossers" have legal documents to enter the U.S.*). Aguilar said Friday that the agency "strongly discourages citizens from taking the law into their own hands." -

What wasn't reported by anyone in the media was the fact that when those groups conducted vigils on the border, the number of illegal alien crossings dropped approximately 60%.

December 2000 - Significant Event Award awarded to Mike Ligon in recognition of your life saving efforts in the month of October, 2000 at the Douglas Port of Entry presented by the Department of Justice, Immigration and Naturalization Service.

One of my best friends at the Douglas Port of Entry , who was raised in Mexico, was roving the line and approached me at vehicle inspection lane 5. We began sharing notes on the spotters across the line while I inspected incoming vehicles and occupants. During an interval between vehicles I was looking past C****'s shoulder as he was talking and saw a group of about ten people walking north on the pedestrian lane. They had already passed inspection inside the inspection area and were just casually proceeding on their way. Suddenly a man at the rear of the group collapsed onto the sidewalk. Five lanes of traffic were passing between me and the pedestrian lane but no one else noticed him fall. I ran past my buddy telling him to call 911. By the time I arrived at him he was slumped against the main office wall with no one around him. His chin was on his chest and he didn't appear to be breathing. Other inspectors were arriving as I checked his carotid artery for a pulse. Nothing. My buddy arrived then and knelt at my left. I pulled on the man's shirt to turn him so I could lay him down on the sidewalk. It took some effort to move him and his head bounced on the pavement when I laid him down. I tilted his head back to open his airway and smelled alcohol. I turned my head to see if his chest rose and feel any breath in my ear. Nothing. I felt again for a carotid pulse and, again, nothing as I looked at my buddy. "I don't see or feel any response." One smart- ass inspector standing in the crowd said "Oh, that's old so-and-so he's just passed out." I gave him a puff and started compressions. The man came to just as the paramedics were arriving. One or two of the local inspectors sarcastically remarked he was just a local drunk and had probably just passed out. The paramedics told our supervisor he was also an epileptic with a bad heart problem.

10 February 2001 - For a day that started out with a cartoon it certainly ended up being a very bad day. I thought I had become inured to the petty accusations and serious though flatulent efforts to get me fired by the Douglas clique until today. A day or two before, I arrived at work to find copies of a political cartoon showing the Dade County, Florida ballot. The ballot had an arrow pointing directly toward Bush's name but a twisted knot of arrows from the other candidates. There were about twenty copies of the cartoon strewn around the office. A Douglas Clique inspector walked up to me, pushed it in my face and asked "What do you think of THAT?" I wrote "Results of ESL!" (English as a Second Language) at the bottom of the cartoon. Immigration assistant Velasco and inspector Mora accused me of racism.

What was interesting was that, in a moment of civility, Velasco, me, and a few others had calmly discussed the problems with how ESL was being administered in local schools – and Velasco had agreed with me. But, of course, she claimed to be Italian – NOT Hispanic (that day).

So shortly after arriving at work today, supervisor Lopez, a 400-pound former Border Patrol agent, sat me down in an office, placed me under oath and read me my rights (Management Inquiry #01X00961). Lopez had either eaten his way out of a Border Patrol job or left for some other inexplicable reason and been promoted to immigration supervisor after filing an EO complaint of discrimination while at the Naco Port of Entry. I had carpooled with him a few times while he was giving a gay secretary a ride to work. We three lived in Sierra Vista and the gay secretary had his driver's license suspended for a year. Lopez appeared to be a good family man who doted on his daughters. He was not educated to any functional level. It was soon to be painfully clear how uneducated "JayLow" was. His father had been indicted for corruption with INS in Texas. His stated goal while at Douglas was to get transferred to Texas. He felt personally responsible for righting all the wrongs committed against Hispanics.

Supervisor Muncie, another willow-with-the-wind supervisor from Naco Port of Entry sat in on the "interview" as did our eunuch union representative S*****– who was as ill-informed of the union contract as Lopez was with the rules for conducting such an interview. For quite a while the position of union representative was considered a stepping stone to promotion to senior inspector – being coopted by management. Neither of them said a word during the interview.

Lopez began the interview by showing me the cartoon and asking if I had "done that". I said I hadn't. He asked me three times if I had "done that" and I said no each time. I told him I had seen it strewn around the office when I came to work and someone had thrust it in my face but I hadn't brought it to work. Lopez pointed at my ESL comment and asked if I had written that. Yes I had. "What did you mean by that?" I meant that ESL was failing to teach children English well enough to understand a simple ballot. Lopez told me some inspectors had been offended by my comment and that he too had been offended. I immediately asked him to recuse himself as being unable to impartially conduct the investigation. He refused – after I explained what "recuse" meant. I asked to have an attorney present as the investigation could result in disciplinary action to include removal from employment. He said an attorney wasn't allowed. This was refuted by our real union rep James Dayhoff in Nogales later. As Lopez asked questions he was typing his questions and my answers. He was having a painfully difficult time doing so. He told me to keep my answers to "three or four words." Seeing his difficulty typing I asked to have a competent, impartial transcriber record the statement. He refused. I asked to have the interview tape recorded. He refused. I was becoming very concerned my responses to his questions weren't going to be recorded in any accurate manner.

My objections that the life style questions he was asking were irrelevant – and illegal- were ignored by Lopez. "Do you live in Douglas? Do you socialize with anyone in Douglas? Do any of your kids go to school in Douglas? etc." Lopez failed to realize the irony that he did none of those either. But his most egregious question was "How many IG complaints have you filed against people working in Douglas?" not only violated Privacy Act and whistle blower protection laws (which protection I had sought and was ignored) but my right to file such complaints of perceived violations of law, policy, and ethics _without reprisal_. Its relevance to a political cartoon had long been discarded. I refused to answer. I was beginning to see he had been fed an agenda by Stemple and Mexican Moses Morris. Lopez was their mouth piece. This was confirmed when he reached down, placed a stack of personnel files on his desk and said, answering his own question, "ALL THESE!" After recovering from the shock that he, Stemple and Mexican Moses' ignorance or belief they could get away with asking such a question, I actually began to have fun with this feeble attempt at a kangaroo court. Lopez continued to exhibit both his ignorance and bitter bias by repeatedly going "off record" and making comments like "I guess in a perfect world we could get someone from the other side of the country," "In the seven years I worked at Calexico I never reported anyone for corruption, filed any complaints or had any filed against me!" and "OH! So MIKE can complain but NO ONE ELSE CAN?" and "Anglo-Saxons don't get treated like that!" (when being asked citizenship on the line).

When the interview was over Lopez handed me the printed Q & A and told me to sign it. I corrected so many spelling and grammatical errors it looked like someone had sneezed blood on the document. I refused to sign it.

I pointed out that this complaint was more appropriately within the venue of EEO and that the first required remedial action in such a complaint was for the complainants to confront the offender and state their objection to the offensive action. Try to resolve it at the lowest level. This was not done. It went immediately to a management inquiry at District.

Velasco and Mora vigorously solicited other inspectors sign the complaint against me portraying me as a racist. Not one did. In fact, just the opposite occurred:

"February 8, 2001, To Whom It May Concern: I have known Michael Ligon and worked with him at the Douglas, Arizona Port of Entry for almost three years. While we have had our differences of opinion at times, I have observed him to discharge his duties as an Immigration Inspector in a professional and objective manner, affording everyone his due respect regardless of race, color, religion, or ethnic background. I cannot think of a single individual who has not, at one time or another, made some remark or comment which could be construed as biased or racist; however, the comment or remark is taken in the context in which it is intended or delivered and hardly and eyebrow is raised. In my opinion, a charge of racism against Mike Ligon is without bases, and an investigation based on such charges is unwarranted. Respectfully, B.R. Martinez."

"February 06, 2001: To Whom It May Concern, I can attest that I personally have not heard Michael Ligon make racial statements against Hispanics or any other racial groups at work. If Michael Ligon did make a statement against ESL Classes I do not believe he did so in a racially biased way. I believe he may have done so in a political sense as he has had political discussions with other employees and done so in a none racial way. All employees at work make political statements. If some other employee such as myself had made the statement Mike made about ESL, I am sure nothing would have been said about it. In the past, anytime Mike had a misunderstanding with any employee I do not believe he did so along racial lines as he has dealt with Hispanic and Anglo fellow employees in the same manner. I believe this may be a personal dispute and not a racial dispute. Harry E. Bailey"

"February 22, 2001, To Whom It May Concern: I am pleased to write a character reference for Mr. Michael Ligon. I worked closely with him in my capacity as a fellow immigration inspector at the Douglas, Arizona Port of Entry. During my association with Mr. Ligon –for the past three years, I observed Mr. Ligon's work ethic as well as his interaction with co-workers and the public. His interaction with co-workers was open and authentic – never any surprises. His interaction with the public was forthright, but never intimidating or intrusive. I have always known Mr. Ligon to treat all individuals with respect regardless of race, religion, sex, or national origin. Mr. Ligon was extremely competent and enjoyable to work with, someone I always knew I could depend on. He always completed assigned tasks quickly and efficiently. His investigative skills were particularly noteworthy. Mr. Ligon and I also conversed privately on a variety of topics, to include Mexican history and culture and the plight of the illegal immigrant. I found him to be very well versed on the latter subjects and found his concern regarding border issues genuine. Mr. Ligon has my unqualified professional endorsement and my personal respect. I would without reservation work side by side with Mr. Ligon in the future. Sincerely, Lauri A. Sanchez"

"February 8, 2001, To Whom It May Concern: Mike Ligon and I have been Immigration Inspectors at the Douglas, Arizona Port of Entry together for over four years. All of us work in close proximity to one another for often extended periods of time. We, as others, have had our differences of opinion at various times but we always get over it and NEVER let it interfere with the performance of our jobs. When my wife and I were considering moving to Sierra Vista, Mike and his wife Susan showed us the house next door to theirs that was for sale. At times we have shared food – my wife has cooked extra and brought it to work for us when Mike didn't have anything to eat. I have never considered Mike to be racist by any means. Controversial subjects are discussed in the office – often started by Bonnie Velasco- but most employees are mature enough to participate in the "give and take" of the conversation and go on about our work. Mike has never made a racist comment in my presence. In fact, I understand his stepmother and stepbrother are Japanese. I know he has been in Special Forces in the Army – and I don't think a person would volunteer for such a job requiring travel to Africa and Latin America – as he has – if he were a racist. Respectfully, Alvaro Aros, Immigration Inspector"

"(undated) To Whom It May Concern: I give forth a letter of character reference on behalf of immigration inspector Mike Ligon. I believe my introduction to the above mention II Ligon is approaching four years ago. Since that time I have experienced an honest, friendly man of integrity. II Ligon and I are employed both at the Douglas Port of Entry, but by different agencies. There for protocol would dictate only small professional greetings when the course of our daily activities intersect. II Ligon behavior has been this, plus courteous, professional, friendly and interactive. II Ligon and I have conversed many times to share both information of both work related activities, and of past military experiences, family, financial and current worldly events. I believe the above stated is not the actions of a racial man. I have found our conversations and comments to be of the upmost honest, open-minded, and unbiased nature. I have never experienced any implications of racism. II Ligon also assisted me in my families residential move. Offering me personnel time and effort. I believe the above mentioned are not the actions of a racially biased man. I, Senior Inspector Arellano, being of Hispanic, and Native American decent [sic] have found II Ligon to be of upmost respectable character. Sincerely, Jesus G. Arellano"

It was, by far, no secret to anyone at the Port of Entry that management wanted me gone. For the last five years they had been trying to get me fired or make me quit. It is particularly amazing to me that, in view of the managerial bulls' eye I was in that fellow inspectors would step up and write such kind words for such a pariah as I was being made out to be. Some who told me they would write character references shrank from fear of management's wrath and didn't deliver. These inspectors stood up for me. I'll never forget it.

The charge of my being a racist was found without merit – again.

Immigration Assistant Velasco's racial sensitivity was very selective. One evening when I first arrived at the Port – and we were still "friends" (or more accurately she was still pretending to be my friend) - a distinguished looking, older Mexican gentleman entered secondary requesting a permit. While issuing him one I learned he was a widower. I got Velasco's attention and winked at her nodding toward him. She was a divorcee and I thought they would make a good couple. Immediately after he left the office, Herlinda "Bonnie" Velasco exclaimed *"Mike! I would NEVER date a MEXICAN!"*

When a cartoon comparing President Bush to Timothy McVeigh was distributed around the office no one complained. In fact it was copied and strewn around the office too. Not one supervisor inquired into who brought it work and no one was disciplined. While Clinton was president there was a Mao-sized photo of him prominently displayed in the staff and customer rooms. When Bush was elected he rated an 8" x 10" photo in a hallway.

If "JayLow's" investigation was the best the Douglas management could throw at me I was assured retirement......barring assassination...because I wasn't going to quit.

Maybe I should have.

15 February 2001 - Marcos S****** requested entry into the United States through the Douglas, Port of Entry driving a blue, 1990 Chevy Astro van. As he approached the inspection booth I recognized the vehicle and general description of the driver as that of a BOLO issued by supervisory Customs Inspector Austin earlier in the morning. S*** stated his US citizenship and was bringing nothing back from Mexico. When asked for ID, S**** said he left his driver's license and his wallet at home. When asked to turn off his engine he said he didn't have the ignition key for the vehicle. S***** eagerly volunteered that he was "bringing nothing illegal back from Mexico." His purpose in going to Mexico was "to just cruise". He said he neither gotten out of the car nor left it unattended while in Mexico and that everything in the car was his. I escorted S***** to Customs secondary where two large bundles of marijuana were found concealed in the rear passenger area of the vehicle.

22 March 2001 - I requested another management inquiry into immigration assistant Herlinda Velasco's interference with inspector's adjudication of permits. For the last four years, Velasco's meddling in inspectors responsibilities had created a hostile work environment. Inspectors M*, C****, A***, and M**** had also complained about her interfering with their inspections. The problem was the request went directly to Velasco's mentor and protector, Mexican Moses, who had now been promoted to Acting Area Port Director. I saw the paper work from District headquarters that denied Mexican Moses provisional appointment to Port Director. She had not passed any promotion exams. But of course those exams were "discriminatory" so those had been thrown out. So, miraculously, a woman who had started out as a secretary "serving" the Border Patrol after duty hours at the Port of Entry and had put in her time opening the floodgates to every Mexican who asked to enter the United States was promoted to Acting Area Port Director (the area included Naco). Her position was finally determined to be the Assistant Area Port Director - the number 2 position at the Port of Entry. It boggled our minds that someone who refused to enforce the law on a daily basis was able to rise to such a level. It gave a whole new perspective to the Peter Principle – except Ernestina Morris was not only incompetent but corrupt and grossly anti-American.

Ernestina Morris, "Mexican Moses", took very good care of those she used as snitches – snitching on the inspectors that were rebelling by trying to enforce the law. She also strenuously tried protecting a Hispanic female from being fired who had lied on her employment application. This inspector had previously worked at the local state prison. She failed to mention she was fired from that job –or given the option to resign- because she was under investigation for having sexual relations with prison inmates. However, because she could type and write a coherent sentence, Mexican Moses, adopted her into the main office and had her work directly for her. The two very capable office secretaries were offended by the preferential treatment given this inspector. It appeared to everyone that Mexican Moses lobbied enthusiastically to retain this inspector. Perhaps it's because they had so much in common. The inspector was eventually fired but she left with a nice cash bonus for doing such an "excellent" job for Mexican Moses.

23 March 2001 - We had an "SRI" inspector whose job was to process the vehicles we seized from smugglers or fraud cases. I never knew what the acronym "SRI" officially stood for (a guess would be "Seizure & Recovery Inspector?"). It appeared to mean "Sit, Relax In his office and do nothing". Although processing vehicle seizures was his main job, he rarely did it. INS – and subsequently CBP- had quit seizing vehicles used by smugglers for several years. We could almost hear them celebrating across the line - having just cut smugglers' operating costs in half. Evening and midnight shifts he never answered his phone and he basically got by doing literally nothing.. He was an inspector like us and could have helped during the flood of cases when we were doing 250-300 cases a month but instead he was invisible. Management finally forced him to come out of his office and work as an inspector. He was lost. He hadn't done any real work in so long that the expedited removal process was quite new to him. He had been a border patrol agent for a few years prior to getting the job as SRI. His Spanish was perfect. His English and tone of voice was exceptional – he should have been a disk jockey - but sense of opprobrium was atrocious. For example, as mentioned, I got two days on the bricks for telling Velasco to kiss my ass after she told me to go to hell. Our SRI had no qualms about his profanity in front of the public or subjects. He would loudly call our gay secretary a "turd burglar", Mennonites as "cross-breeders" and ask inspectors in front of their subjects "What does this asshole need?" Velasco went along. No days off for our SRI. No complaints by Velasco. His routinely brazen use of profanity without in-kind disciplinary action was a wonder to me. Rather than do actual work he would stand at the permit counter and tell –often racist and sacrilegious jokes. He had new jokes every day – to the point of distraction. He was an amicable, big, Minnesota guy who fondly remembered going hunting with his dad. He was very familiar with guns, pro-American, law enforcement minded - and a ROAD Scholar (Retired On Active Duty). He finally officially retired. I think he was so disgusted with the way things were being mismanaged he shut down – for several years.

Chapter 6. Appraisal

31 March 2001 - Performance Appraisal Record Rating Period April 1, 2000 to March 31 2001: The below is how immigration inspectors were evaluated prior to being combined with Customs into CBP. Pardon the grammar - I've transcribed this verbatim. The appraisal consisted of five Job Elements each containing four Parts. The Part IV ratings for each Job Element consisted of: "Outstanding", "Excellent", "Fully Successful", "Minimally Satisfactory", and "Unsatisfactory". Based on things so far, one would think my appraisals would be at the bottom of the septic tank. Part IIs in each Job Element were written by my immediate supervisor "JayLow" Lopez. Part IIIs are written by the Port Director Charlie Stemple.

Job Element 1: "Contributes to good public relations and agency teamwork."

Part I: Critical

Part II: Progress Review Record: Inspector Michael Ligon treats the traveling public and his fellow inspectors courteously. Inspector Ligon is a diligent individual who seeks to improve himself constantly. Inspector Ligon interviews a great deal of persons seeking permits to travel in the United States and in doing so he continues to hones [sic] in his proficiency of the Spanish language. Inspector Ligon constantly maintains a clean appearance.

Part III: Inspector Michael Ligon has had several complaints from the traveling public during this second half of his rating period. Inspector Ligon has had one oral counseling this year. Inspector Ligon has continued to maintain a tidy duty uniform. (interesting word "tidy"!)

Part IV: "Fully Successful" (the middle choice)

Job Element 2: Conducts Inspection [sic] of Applicants for Admission to the United States

Part I. CRITICAL

Part II. Progress Review: Inspector Michael Ligon makes timely independent decisions as to the admissibility or inadmissibility of individuals applying for entry into the United States. Inspector Ligon has been extremely successful in searching the contents of individuals. In doing so he has found counterfeit Immigration Documentation, which yielded two Expedited Removal Cases (are you kidding? In the last year? More like almost 200! Shows how little they either pay attention or give credit where it's due). Another case involved a person applying for a Visa Waiver. Inspector Ligon asking to search this person from the Netherlands contents, he discovered this person was residing and working in the United States for the past five years. Inspector Ligon conducts a great deal of Sworn Statements with no apparent errors.

Part III. Performance Achievements: Inspector Michael Ligon continues to make timely independent decisions as to the admissibility or inadmissibility of individuals applying for entry into the United States from Mexico. Inspector Ligon has had one improper seizure of a border crossing card from an applicant who's [sic] (I-586) Border Crossing Card had expired. Proper procedures were not used in the confiscation of the applicants Border Crossing Card. Inspector Ligon continues to conduct significant sworn statements in a rational amount of time. [It must drive Stemple crazy to write I "continue to make timely Independent decisions. He, Mexican Moses and the rest of INS management were doing everything in their power to prevent us from making "independent decisions regarding admissibility" . This was written proof that it was actually our job to do so! For example, the "improper procedures" I failed to follow in seizing an expired Border Crossing Card. The card was not only expired but I had written on the card the date he was told to renew it. They are usually given six months to do so. He hadn't so I seized it – without their "permission".

Part IV. "Outstanding"

Job Element 3: Performs Administrative Duties

Part I. NON-CRITICAL

Part II. Inspector Michael Ligon Performs his administrative duties (POMS Express) in a timely manner. His memorandums/reports are concise yet at times extraneous of his beliefs. Memorandums should address only facts and should be free of opinions. Inspector Ligon maintains his ccmail and or mailbox on a daily basis. (I was expressing my irritation at Douglas Clique inspectors giving Mexicans back their cards without ensuring they provided the demanded comprobantes)

Part III. Inspector Michael Ligon continues to perform his POMS Express duties and has been advised to update his POMS daily activities for the month of March 2001. Inspector Ligon maintains his ccmail and mailbox. Inspector Ligon reports and memorandums are submitted in a timely manner.

[POMS was a complicated time sheet that hardly anyone –any line officer- knew how to complete without the assistance of a supervisor. Supervisors received training on how to keep track of inspectors' hours when they went to supervisor school. We never got that training. POMS died a slow painful death and we were no longer required to keep track of our own hours]

Part IV. "EXCELLENT"

Job Element 4: Cross-Designation Responsibilities (Applies Customs & Agriculture laws)

Part I. CRITICAL

Part II. Inspector Michael Ligon uses regulations and policies when conducting his duties and or conducting cross-designated duties. Inspector Ligon has utilized IDENT and in doing so this resulted in a positive hit for prior deport. ("A" positive hit? I was getting "positive hits" on an almost-daily basis! ….and was continually harassed and overruled by management for using that information to cancel border crossers' cards for entering illegally).

Part III. Inspector Michael Ligon works well with other federal agencies at the port of entry and continues to use regulations and policies when conducting his cross-designated duties. Inspector Ligon has referred quality referrals to INS and Customs secondary for further processing.

Part IV. "Excellent"

150

Job Element 5:   Expedited Removal/Withdrawals

Part I. CRITICAL

Part II. Inspector Michael Ligon has referred eleven [really over 100 in the last year –not counting the ones management let in- but why quibble?] would-be applicants to INS secondary who presented fraudulent Immigration documentation to enter or reside in the United States. He has completed extensive I-213s, Sworn Statements, (I-867) and has had several withdrawals of applications (I-275's). Inspector Ligon when assigned to be a lead inspector has performed his duties Successfully [my shifts held the record for the most cases done in the least amount of time].

Part III. Inspector Michael Ligon continues to perform his duties in expedited removal cases efficiently. Inspector Ligon is highly proficient in all phases of the expedited removal process. Inspectors [sic] Ligon when tasked with the lead inspector position has performed admirably.

Part IV. "Outstanding"

Overall Performance Rating: "Excellent"

This annual performance appraisal for the period between 1 April 2000 to 31 March 2001 was the best I remember receiving – not what I deserved based on number of cases I made but better than the slam I received from Chavez. If an inspector got "outstanding" in four of the five categories, that inspector got a significant cash bonus. You can imagine who got those. Supervisor Lopez was illiterate and Port Director Stemple hated my guts. Only while writing it down now did I realize the only person capable of writing this kind of appraisal was –my nemesis- Ernestina Morris. She was a secretary when she first started out at the Port of Entry so she was the most literate in immigration management. She couldn't read the U.S. Supreme Court decisions I gave her regarding the use of ruses and we totally disagreed on whether to enforce the law. But from infrequent favorable comments she made to me about my work and her background as a secretary I believe she actually wrote this appraisal and gave me at least begrudging major credit where it was due.

Even though the appraisal period ended on 31 March 2001, "JayLow" Lopez didn't sign it and Port Director Stemple signed it June 1, 2000 when he meant 2001.

The fact I had been a shift/team lead during this period was also surprising considering how much management was trying to make me quit. I absolutely loved being a shift/team lead. When I had good inspectors and a good supervisor – usually a Customs one- we could operate like a pit crew in the Daytona 500. Instead of one inspector taking 3-5 hours to do one Expedited Removal case (this milking of overtime is done thousands of times a day throughout the country costing taxpayers a lot of money) I could task organize and get one done in about 45 minutes to an hour. This included covering the permit counter, secondary referrals and rotating out to the line. We took great pride in getting them all done before the shift was over without anyone having to stay late or dumping it on the next shift. My real reward was hearing the good inspectors tell me they enjoyed being on "my shift". They knew I'd back them up and jump in and work with them. Everybody cooperated and covered for each other. That's team work.

16 August 2001 - Emma L**** de R***** entered immigration secondary and requested a "6-Month" permit to travel to Los Angeles. She didn't present any proof of residence or employment so I looked in her purse. I found U.S. documentation that she had been living in L.A. illegally for the last year. She admitted to having done so during the subsequent interview. Acting Area Port Director "Mexican Moses" Morris told me I couldn't cancel her visa. MM was on a crusade of repeatedly telling inspectors we can't cancel visas of persons admitting to having lived illegally in the U.S. *if we couldn't get them to admit that they were requesting entry at this time with the intention of returning to live illegally in the United States*. Again, we were all astounded at her audacity to implement a personal policy in direct violation of Section 212(a)(9)(B)(i) and (ii) of the Immigration and Nationality Act (INA). Of course when we asked her to show us her policy in writing she would ignore us. It would take a real idiot to admit to an immigration inspector they were intending to live in the U.S. illegally while asking for admission into the USA. A lot of them may be dirt poor (or not) but they aren't stupid people. Neither are we inspectors. Mexican Moses was consciously, again, preventing us from enforcing the law. All of us line officers continually wondered how she could get away with all her "local" policies that seemed to always favor the illegal alien – never toward stricter enforcement of the law.

That was going to be forced upon her and all the other POE fiefdoms in less than a month.

Apparently "Mexican Moses" Morris wasn't the only one in INS management allowing everyone in. The following is a copy of an email sent by one of my fellow Douglas inspectors to a friend working the El Paso Port of Entry and his El Paso buddy's response (the names have been redacted to protect the truth tellers):

Subject: New Guy

Author: *name redacted* at WRO-PHO-DOU-001

Date: 08/07/2001 2:35PM

"*name redacted* (beer man) their (sic) is a new guy going down to El Paso if he ends up in your area take care of him. He didn't like it here and he is going over their (sic)."

The El Paso inspector's response to my friend's email was especially revealing:

Author: *name redacted* at SRO-ELP-BOA-001

Date: 08/16/2001 9:06 AM

Normal To: *name redacted* at WRO-PHO-DOU-001

Subject: Re: New Guy

"I'm currently working at the airport here and was unable to read my CC mail so what is the new guy's name, I be [sic] on the lookout for him. This places is really going to the dogs, *__they don't even allow us to check documents any more its just give the permit if the applicant has a BCC. He might not like it here either. This district cares more about the aliens then its own workers.__* But I guess it's a job....How's life in AZ."

September 11, 2001 - The reaction of the Douglas Clique to 9/11 seemed to be that it happened in another country – which, to them, it was. I opined on the evening shift that the federal government will implement their usual knee-jerk reaction by throwing money at "the problem" and form a new bureaucracy without making America one scintilla more secure. That's exactly what they did.

Charlie Stemple epitomized his ignorance and INS management's mentality by issuing a memo to all inspectors that no military leave would be authorized during the period of increased security. Stemple's ego convinced him he could usurp federal law regarding the activation of reserve soldiers. Of course they put more line officers on overtime and gave us shotguns. That really increased our national security. Oh! I forgot the national guard! They were activated and got more credit toward retirement while standing around clueless and getting in our way. That was money well spent. We were eventually issued small radiation meters that would pick up radiation from people who had recently been X-rayed five cars away but no nuclear weapons were ever detected coming through Douglas.

Stemple asked me to prepare a class of field expedient explosives so line officers would have an idea of what kind of common materials in combination could be made into explosives. I went through my house and garage and collected enough stuff to cover my kitchen counter. Just before I told Stemple I was ready to give the class, he approached me (sweating as usual) excited about "us" taking this class "on the road". I had no intention of going "on the road" with a man who had made my life miserable for five years so he could look good to higher ups. I had also considered who my audience was and didn't feel comfortable teaching sensitive Special

Forces explosive techniques to the Douglas Clique. I told Stemple I wasn't going to give the class – to anyone - ever. He didn't take that too well.

It reminded me of a visit a buddy of mine and I made to a used book store just outside Ft. Bragg off All-American Boulevard. The store owner was a large, former biker with a great full beard. He knew us and what we usually looked for when we came in. "Hi guys. Come on in. I have two copies of it left and I held it for you two" he said. The "Anarchist's Cookbook" had just come out and was hard to get. "One scary-looking young punk came in asking for the "ANTARCTIC Cookbook". I figured he'd be better off without it". We got a lot of laughs out of that one.

Things we could get off the internet in that subject were common before 9/11. My first step when Stemple asked me to give the class was to go back to some of those web sites. They were all gone. After trying to find the third or fourth website, a red banner filled my computer screen with the message "The websites you are trying to access have been shut down. The FBI will be notifying you and your employer ...." They never contacted me. If they had contacted Stemple he could have burned me big time by denying he asked me to give the class. He was too occupied with visions of glory.

Which reminds me of another of fantasy of Stemple's: He asked me and Del Rincon about the feasibility of buying an airplane fuselage to train Douglas immigration inspectors on how to take back a hijacked plane! Yeah! Like THAT was going to happen! If Stemple wasn't on crack I don't know <u>what</u> he was smoking! This was our Port Director!

15 October 2001 - Benito Rojas T****** was referred to secondary where I obtained an admission from him that he had been living and working illegally in Oregon and California for the last two months. His six-month permit was issued on May 6, 2001 so he was probably living and working there illegally since then. Ernestina Morris let him keep his DSP-150 Border Crossing Card and allowed

Benito to disappear into the U.S. to continue living and working illegally.

26 October 2001 -   1100hrs. I interviewed Luis Mario Mxxxx Rxxxx and his son, Sammy Mxxxx Gxxxxx who had been referred for a more intensive inspection in secondary. After finding Arizona driver's licenses on both, I obtained confessions first from the son, then the father independently that they had living and working illegally in Phoenix for over a year and the purpose of their entry today was to return to work and live illegally in Phoenix. Since I had been accused of lying by Douglas senior inspectors and management was accusing me of being a "trained intimidator" and coercing confessions, I asked both to write their admissions on pieces of paper.   When I showed the written admissions to Ernestina Morris she "deferred" their inspection by requiring them to return to Mexico – with their Border Crossing Cards. This allowed them to enter at a different Port of Entry or later through Douglas with a friendlier inspector. No amount of evidence was sufficient for the Mexican Moses to cancel a Mexican's document or impede their entry into the United States. After all, according to her and her clique, it was a Mexican's "right" to enter the United States – and apparently to live and work here illegally.

29 November 2001 -   I wrote another letter to Office of Internal Affairs in Washington, D.C. informing them that Area Port Director Stemple had given a Border Crossing Card back to a convicted drug dealer. I had been called out to the pedestrian lane to escort a suspect into the office. The referring inspector told me the man had been convicted of drug smuggling and presented his Border Crossing Card – which should have been cancelled. En route to the office I asked if he had ever been arrested (in spite of MM telling me I couldn't). He told me he had served six years in the New Mexico state prison for smuggling 10,000 pounds of marijuana. I asked how he got his card back. "Charlie Stemple gave it back to me" he replied. While I was running his name on the computer to verify the information, inspector Eddie Hurtado, Sr. came up behind me and said, "You don't need to worry about him. He's alright." I asked Hurtado how he knew that. Hurtado replied "I rented a house in

Douglas to him for several years." This Port of Entry just couldn't be more corrupt! I asked Hurtado how he rented a house in Douglas, AZ to a person who wasn't supposed to be living in the United States? He scurried out the side door of the office. When I informed supervisor "JayLow" Lopez about the situation, he said "Stranger things have happened at this port of entry."

The power went to Charlie Stemple's already sizeable head when he became Area Port Director. In addition to giving (at least) one convicted drug smuggler his Border Crossing Card back, he began issuing "X Application" I-94s to some questionable characters across the line. "X Application" I-94s are a paper entry document. The holder shows this form to the inspector on the line and allowed entry into the United States. It has no photo and no fingerprint showing the holder is that person. The "X Application" notation in the "Purpose of Visit" block on the form means the holder is a confidential informant – normally for Customs Special Agents. Customs inspectors who knew Charlie's history began running checks on those "X Applicants" who began crossing the border. They started coming up with information these applicants were being arrested elsewhere for drug smuggling. Stemple became aware of the cross-checking and, instead of ceasing the practice, threatened to fire anyone who questioned his authority on issuing the documents.

Douglas, Arizona Port of Entry: For Outstanding Shooting Performance Presents the Firearms Award 2001 To: Michael Ligon, Immigration Inspector, signed Paul Del Rincon, Senior Firearms Instructor Paul Del Rincon was the "Perfumed Prince" of the Port. He was born and raised in Douglas –by his grandmother- and was always perfectly groomed and articulate. I'm always suspicious of guys who are always perfectly groomed - particularly when they are too good to use the common bathroom with the rest of the inspectors. It was hard not to like Paul because he made it a point to be liked by you – very Clintonesque. One thing I did appreciate was he organized our firearms training and improved the quality of it to the point that, once I became aware of how poor the other agencies firearms training was, I was rather proud of. Our firearms qualification course was the most rigorous of the federal agencies. As I remember it, it required us to fire from the hip at three feet within three seconds, from five, ten and fifteen feet alternating hands while standing and kneeling and from twenty feet standing and kneeling at both sides of a barricade – all timed while changing magazines. It was good training at the academy and once Paul took over it was good training at the Port of Entry. He had us firing from all kinds of different positions we might find ourselves in. Paul married well and has beautiful children. He is a big fish in a very small pond. But he is smart and will be a port director someday. I hope he can overcome his propensity to let his high school chums get away with things they should be prosecuted for when they cross the border. Besides, by the time he's eligible, CBP will have begun removing locals from working at the POEs they were raised by ……….when pigs fly! And to top it off he's a 1 or 2 handicap golfer who missed qualifying for the Amateur Tour by one stroke.

But to get back to firearms qualification: Paul instituted a firearms award program to boost morale among the troops and he did just that – at least among those who cared about firearms training. In order to earn the award I believe one had to be one of the top three scorers on the course. This usually meant a score of 355 (or higher) out of 360 – excluding the firearms instructors. Paul is a very good shot and Ray Chavez, the old Vietnam vet, was a cold-blooded dead shot. He usually shot 359 or a perfect 360. The story goes that back in the day when inspectors weren't required to carry weapons on duty (hard to believe now) Moses Dominguez wasn't wearing one when an old geezer reached under a newspaper lying on the seat of his truck and pulled out a gun. Mo, a Customs inspector, took off at a fast trot as Ray Chavez, an immigration inspector who carried a revolver, fired a few rounds at the guy but didn't hit him.

Firing a weapon on the line was a dangerous course of action in several ways. As anyone who has driven through a Port of Entry knows, it's crowded with pedestrians and vehicles full of people. If a suspect was discovered smuggling and chose to shoot his way back to Mexico the potential for by-standers getting killed or wounded was almost assured. Luckily it rarely happened. The smugglers knew we wouldn't shoot them if they just ran because of that risk and, if they thought they were faster than us, would occasionally make a run for it.

I was walking a driver back to secondary because I was pretty sure he was "wrong" some way or the other. He fit the profile of a runner if he was caught – young, male and alone. He presented me an Arizona driver's license with a dark, smudged photo. His story for being in Mexico and for being in that car didn't measure up so I told him to stay next to me as I walked him in his car back to secondary. I started out next to his door – to keep him from bailing out on me. While scrutinizing his smudged driver's photo to ensure it was his, I suddenly realized I was walking next to his headlight. "Kerchunk" went his transmission and, as I turned back toward him, he was bolting out of his vehicle. I ran after him but he executed a perfect swan dive between the bars of a closed gate, did a perfect landing roll to his feet and was back across the line in a New York minute. I stepped half-on, half-off a curb around the inspection booth and twisted my left ankle while running after him. We had the car though and when the Customs inspectors opened the trunk the dope was there. Normally that would be it. Just process the drugs and close the case. For some reason, the Special Agent on duty filed an arrest warrant for the driver since I had his driver's license and had confirmed that the driver was the person on the license – the idiot used his real ID. Kudos to the special agent for going the "extra mile"!

About seven months later I received a letter from the Assistant U.S. Attorney's Office in Tucson informing me of my required presence at the trial of the idiot who ran from me! One of the pieces of direct evidence they required was the guy's actual driver's license. The only thing that made it to the AUSA's office was a Xeroxed copy – a barely discernible copy. Somehow the actual license disappeared after the acting port director, Jesus Jerez, reviewed the file. I had given it to him personally because he was standing in the primary traffic area as I returned to the line. When it was determined the license itself couldn't be retrieved the AUSA petitioned the federal judge to accept the copy. That was a close one. The whole case could have depended on having the actual license. Otherwise the defense attorney could claim his defendant wasn't the person I attempted to arrest – a case of mistaken identity. The judge accepted the copy.

The "idiot" had been apprehended during a traffic stop by the Border Patrol northeast of Phoenix. The BP agent had all the passengers on a Denver-bound bus off-load and when he told my idiot to go over and stand by the side of the bus the idiot went over to the side of the bus, faced it and put his hands on the bus! That's called an indicator. The agent went over and cuffed him –so the idiot wouldn't be disappointed- while he ran a records check and found the outstanding warrant from my drug bust.

There was only about 250lbs of marijuana in the guy's trunk when we confiscated his car. The reason I say there was "only" that much was because the Asst. US Attorney was putting out "prosecutable limits" on the amount of drugs her office would prosecute. I don't remember how much it was at that time but by the time I left CBP in 2006 the limit was 500lbs. That meant that in order for them to prosecute a drug case we had to have seized more than 500lbs of marijuana. Anything less was just seized, a file was created on the smuggler and he was released back into Mexico. It was a coin toss if Douglas immigration management cancelled the smuggler's Border Crossing Card or visa.

I asked the attorney assigned to the case why they were going to such lengths to prosecute a relatively small amount of drugs. In addition to me and the BP agent they had sent for a criminal lab specialist – a cute young lady – from San Diego to testify about the drugs. The attorney's response was "We're making a point with this guy." I interpreted this to mean he had prior involvement with their office and had gotten off easy. Then she showed me the file cabinets aligning one whole wall full of pending drug cases. One whole drawer was a pending drug case a buddy of mine at the POE had made over a year ago. The AUSA's office is so overwhelmed with drug cases it will never catch up without additional funding for additional attorneys. She went over the case with me and concluded saying "When he walks into court if you aren't totally sure it's him let me know immediately. We don't have time to pursue this if you aren't sure."

Well we all showed up at court on the appointed date and time and sat at the back of the courtroom waiting for the judge. The BP agent and I were shooting the breeze when the judge walks in and the court gets quiet. The judge looked exactly like James Earl Jones as the high priest in Swartznegger's movie "Conan" – only he has a white and pink camouflage-looking birthmark over his face so large it's hard to make out his features from the back of the court. This made him seem even more formidable than he already was! He sat down and stared directly at me then the BP agent. I whispered to the agent "He's sizing us up to see what kind of people we are." It was just a guess - but I wouldn't have liked to have been one of his kids caught in a lie! The thought made me grin and, luckily, the idiot was brought into the courtroom diverting the judge's attention from us. When the idiot looked at me I almost involuntarily said aloud "Oh! Yeah, that's him!" It could be heard at the front of the room by everyone including the judge. The idiot's shoulders' slumped when he heard me. His gig was up.

I was the first witness called. The defense attorney grilled me on how I could remember the defendant's face after processing several hundred people a day entering the United States for seven months after the incident. I told her I remembered his face every time my ankle hurt for five months. "No further questions, your honor!" Our attorney just told me to relate what happened. When I explained how he escaped diving through the gate, the judge said "A swan dive?" I described the gate in detail explaining that in order not to offend Mexican "sensibilities" management had left large gaps in each lane's gate to be more decorative than secure – and the subject had dived through one of the large gaps. "It was a 9.5 your honor!" He looked at me quizzically for a moment then grinned and said "Oh!" My idiot received 14 months in prison.

Things didn't usually go this far when we had runners. Mainly because the documents we were left holding weren't actually the subject's! Not having any way of identifying those who fled it was chalked up to experience - trying to be more in control of the situation and aware of the subject's demeanor the next time. Customs and immigration inspectors are real good about backing each other up when one is confronting a subject.

I was going out to a shuttle van in secondary one day with a relatively new rookie. He taught me something. I was observing him conduct an inspection on each passenger in the shuttle van. The first thing he did was take all of their documents. He mixed them up in his hand while looking at everyone's faces then tried matching the owner with the random document. I thought I was pretty good at identifying imposters – and I was- but he showed me a new way to do it. I like it when motivated rookies impress me. He asked one very short, older Mexican woman to step out of the van. I got closer as he is explaining to me his technique. Then we see the little mamacita starting to walk away! I look at her slowly shuffling away and ask the Rookie "Where is she going?" He replies "You don't think she's _leaving_ do you?" and we both laughed in disbelief – just as she starts running! A vision of one of Cinderella's mice running across the castle kitchen floor flashed through my mind. She was a little disoriented and had started running northwest toward the southbound pedestrian sidewalk. While the rookie was catching up to her by a direct route I had leaped over the southbound guardrail resulting in a not-so-coordinated roll on the ground. I added that knee scar to many others. She was caught by the rookie and deported as an imposter. A Customs inspector had jumped that guardrail chasing a suspect a few years before and ended up being medically retired for a trashed knee.

06 February 2002 Department of the Treasury, United States Customs Service, Douglas, Arizona "DOPE BUSTER" presented to Mike Ligon, Immigration Inspector, In recognition of your outstanding enforcement action and seizure of 53.29 pounds of marijuana on February 06, 2002. Signed James Y. Tong, Jr. Port Director, Douglas, Arizona.

The "poundage" wasn't a lot to brag about but I sincerely appreciated this certificate because it was presented by Jimmy Tong. At that time the Douglas Port of Entry had two port directors – one Customs and one immigration. I liked Jimmy the first time I saw him. As his name suggests he is of Chinese descent. I and my Okinawan step-brother had started taking martial arts on Okinawa when we were about 13 years old. I immediately recognized Jimmy's gait as a judoka or some other type of martial arts participant. This told me already he wasn't the typical government bureaucrat. As time went on I saw that he was quick to smile, explain and praise, slow to criticize and supported us troops working the line. Immigration management did none of those. I consistently received more back-up from almost everyone in Customs than I ever did from immigration management. He never knew it –we only talked face to face maybe once or twice - but I thought of Mr. Tong as my sensei.

15 February 2002 another "DOPE BUSTER" award for the seizure of 74.9 lbs. of marijuana. Again signed by James Tong.

28 February 2002 another "DOPE BUSTER" award for the seizure of 185.72 lbs. of marijuana. Again signed by Jimmy Tong. (starting to see a pattern here?) I was on a roll catching drugs for a while – until the spotters across the line figured out I knew what I was doing. That's not to say they didn't get any loads past me. No honest inspector will ever claim that. But it seemed to dry up for me for a while after these seizures.

Regarding martial arts this seems like a good time to include this almost totally irrelevant award:

"Department of the Army: This is to certify that the Secretary of the Army has awarded The Army Commendation Medal TO: Corporal Michael Richard Ligon, United States Army FOR meritorious achievement during the period of 2 November 1983 through 2 December 1983 while serving on a classified overseas mission. As the junior communications specialist on operational detachment A 572, Corporal Ligon was responsible for intensive training of a 100-man company in patrol bases, control measures, and crossing danger areas. As an instructor in hand-to-hand combat, Corporal Ligon's comprehensive knowledge and technical skill brought unstinting praise from both American and Allied officers. The initiative, sound judgment, and devotion to duty displayed by Corporal Ligon contributed immeasurable (sic) to the success and prestige enjoyed by this unit and reflects great credit upon himself, and the 5th Special Forces Group. Given under my hand in the City of Washington this 5th day of January, 1983 signed James A. Guest, Colonel, Infantry, Commanding and John O. Marsh, Jr. Secretary of the Army."

I appreciated the recognition of this award not because I thought I did anything special. I appreciated it because both men who signed it were decent, honorable men. And it reminded me of what a great team I was on. And of what a great organization the 5th Special Forces Group is. That Mobile Training Team (MTT) trip was the most enjoyable of several during the most enjoyable time of my military life. I'm still telling students about that trip. Yet I've often wondered since how I could be a good soldier and officer then – and such a dirtbag immigration inspector now. It has been said that you may know a man by his enemies and by what's in his library I was proud of both my enemies and my library.

13 March 2002 - MEMORANDUM FOR: Port Director James Tong (Customs)

FROM: SI Steven Phillips

SUBJECT: Imposter with I-94

".....at approximately 2020hrs. a Toyota pickup was referred for a Customs secondary inspection. The vehicle was occupied by a driver and a passenger. The passenger presented a Mexican driver's license and a temporary immigration document that said "Public Interest" in the upper right hand corner. The document also had the initials "CAS". I recognized that an individual with this type of document would be a Confidential Informant. And to add to this, I recognized that the initials were those of immigration Port Director

Charles Stemple. The document had the name, S****-B****, Enrique, DOB: ******.

After asking subject a series of questions, biographical and questions concerning the I-94 and where it was obtained. SCI Harnett was called to secondary and informed of the situation. Customs inspectors felt that the subject was an imposter and that INS inspectors and immigration supervisor Lopez did not want to deal with the situation because the individual was an informant and the I-94 had immigration Port Director's Charles Stemple initials on it. This is an important fact, because approximately three weeks ago, during a joint shift briefing, Immigration PD Stemple threatened each Immigration Inspector and Customs Inspector. Stemple said that if any Inspector questioned a Confidential Informant that either OIG or IA would be called and that Inspector would have to face an investigation.

SI Phillips and SCI Harnett then called the subject into the building and began to question his entry document. The subjectd finally confessed that the document did not belong to him and that he was not born in Agua Prieta. SCI Harnett then turned the subject and all information back over to INS for further processing."

I was in the immigration secondary office when Harnett brought the subject and his document in and gave it to "J-Low" Lopez. I further identified that even the Mexican driver's license was fake. I don't remember what Lopez did with the case. He was very enforcement-minded when he first arrived but was soon co-opted by the Douglas "Pasale" management. The significant thing about this incident was Stemple's terrorizing inspectors to avoid scrutiny of whatever under-the-table operation he was running – an operation in which all of his "Confidential Informants" were usually caught smuggling drugs or committing other illegal acts.

Running "CIs" was not an activity available to just anyone. Having people inform on drug smugglers on the border was risky business for the informant. To avoid exactly the type of "unofficial" informant activity Stemple was running INS had specific procedures in place before anyone could run an informant. Stemple assumed because he was the Port Director he could arbitrarily recruit informants without official blessing by higher. He was wrong. Not that he cared or would have sought approval considering what appeared to be his real agenda for doing so. Remember the mayor's son I approached as a potential informant? Wayne Morris, the Port Director at the time, had to notify District for approval to do so.

Since half the immigration staff were born and raised in Douglas – and Mexico, it was natural to have family and friends across the border. It was also natural that these contacts would provide information to their friends and family working at the POE regarding observed drug activity and identify smugglers – just as it was natural to ask for "favors" on getting admitted into the United States. This was risky for the informers because they had no way of knowing if the inspector they were reporting to wasn't bought by the drug smugglers.

There was a Customs inspector who was "getting a little on the side" with a Mexican female across the line. She was his informant. He was "taking care of her and vice versa" - until she was killed. He conveniently transferred to California.

I thought it was tragically funny the first time a Mexican approached the pedestrian lane and asked to speak with a Special Agent. He had to wait there in plain view of both the public and the spotters across the line until a SA arrived who then took him into the immigration main office. The informant would also leave by the same door from the main office back into the pedestrian lane – usually with an I-94 "Public Interest" clutched in plain view in his hand. Everyone on both sides of the border knew what a "Public Interest" I-94 meant so having one either meant having a "Kill Me" card or it was a way to play the system against the agents. Take your pick which it was. In my opinion, the "CI" program run by immigration staff at Douglas, including Stemple, was just an extension of the abuse of their authority to circumvent the law – at best. At worst money was being made.

During one of the anthrax mail scares, Stemple and Customs Port Director Molaski told us in a staff meeting to not have our personal mail delivered to the Port of Entry. I thought anyone would be crazy to do so but I guess it was the same as on an SF team in the army – there were married inspectors getting mail from paramours sent to their work addresses. Both Stemple and Molaski told us if personal mail were received at the POE it was going to be opened by them. I responded by stating the obvious – opening personal mail not yours was a violation of federal law. Stemple reacted as expected. His bulbous eyes bulged even more and he asserted his right to, not only open our personal mail, but to stamp it "Return to Sender". After the meeting our union rep told me Stemple had already told his secretary to open inspectors' mail. She rightly objected to this.

Stemple's and Molaski's ignorance shone brightly in their claim to open mail. I wish they both personally _had_ opened anthrax letters – and taken _deep, deep_ breaths!

23 May 2002 - At approximately 2040hrs Jorge Alonso V****** - C**** entered vehicle lane 3 driving a 1992 Ford Aerostar (AZ ZVW ***). Due to behavioral anomalies I referred him to Customs secondary for a more intensive inspection. Customs inspector V***** discovered 52.3 pounds of marijuana secreted in the gas tank of his vehicle. When I refer people and vehicles from the line to secondary I can assume Customs will give it a good looking over. With immigration it depends on who is working back there and who the supervisor is as to whether the drug smuggler's entry documents are cancelled.

29 May 2002 – Inspector ***** referred Francisco Ernesto N*****- C*****, a Mexican citizen, to secondary for an IDENT check. IDENT was an automated system finally installed at all the Ports of Entry that enable us to take a photo of their face and a right index fingerprint to match with the National Crime Information Center (NCIC) and the immigration (border patrol) data bases for prior arrests, convictions and warrants. When IDENT was first installed, over 40,000 criminally deported aliens were apprehended trying to re-enter the U.S. in just the first year. During Vice President Gore's program to grant citizenship to 500,000 aliens prior to the 2000 elections INS management was telling adjudicators not to bother with the "routine" process of an interview in English and a criminal check. After the election over 65,000 aliens who were granted U.S. citizenship had their citizenship revoked for having prior criminal records. The efforts to subvert the electoral process by the Democrats continues to this day. It's called "swarming" and is discussed on the website "DiscovertheNets.org". Senator "B-1" Bob Dornan, of Orange County, California was voted out of office by illegal aliens voting in the '80s. The FBI – or whoever investigated it- quit counting fraudulent votes after the tally reached over 150,000.

Cebreros admitted he had been caught by the Border Patrol as an EWI (Entry Without Inspection – jumping the line) six months ago. When I informed senior inspector Acuna, shift leader that day, of the impending Border Crossing Card cancellation Acuna said "Not necessarily. Do you know how many Border Crossers jump the line?" Acuna was telling me that because a lot of border crossers jump the line illegally – and are probably coyotes smuggling either people or drugs across – we don't cancel their entry documents. That was in contradiction to the law – and he knew it. So Acuna went to discuss it with Mexican Moses. He returned and said "We don't _want_ to cancel someone's visa without _proof_!" I had heard those exact words out of "MM's" mouth multiple times. I said _there was no more direct proof than a freely given admission and the IDENT hit_. Acuna said "I mean _other than that_!" I told Acuna to do what he was going to do – and I was going to do what I was required to do. He asked what I meant by that but I declined to elaborate. Acuna went to tell Mexican Moses of what I had said. When he returned he told me Cebreros was a TECS hit with five EWIs – and we were cancelling his card. If I hadn't inferred I was going outside channels Cebreros would have been "down the road" into the U.S. . Acuna said exactly what he meant – and, in doing so, articulated the philosophy of the Douglas clique: "We don't _want_ to enforce the law. It's the Mexicans _RIGHT_ to come into the United States." I was reduced to having to threaten to go to higher in order to do my job.

The trouble with Joe Acuna started when I took a rookie inspector out from the immigration office to check out a suspect's car. The referring rookie immigration inspector had spent some time in the interrogation room with the suspect but came out with nothing. "I know something's wrong with this guy but I can't put my finger on it" he said. I was sitting at the permit counter with Lauri Sanchez and said "If it's not him it's the car" and took her out to the car. As we're leaving the office Bonnie "the Italian" Velasco and Joe Acuna repeatedly said "Why are you harassing that man? It's Inspector ****** who's wrong!" Joe Acuna followed us to the car and continued telling us nothing was wrong with the suspect's car. Sanchez took the driver's side and I took the passenger side as I began to explain how to conduct a methodical car search. With Acuna standing at the right front headlight I told Sanchez "When one inspector tells you another inspector's instincts are wrong and to not bother looking you should have a red light go off in your head about that inspector". I had cleared the inside of my side of car and told Sanchez I was going into the office to get the keys to the trunk. En route to the office I asked a Customs K-9 officer to run the car. When I came out of the office with the keys, Customs officers had handcuffed the driver and were escorting to the holding cell. K-9 had alerted to the marijuana concealed in the rear quarter panels of the vehicle. Sanchez was approaching the office and confirmed the find. Joe Acuna was standing just outside the door and almost literally tap dancing. "The Italian" Velasco was stuttering inside. Sanchez and I went inside to tell the Rookie his instincts were right on. When I turned to look through the plate glass window to secondary, Acuna was talking to supervisor Choate. I walked outside to involve myself in this interesting conversation. My mouth dropped when Choate told me "Well, Mike, we need to keep this between ourselves". "You two do whatever. I'm going to do what I have to do." I said – and walked back into the office. As I entered two contractors working on the ceiling (where one of the Customs inspectors had fired a round into it) came through and asked if we had a copy machine. The only one we had at that time was in the main office across the street. I told them to follow me and proceeded out the side door. I happened to come up behind Choate and Acuna heading the same way. I heard Choate say "Ligon's been a pain in the ass since he got here. He needs to keep his mouth shut about this." To which Acuna agreed. "So! I have to keep MY mouth shut do I?" I asked. They almost jumped out of their skins but continued on without saying anything else.

I had the next two days off. When I came back to work I attended another one of those useless "mini-musters" during the first thirty minutes of each shift (I believe the real reason for them was to get overtime for the departing shift). During the meeting mention was made of a drug bust made in front of one of the vehicle inspection lanes. A Mexican man had driven just across the red line where our jurisdiction began, put the car in park, got out and walked back into Mexico. Joe Acuna walked up, drove the vehicle to his inspection booth and "found" the drugs. A Customs inspector saw the bundles of marijuana lying on the floor in the back seat, in the open in the trunk, and on top of the engine. "It looked like they didn't even try to hide it" he said. It was Joe Acuna's lane. In espionage that's called trying to re-establish your bona-fides with those you're trying to deceive. You need to know someone in the drug business in Agua Prieta to set that up.

I sent a memorandum for record up to District about Acuna's interference with the inspection – the whole thing. About a week or two later, Port Director Charlie Stemple walked out onto the vehicle primary inspection lanes to tell Joe Acuna loudly enough for me to hear "Don't worry about Ligon's complaint. You'll only get a letter of reprimand".

This reminded me of another incident that occurred shortly after I started working at Douglas. I had obtained an admission of living and working illegally in the U.S. from a Mexican man in his late twenties or early thirties. He was the son of the former mayor of Agua Prieta just across the line. Since he was facing deportation for at least a year, he was intelligent, articulate and well-placed, I thought he might make a good confidential informant. I left the interrogation room and crossed the street to bounce this off the Port Director, Wayne Morris. He thought it had potential but he had to bounce it off District in Phoenix. While he called them he told me to go back and get more information from him. When I got back to the office the door was closed and locked. I could see Joe Acuna through the window talking to my suspect. I started rattling the door knob until Acuna opened the door. "What's going on?" I asked as I pushed past the departing Acuna. "Nothing" Acuna said and walked away. My potential CI - who had been warm to the idea of getting his Border Crossing Card back in exchange for information on alien and drug smuggling in AP. He wouldn't even open his mouth to talk to me. We cancelled his Border Crossing Card and walked him back to Mexico.

A few days later I was on the line and a guy who told me he worked for "various agencies" in his time came through my lane. I asked if he knew so-and-so - the former mayor's son. "Oh sure! Everybody knows him! I heard you cancelled his card! Well, he's back working in Tucson. One of your inspectors let him through his lane – the one that's played handball with him for years" he said. It was Joe Acuna.

24 June 2002, 0220hrs. - I referred a Ford truck to secondary for a more intensive inspection. The driver, Victor Hugo O*****-M******, a Permanent Resident Alien was found to have approximately an ounce of cocaine in his truck. He subsequently admitted to me that he was a regular cocaine user – the most recent being three hours ago. I also found cocaine in his pocket. Customs tested the material and found it positive for cocaine but refused prosecution. Immigration District Headquarters had issued directions requiring us to hold onto persons found with narcotics whether Customs prosecuted or not to see if we could take immigration action against the subjects. Our shift leader informed Ernestina Morris of the discovered cocaine and subject's admission of routine drug use – grounds for deportation of a Resident Alien. Instead, "Mexican Moses" Morris told us we could not serve Mendoza with a Notice To Appear (NTA) before an immigration judge for a hearing on deportation because *we had no evidence*! Title 8 of the Code of Federal Regulations states *any* drug use is grounds for deportation. Our Acting Area Port Director was prohibiting us from enforcing Sections 212(a)(1(A)((iv) and

171

212(a)(2)(i)(II) of the INA. She let the Resident Alien drug addict enter the United States.

24 June 2002 (same day as above) - **Inspector Malfeasance/False Official Statement - 0435hrs.:** I emailed the INS District Director regarding an incident on 10 June. I had just returned to the secondary office from the line and was told to conduct an I-867 Sworn Statement from a Mexican man for requesting entry after deportation. During the interview he told me he was not requesting entry. He came into the office to inquire about the possibility of obtaining amnesty for his previous deportation. He showed me the Form I-94 he had been given by senior inspector Luna. He had written "ask about amnesty – Form 212" for purpose of visit. Only those who have been deported know of that form. It is their only chance of overcoming a mistake and being able to enter the United States again. He was trying to obtain amnesty through the legal process so he could return to his family in Phoenix who were all U.S. citizens. Luna had made a major leap to an incorrect conclusion as to the man's purpose for entering the office and had told me to prepare an expedited removal case on the man for something he wasn't doing. I told supervisor Chavez who went to tell Mexican Moses. Instead of giving the man the appropriate assistance he asked for regarding his completion of the amnesty form, MM told Luna to conduct another interview instead of me! I was taken off the case and Luna conducted another case behind closed and locked doors. Inspector A**** had been at the counter and witnessed Luna jumping to the wrong conclusion. Luna may have wanted to make a case or two after I complained about her never being in the office to help with cases. When Arvizu saw Luna conducting the case "in camera" he said "Now she's _badgering_ him into a confession!"

I am a very law enforcement-minded person and I will do everything within legal procedures to catch illegals from entering the United States – drug smugglers, alien smugglers, child smugglers, oral and documented false claims to U.S. citizenship, - the whole gamut. I take the security of the United States personally. But I won't burn a person who has paid for his mistake and is trying to

172

abide by the rules to be reunited with his family. I'm pretty good at lie detecting and this guy was legit. Plus he had the documentary proof. Mexican Moses was assisting Luna (Victoria Secret party pals) in covering up her error. This man was going to be permanently banned from the U.S. because Luna was going to cover up her mistake with a fraudulent case. The cover up didn't stop there. About two weeks later......

@ **14 July 2002** – .... Special Agent Oberly read me my rights and told me I was being investigated for "going outside the bounds of a normal interview" in the Mendoza case. He looked a little sheepish after I told him what had really happened regarding Morris and Luna covering up Luna's error. I asked if there were any procedures for false accusations by management – or covering up for an inspector's fraud. The Acting Area Port Director Ernestina Morris, the Mexican Moses, was trying to protect her Victoria Secret buddy's outright perjury for submitting a signed sworn statement in a federal prosecution case she knew to be false. And the vindictiveness didn't stop there either. ***The very next day***........

@**15 July 2002** - ......Special Agent Oberly returned and again read me my rights in order to conduct another management inquiry – two within two days. This time I was being charged by Douglas INS management, Stemple, Morris, Glass and Luna for "use of derogatory and/or abusive comments in the work place towards fellow workers" on April 29, 2002. Those people calling for a management inquiry into that kind of charge is not only the ultimate in hypocrisy but the immigration version of issuing a speeding ticket at the Indianapolis Speedway.

I knew I had hit a nerve by how much heat they were trying to bring down on me. The District Directors, Donna De La Torre or Roseanne Sonchik, didn't care enough to come down and get to the bottom of what several of us inspectors were complaining about. They were just political hacks who were trying to collect their paycheck and retire. It was easier to go along with the specious and false accusations by the Douglas clique against me and others than reprimand, transfer or fire them despite the volumes of complaints by many inspectors - against Morris particularly.....especially when none of our rebuttals seemed to make it to District at all. Either one of the District Directors could have solved most of the problem by transferring Ernestina Morris – the Mexican Moses. By virtue of succeeding Stemple as Acting Area Port Director, she was the successor ringleader of the corrupt Douglas clique. She and Stemple were of the same rotten bolt of cloth. Morris was management and therefore not "protected" by the union. She could have been transferred anywhere at any time for "the needs of the Service". She wasn't transferred because she knew where all the skeletons were buried. For example, an inspector who had been there a lot longer than I showed me a picture of District Director Donna De La Torre drinking a beer in a booth at a bar with several of the Douglas clique. So there were some social ties there. This is exactly the type of corruption the Border Patrol tries to avoid by not letting agents work in the same locations they grew up in.

In this incident District Director Sonchik ordered a management inquiry regarding my alleged criticisms of Luna. I fully admitted making critical comments about senior inspector Luna. I made them during a closed-door discussion with our supervisor that night – Ann Glass. She had come aboard the Douglas Port of Entry from Seattle where she had been an adjudicator of citizenship applications. She was the one who told us of Vice President Gore's push to grant citizenship to so many without proper vetting. Glass, like most of the immigration women at the POE, was a Lilliputian-sized supervisor who was trying very hard to be liked by the DC (Douglas Clique).

She was a strange person in many ways. She brought several books to work dealing with magic potions and spells. She wore a ring on her finger that, according to her, was capable of carrying poison. She wore the worst wigs any of us had ever seen. She also had a drinking problem as well as a problem keeping information discussed during rater/employee consultations confidential. This was not only an expected professional characteristic it was required under Article 41B of the Union Agreement.

Supervisor Glass and I were discussing behind closed doors in her office an incident I had been involved in with senior inspector Luna. It was during the period we were processing 250-300 Expedited Removal cases a month. Luna was our shift leader one evening but, again, was disappearing into the offices across the street to schmooze with her favorite Customs married playboy or stroking the stomach of a grossly obese, married immigration supervisor while smiling demurely and pressing her body against his in an empty hallway. That's how she kept her job: flirting with the males at work and inviting various key individuals to her Victoria Secret parties. She certainly didn't rise "meteorically" to senior inspector by her intellect and dedication to duty. I was complaining of just such of Luna's behavior to Supervisor Glass in hopes of Glass taking whatever action required getting Luna to actually work with –much less actually lead – the shift team while we were so busy and short-handed.

I also told Glass of an incident in which Luna and I were sitting at the permit counter and she provocatively bumped me with her hip. When I didn't respond with the expected interest, she blurted out in the middle of a discussion between other inspectors and me that I had been trying to get in her bed for years. That was a damn lie and I told Glass so. I believe it embarrassed Luna when I responded "that's wishful thinking on _your_ part - and that will never happen!" I told Glass during our discussion that I had become aware of Luna's "Black Widow" enticings years ago and had no intention of getting snared in her web. I warned Glass to not get drawn into Luna's offers of friendship and how I had heard her and Herlinda "Bonnie the Italian " Velasco conspiring to "get to know them so we can get the 'goods' on them and use it against them later." I also told Glass I was considering filing a sexual harassment complaint against Luna for stating such a lie. She was defaming my integrity to my wife and family. The reason the other inspectors laughed was because they knew it was so untrue – both because I was faithful to my wife (I had never socialized with anyone outside of work) and Luna's character spoke for itself.

When I pointed all this out to Special Agent Oberly, he just sighed. He tape recorded it and said I would hear the result of the management inquiry in a month or so. I never did.

Two management inquiries in two days. Two days in a row I was read my rights and threatened with loss of employment based on groundless, specious charges. By this time other inspectors were telling me management was just trying to make me quit because I wasn't "one of them." Duh! The honest Douglas native Custom and Immigration inspectors –and there were a few- told me management was trying to make all of us who weren't "going along with the program" quit.

9 September 2002 - Rosa Emma G*****-R**** entered the INS secondary office and requested an I-94 permit. She appeared to be a poor, humble woman much worried about the health of her daughter. She had no comprobantes later than July '02. She said she was coming from her small pueblo in Mexico after raising money to pay for her daughter's surgery scheduled to the next morning. Her daughter had epilepsy and was on oxygen in a Phoenix hospital as we spoke. She told us the doctors were going to take her daughter off oxygen and conduct delicate brain surgery in the morning to try to cure the epilepsy. I asked how much money she had raised in her pueblo. She said she managed to raise about $300. I asked her if she was receiving any "public benefit" from the State of Arizona. She said she wasn't – that was why she made the trip home. She told me her husband was in Phoenix with their daughter. This was a difficult call. If you ask anyone at the Douglas Port of Entry I'm sure you'll get pretty much a unanimous "fair but hard" response to what kind of inspector I am - at least from the honest inspectors. If it weren't for her daughter's medical problem and the pious demeanor of the mother I would have had no problem denying her a permit. She showed me a letter from a doctor verifying the surgery in the morning. I called the hospital and they confirmed it. I took her into an interview room and asked inspector S***** to assist me.

"A*****" was a spark plug. I always got a kick out of all the spunky female inspectors who were tougher –and smarter- than quite a few male inspectors (and all of management). A***** was from Douglas and had been an immigration secretary for some years. She made all the male inspectors grin when she announced over the intercom a phone call for so-and-so in her sweet, heavily accented voice. She could have made millions working for a 900 phone line –if she wasn't so innocent! She was all of almost five feet tall and a single mom with a son who is a fantastic baseball player. We older males looked on her as "little sister". She finally took the plunge and submitted an application to become an inspector and graduated from the immigration academy. When I heard her first assignment was Nogales I thought "they are going to eat her for lunch at the Nogales POE!" Nogales was a very busy port of entry. She didn't spend much time at Nogales before wrangling a position back in her home town of Douglas.

Taking "the line" at a Port of Entry isn't as easy as walking up to a booth, waving cars forward and asking "Que trae?" "A donde vas?" "Ciudadano de que pais?" (What are you bringing? Where are you going? Citizen of what country?) In an eight hour shift an inspector could expect to man the pedestrian lane and two vehicle lanes about half the time. During this time each inspector could average inspecting 200-300 vehicles and 600-900 people. I'm guessing a municipal police officer makes about ten traffic stops a day. Every person or vehicle approaching the line at a port of entry has the potential to be a felony arrest just as it does with state and local cops. It takes a certain degree of confidence and maturity to present an authoritative presence to the public and extract the required information. It also takes a good sense about human nature. A**** had all of this and more.

On the other hand I know a male inspector (let's call him "Barney") who became so nervous when confronting the public on the line he stuttered uncontrollably. His hands shook and he couldn't focus on the documents presented to him. This young man was very intelligent. He just couldn't deal with confronting the public who may be wanted criminals, drug smugglers or simply lying to enter the United States illegally. He became so visibly nervous on the line the Mexicans would laugh at him as they drove away from his inspection booth. At the permit counter an inspector was expected to determine if the comprobantes presented were real or fraudulent. I sat next to him at the permit counter one day because I had heard he wasn't really looking at the comprobantes – or more accurately he was pretending to look at them and just issuing everyone a permit. The first person who entered the office and requested a permit gave his documents to "Barney". Barney glanced quickly at the utility receipts and paycheck stubs and reached for his stamp to issue the man a permit. I asked Barney if he saw that the man's receipts were over a year old. The man was probably living illegally in the U.S. Barney began backtracking and rationalizing. It wasn't pretty. The next person to enter the office was a referral from the line. He was referred as a possible Documented False Claim to US citizenship. He handed a U.S. birth certificate to Barney who looked quickly at the certificate in the nice glass frame – then turned it over and stared at the blank back of the frame for almost a full minute. Barney said it looked OK to him. I pointed out to him the erasures on the front of the certificate changing the date of birth. And Barney became angry. I know I intimidated him by sitting next to him – that was half my reason for doing so. None of us senior inspectors would help another inspector –particularly a rookie- who wouldn't listen to someone with experience trying to help him. Others had tried so I just went straight to the jugular with the specific intent of making him quit. He was a very real risk to himself and to the other inspectors. We wore badges and carried weapons for a reason.

A*** walked the woman into the interview room with me. I asked her the same questions again and a few more. She seemed sincere in her effort to raise enough money for the operation and I said so to A*****. Due to her efforts to pay for the medical care with no apparent "public charge" violation, I said I was inclined to issue her a permit. A***** tensed ever so slightly. I sensed she had reservations she hadn't expressed yet – and was professional enough to let me make the call. I asked A**** what she thought. With the right tone of voice even "I don't know" can mean "there's more to this than meets the eye." I stood up to go talk to our supervisor when I saw the woman's purse. The little voice in my head shouted

"*You didn't check her purse!*" The very first thing I pulled out of it was an official letter from the Arizona Cost Containment Health System (ACCHS) congratulating her on qualifying for $140,000.00 in welfare payments to pay for HER AND her daughter's medical issues. She was being treated for diabetes and her daughter was, in fact, going to have neurological surgery – at tax payer expense. Rosa R**** was caught in a lie. It's actually a violation of federal law to lie to a federal law enforcement officer. It's punishable by two years in prison upon conviction. That punishment never happens of course. There's not enough land in America to build the prisons necessary to house everyone who lies to us. Besides, immigration management would be the first inmates. I held onto Rosa's entry document and the letter from ACCHS, told her to spend the night across the line and return in the morning to speak with a supervisor.

The first thing Mexican Moses yelled at me when she entered the secondary office the next morning was "*We don't process public charges anymore! We haven't since 1996*!" Now that everyone in southern Arizona heard her telling me we don't prosecute welfare fraud, I responded by showing Mexican Moses an official INS statement of "Grounds of Inadmissibility for Cases dated April 1, 1997 listing Public Charge (Section 212(a)(4) of the INA as one of the grounds for inadmissibility. This notice was distributed to all inspectors. Her response was incredible for its' lack of logic: "*What would happen to the welfare workers' jobs if we caught all the welfare fraud by illegals?*" Again, I said I was going higher with this if the appropriate measures weren't taken. For once the District Director told her Mexican Moses the woman was inadmissible. It was like stepping on a rattlesnake's tail. Incredibly, the District Director's response was a study in obfuscation. The first two pages of her response were monuments to "well, yes, you're right *by the law BUT not necessarily if you consider district, local policy*" *with the conclusion that I needed remedial training*. She sent an assistant district director down to talk to me. If his intent was to quench my desire to enforce the immigration laws he failed miserably.

The woman didn't have to go without medical help for her daughter nor did she have to live illegally in the U.S. The Shriners routinely visited the port asking if we knew of any Mexican children needing medical assistance. I saw them assist dozens of children every month or so with medical problems. Assisting them in getting the kids to the doctors who could help them was one of the few really rewarding things we did as inspectors – other than catching the bad guys.

The State of California tried curbing welfare fraud in the late '90s by assigning MEDI-CAL(?) staffers at the Ports of Entry with Mexico. The staffers cross checked Mexican border crossers with the MEDI-CAL rolls – of which only U.S. citizens were eligible. Within the first months of the operation they saved tens of millions of dollars. It was so successful a conference was scheduled in Phoenix to discuss Arizona, Texas and Florida doing the same thing. For "some reason" (read "votes"), California cancelled the operation and none of the other states implemented the program.

About 2a.m. on a hot summer night I saw a lump of humanity lying just inside the red line that was the actual delineation between Mexico and the U.S. The red line was painted east-west on the road about 75 feet south of the U.S. vehicle inspection booths. The lump was over toward lanes six and seven - really be in danger of being run over at that hour unless a drunk failed to make the turn or someone was running from the federales (not wanting to pay the 'mordida' - bribe). I walked out to the southbound guardrail and tapped it a couple of times with my baton to wake up the drunk lying on the pavement. Three people stood up.

Actually it was four. The frail woman looked like she was going to have twins – and real soon! Her son was a small six years old. Her husband looked gaunt and worn out as well. They all looked gaunt and worn out. Despite her condition she was carrying the cloth bag with all their belongings and a milk gallon jug of water. "Por que estan dormiendo aqui?" "Why are you sleeping here?" I asked. "It's the only safe place we could find to sleep" he said. I first saw John Ford's black and white movie "The Grapes of Wrath" when I was a kid living in Midwest City, Oklahoma. I remember Tom Joad's "Wherever there's a fight, just so hungry people can eat, I'll be there" speech. As an adult I read John Steinbeck's book from which the movie was taken. I consider it one of the best books I've ever read. I'm from Oklahoma – and proud of it. I also had relatives who left Oklahoma during the Dust Bowl of the '30s as "Okies" and experienced the mistreatment by the California authorities simply because of their poverty. I thought of my Okies frequently as I watched the Border Patrol busses off-load the illegals and point toward the Mexican border on the southbound lane – two or three times in an eight hour shift. And I had lived in roach-infested East Boeing Apartments across the street from Tinker Air Force Base eating oatmeal for breakfast and beans for supper for years after my parents divorced in 1960. I remember being laughed at by my passing high school peers as I emptied trash cans for the Andes Trailer Park in Burns Flat, Oklahoma daily after school for $17.50 a month. None of that was as desperate as the condition these folks were in. "Why don't you ask the Catholic church right over there to help you?" "I did. They said they didn't help our kind of people and locked the doors" he lamented. I still remember the desperation in his voice and their eyes. I gave them what little cash I had in my wallet and told them it wasn't safe to sleep on the pavement either. I could feel their bone weariness as they shuffled back into the clutches of Agua Prieta at night. Agua Prieta, appropriately, means "dark water".

That small family haunted my thoughts for quite a while. And the fact that "the only safe place" they could sleep was on the pavement just inside the border on the American side. It often brought tears to my eyes as I drove home to my four children sleeping safe in their beds – knowing my kids were sleeping "on the American side". And it often made me angry at the Mexican government.

It wasn't until a year or so later that I met an American couple who were serving a humanitarian mission in Agua Prieta for their church. They had set up a comfortable refuge for people just like the family sleeping on the line and Mexican girls caught up in the all the snares of the smuggling world. When they first arrived and entered my lane as strangers I queried their purpose in Mexico. They told me about the refuge. I went to their Casa de Amor (the name connoting something more profitable) in a barrio on the south end of Agua Prieta and found a comfortable and safe establishment. I donated some bedding and kids clothes after the divorce – and kept their business card. They told me if I ever found a girl sincerely in distress or a family like I had told them about it didn't matter what time of day or night they would be there. And they never failed to show when I did. I often gave Mexican females we deported their phone number if I felt the girl was in dire straits. You could tell if they had been through hell getting to the border. They didn't talk much - or flirt. The stranded were allowed to stay a while, perhaps contact family for money to get a return bus ticket home or stay long enough to learn a simple trade. We need many more people like that - God's angels quietly doing His work.

14 September 2002 -   Just five days after being "corrected" on the Public Charge law, Mexican Moses asked supervisor "J-Low" why he cancelled the laser visa of a Mexican female who was found with Arizona welfare checks in her purse. "J-Low" told MM the woman admitted to having received welfare from the State of Arizona for the last six months and having worked illegally in the state during that time. MM told "J-Low" he violated "Port" policy by cancelling her visa. She also criticized "J-Low" for letting inspectors adjudicate the cancelling of visas by agreeing with them. Basically, she was criticizing a supervisor for allowing the inspectors to enforce the law.

18 September 2002 - Immediately upon arriving at work for the midnight shift supervisor "J-Low" counseled me in writing for two emails found lying in the secondary office area. One email contained cartoons mocking the Taliban and Al Qaeda. The other email contained excerpts from old Hollywood Squares shows. As mentioned previously on the "English As a Second Language" caper, the first step required if "someone" takes offense at something appearing to be an EO or EEO complaint is for the offended person to confront the alleged offender. I had seen these emails off-duty. I did not bring them to work. Someone else had. But one of the Douglas clique, again, took "offense", blamed me for their presence, and the emails were faxed directly to Phoenix headquarters.

The fact that one of the Douglas clique "took offense" at cartoons mocking the Taliban and Al Qaeda only proves my perception of their reaction to the 9/11 attacks by those terrorists. The Douglas management and their sycophants felt 9/11 happened to a country other than their own. There was no outrage, no horror – just mild curiosity as someone from a foreign country would react at seeing it on the news. The only obvious response I perceived at the Port of Entry was almost literally hearing the thunder of thousands of Resident Alien feet running back into Mexico at the thought of possibly being called up for duty in an American war.

They wanted all the benefits of American citizenship but none of the responsibilities or civic duties like military service. That's what I saw at Douglas. The military and Congress made it easier for resident aliens to obtain citizenship after serving in the military and I was glad to see that. My Okinawan step-brother joined the navy as a Resident Alien. He participated in the evacuation of Saigon pushing Vietnamese helicopters off the deck of the USS Midway (or the "Connie"). For several weeks a young Mexican man would daily approach the pedestrian lane inspection counter and ask if he could join the American military. He felt it was wrong for us to be attacked and volunteered every day to serve. Soon after he quit coming, two young Resident Aliens, a 20 year Hispanic girl and her 18 year old brother, entered immigration secondary to get the forms to adjust their status to U.S. citizens. Every inspector sitting at that counter at the time was a veteran. Someone gave them the forms and, as they were looking them over, I mentioned to the young man that being 18 and a Resident Alien/U.S. citizen meant he was required by law to register with the Selective Service. "What's that?" he asked. Mo told him it meant if the U.S. went to war he could be called up for service in the military. The young wimp literally dropped the form on the counter like it was red hot. I told him if it were within my power I would cancel his Resident Alien status and give it to the young man who came to the pedestrian lane every day asking to serve in our armed forces. The wimp became a U.S. citizen anyway – just one of many of the 97% of American males who haven't served their country.

30 September 2002 0230 hrs. - Customs inspectors Bxxxxxx and Hxxxxx remarked they could smell alcohol on immigration supervisor Glass' breath during the midnight shift two nights ago. I had taken her phone call at 1155hrs that night saying she would be late because she had "fallen." Her speech was slurred. She finally arrived at 0115hrs and couldn't stop talking and laughing. At approximately 0200hrs she fell off a curb on the line chasing a cat. She is drinking buddies with Acting Port Director Morris and senior inspector Luna – two members of the "Victoria Secret" club. Supervisor Glass had been invited by Morris and Luna to go drinking with them and Port Director Stemple at "Shooters" bar where they all complained very publicly "what assholes they had to work with." This was the same night that Port Director Stemple was kicked out of his house by his wife for sleeping with Mexican Moses. I guess Mexican Moses had an "open" relationship with her married, Mexican rancher boyfriend. The moral bankruptcy of Immigration management at the Douglas Port of Entry boggles the mind. We all wondered why the higher chain of command not only tolerated it but promoted them in spite of it. It was humiliating to be wearing the same uniform as them.

01 October 2002 – Customs inspector L**** informed me senior immigration inspector Joe Acuna told him it was a Mexican's "right" to enter the United States. This idea dovetails with Mexican Moses' opinion that inspectors have to prove Mexicans aren't eligible for permits – not the other way around as required by law. MM was informed she was wrong in 1997 – but apparently she and the rest of the Douglas clique have ignored it.

Also occurring that evening:

"TO: U.S. Customs Supervisor Villareal

NTEU Chapter 116 Representative S**** C******

FROM: Senior Inspector J***** M********

SUBJECT: Officer Safety / *Directed Re-write*

Gentlemen:

I am writing this to protest in the strongest possible terms an incident which occurred during my midnight shift, Friday, September 27, 2002. At first issue is officer safety. The other issues are painfully obvious.

During my primary lane one assignment, duty USINS Supervisor Glass was staggering around in and out of the pedestrian lane door into lane one trying to coax and catch one of the scroungy stray cats that inhabit the area. I am aware she has a problem with her knee. I observed her fall off the curb exiting the pedestrian lane door and fall into vehicle lane one. She slowly dragged herself up on the open gate against the building and hung there draped over the rail at nearly waist height. When I noticed she did not move for a minute or two I went over to her and asked if she was all right. She mumbled she was and continued hanging onto the gate.

While I am "neither trained nor inclined" to assess the state of intoxication of others, it was obvious that she was impaired. She smelled of alcohol. Subsequently other employees stated she is often impaired by alcohol in the workplace. Her fellow INS employees report that they have been told "don't worry about it" when they've reported similar conduct to management before.

I accept the responsibility for back up and support of my co-workers. I do not, and will not, accept responsibility for an ARMED, falling down drunk, who is a danger to herself, the public, my co-workers and me.

The new INS uniform (all blue), in which she was clothed, is strikingly similar to the uniform worn by the Customs Service. The previous uniform distinction (white shirt, black pants) has been integral to the identity of the offending organization employee when processing a public complaint as either Customs or Immigration.

I am prepared to go to USINS Inspector General if this is not handled appropriately at the local level. Additionally, I am alert for, and will not tolerate, any retaliation for having made this complaint.

Respectfully submitted, J***** M*******"

I can't begin to tell you how much most Customs inspectors and supervisors hate Immigration staff in general. They work hard to prevent drugs and other contraband from entering and leaving the United States. Many are also very good at detecting if something else is wrong with the people requesting entry into the United States. Many times the smugglers and illegals they catch are released into the United States by immigration inspectors or supervisors. Customs inspectors are justifiably angry and distrustful of many immigration staff. Most Customs personnel are "pure" enforcement minded. Most immigration inspectors and almost all supervisors and management-level staff couch their refusal to enforce the immigration laws as being "service" minded.

14 November 2002 -

RE: Office of Internal Audit (OIA) Case No. 02X03462

Dear Mr. Ligon;

An inquiry has been conducted under the auspices of the OIA concerning allegations that on June 10, 2002 you were assigned to complete a Question and Answer (Q&A) statement on an individual seeking entry into the United States. It is alleged that during the Q&A session, you asked questions that were out of line and not part of the test to determine admissibility. The inquiry did not disclose information to substantiate allegations of willful misconduct. Accordingly, we have closed our file in the matter and will not pursue it any further. In accordance with Service policy, no record of this inquiry will be placed in your Official Personnel Folder.

Sincerely,

Sue E. Armstrong, Assistant Director, Internal Investigations Branch

It was nice to receive written proof that I was correct. I wonder if anything was done to Luna and "Mexican Moses" for creating a false case and then covering it up by charging me with malfeasance. I doubt it. In view of what Customs inspector Spring told me about my file in D.C. having a "red flag" on it, I also doubt "no record" was kept in my official file.

22 November 2002 - "Dear Inspector Ligon, I would like to take this opportunity to recognize you for your outstanding cooperative efforts with the United States Customs Service. On November 14, 2002, you were involved in an incident with an armed passenger at the Douglas, Arizona port of entry. Your actions ensured the safety of your fellow officers, the victims, and others as this confrontation developed. Your exceptional judgment, restraint, and professional demeanor in resolving this precarious situation without incident is noteworthy. Please accept this letter and the enclosed "buck-knife" as a small token of appreciation for your actions. Thank you for a job well done and best wishes for your continued success. Sincerely, Jayson P. Ahern, Assistant Commissioner, Office of Field Operations, U.S. Customs Service, 1300 Pennsylvania Avenue, N.W., Washington, D.C."

It was Customs inspectors who saved my job in 1997 when I "violated immigration policy" backing up Customs during a felony drug bust. Customs' chain of command doesn't hand out accolades like this liberally. The man's signature on the bottom meant something. And they went above and beyond a form letter by giving me a buck knife. Immigration followed up a week later with a nice letter of commendation (below). Thirdly, it reminded me how close I and J**** B**** had come to blowing that guy's brains all over his baby lying in the bassinet in the back seat behind him. That kind of stuff keeps you awake for quite a few nights.

09 December 2002 - "Dear Inspector Ligon, I would like to commend you for your actions of November 14, 2002. At that time you and your colleagues were confronted with an armed traveler who unexpectedly drew a weapon placing his family, the travelling public and you in serious danger. You responded immediately with quick thinking, exceptional skill, and sound judgement. As a result you were able to defuse a potentially life threatening situation. I am extremely proud of the manner in which you managed the situation. You demonstrated courage, professionalism, and restraint throughout the entire confrontation. Your actions are a credit to you, the Port of Douglas, and the U.S. Immigration & Naturalization Service. Please accept my personal congratulations for a job well done. Sincerely, Donna De La Torre, Director, Field Operations, Customs Management Center, Arizona"

The funny part of all this was I had been working the midnight shift for about two solid years *specifically to get away from immigration management*.

There was no doubt in my mind I would have blown this guy's brains out. Just as I knew in '97. I was very calm as I sighted my weapon on the man's forehead. It was a moment frozen in time. I think all of us were yelling "Manos arriba! Manos arriba!" I wasn't even really aware of his wife sitting in the front passenger seat next to him. Both J*** and I were squeezing our triggers when he opened his door and placed the gun on the ground (with the barrel pointing at them) raising his other hand skyward. If any of us had squeezed a bit faster his surrender would have been a moot point.

In fact, I was the last one to arrive on the scene. But let the primary officer on the scene tell it:

MEMORANDUM TO: Douglas Port Director Charles Stemple

FROM: R**** H*****, Customs Inspector

SUBJECT: Armed Assault Commendation

"On 11142002 at 0532 hours Immigration Inspector Michael Ligon showed exceptional courage, skill and judgment in assisting me in taking down an armed assailant at Douglas POE. Inspector Ligon was not immediately present in the first seconds of the incident yet upon his arrival in primary he saw other inspector's at gunpoint and immediately drew his weapon taking a position to provide me and

Senior J*** B***** with tactical cover. At the time I extricated the assailant Ramiro Rascon Escalante from the car Inspector Ligon took the initiative of stepping forward grabbing the assailant's right arm and hand and assisting me in subduing the assailant and handcuffing him. Even though Rascon had put down his loaded 9mm Browning before he was extricated there was still the danger of that he had another gun or knife on him. I later discovered that Rascon was under the influence of cocaine and found .5 grams of the substance on his person. By his exemplary actions Immigration Inspector Michael Ligon helped save the lives of Liliana Escalante-Rascon and her two 5-month old babies that Ramiro Rascon threatened with his gun. Inspector Ligon also provided skilled armed backup of me and fellow officers at a time that our lives were in danger. I would like to recommend Immigration Inspector Michael Ligon for a Commendation and cash award for his actions on the morning of 11242002. In gratitude, R***** H*****, Senior Customs Inspector"

R*** had been a social worker prior to coming on board with Customs and had a heart of gold. He gave me a lot of advice on how to cover my back with what he had seen of immigration management in his years prior to my arrival. To be honest I think we were worried the cameras that recorded the incident would show we didn't exactly follow academy procedures in subduing this crack head. When he stepped out of his car he still wasn't complying with Rick's orders to lie down on the pavement. He was wriggling around while Rick was trying to cuff him and I was trying to get him on the ground while holding onto his gun hand. I finally did a judo foot sweep that dropped him like a sack of potatoes onto the pavement. I have always believed judo and aikido should be taught at FLETC. I was the Oklahoma State Junior Division Champion in 1967 and president of the Brigham Young University Judo Club for three years – it sticks with you. It's saved my bacon on more than a few occasions. Anyway, once on the ground, while Rick was continuing his frisk and cuffing him, with my knee on top of his neck, I jammed the tip of my weapon's barrel behind his left ear so hard the slide pushed back about an inch. "Whoa!" I thought "let off a little or his brains will be all over the pavement!" We were also a little concerned management would view the video and disapprove of the way we "transported" him into the cell. Rascon's wife was very appreciative as she held two crying babies. That made it worth all the effort - that and the buck knife Customs gave me.

09 December 2002 - <u>Arizona Daily Star</u> "Program Reveals Anti-U.S. bias" by Luis Steinkuehler.   "Re; the November 25 article "Cultural Connection." The photos of Che' Guevara displayed in the office of Augustine Romero, director of the Tucson Unified School District's Mexican-American/Raza studies, catch one's attention. While there's no denying Guevara is macho, it might be pointed out to Romero that this Marxist was after all an enemy of the United States and, contrary to folklore, hardly an appropriate role model to be offered by a school administrator to our students.

The article noted that Cholla High School students in the U.S. history/Chicano perspective class are learning about discrimination, racism, and civil rights. All this in the full context of the article seems to reveal a decided anti-U.S. bias in this educational program that is supposedly designed "to curb high school drop-outs and raise academic achievement among Hispanic students."   The students (and the United States) would be better served if they were treated to a class in which they learn why we are so privileged and blessed to live in this country of unmatched and unprecedented opportunities."

This editorial opinion in the Arizona Daily (Red) Star reminds me of an incident at the Port of Entry. As you may have guessed by now I wasn't very timid in expressing my opinion of what management was doing to our country by overruling our decisions to send illegals back to Mexico. One nineteen year-old male Resident Alien was referred to secondary for a more "intensive" inspection. He also just happened to have a sticker on his truck's rear window showing the Felix cartoon character urinating on the words "La Migra" – slang for us and the Border Patrol. I told this cocky guest of the United States that he could be fined $500 for violation of Article 213 of the Immigration & Nationality Act - defamation of a federal officer through speech, gesture or signage. He of course expressed surprise (and my fellow inspectors their amusement) and offered to scrape it off rather than be fined. I provided a scraper and after all the "defamatory" mockery was gone released him back into the mainstream of America. We both felt lucky at the outcome. Him because he "avoided a $500 fine" and me because he didn't ask to see it in writing!

18 December 2002   Memorandum to Deborah Rodriguez, District Director, Tucson Field Office: Yesterday at 0805hrs, Supervisor Jose Lopez began harassing me for filing a complaint against inspector Alma Luna. This is a violation of federal law, professionalism, and ethics as well as a breach of confidentiality. Supervisor Lopez told me in an angry tone repeatedly it was HIS decision to incorrectly process an alien who had simply been asking for the proper forms to request amnesty. He, of course, was just covering her. Trying to avoid an argument I tried to move away but Lopez jumped in front of and very close to me blocking my exit. He was exhibiting a very physically threatening and hostile demeanor. Lopez continued to harass me in a hostile tone of voice. I told Supervisor Lopez I felt it necessary to complain formally after seeing inspector Luna take him into an empty office and, putting her hand affectionately on his (immense) abdomen, whisper something to him about her error. Supervisor Lopez was startled and asked "You saw that?" I tell ya. If it wasn't for the responsibility and authority they had, catching them in lies is just like it is with my own children. From previous experience with Luna's ineptitude and conspiratorial nature, I strongly feel inspector Luna is setting me up for another "going outside the bounds" management inquiry for correcting her egregious error on an innocent alien.

Two day ago I advised supervisor Lopez that inspector B***** had not been listed as the referring officer on an imposter case. Inspector Del Rincon (the "Perfumed Prince") listed Customs inspector E*** A****** as the referring inspector. She needed credit for others' cases because she wasn't catching anything herself. I told supervisor Lopez that not listing the correct referring officer on the file was such a recurring problem that perhaps it needed to be mentioned at a staff meeting. Lopez blew it off. This was actually not-so-subtle discrimination. Douglas Clique inspectors were listing fellow Hispanic inspectors as the referring officers – not the white, non-local inspectors who were catching a LOT of fraud cases. If an audit had been conducted the absence of numbers for the Douglas Clique would have proven embarrassing. At one point in time I thought an audit had been done because the clique suddenly became more "enforcement" oriented – temporarily. This wasn't the only discrimination practiced by the clique by a long shot. It was not uncommon for clique inspectors and shift leaders in secondary to release subjects sent to secondary by white, non-local inspectors on the line into the United States simply because the subject changed his story by the time he reached secondary (or was coached to do so – or the Hispanic inspector simply didn't like the white inspector. The same crowd returned Border Crossing Cards that had been placed in the seized document log in the main office without requiring the "comprobantes" from the alien.

Firearms Award 2002, U.S. Immigration & Naturalization Service, Douglas Port of Entry, to Michael R. Ligon, II, signed Ernestina Morris.

One might ask why wasn't I also a firearms instructor before this? I'm glad you asked that. During the painfully short duration that Jesus Jerez (of "my father has twenty businesses in Mexico" fame) was acting Port Director, "someone" –and I'm not saying who- drew a cartoon moustache on President Clinton's picture. You know the thin, curly, waxed moustache of the bad guy in the Perils of Pauline silent movies and cartoons back in the day? Now, this wasn't just a picture of the president hanging prodigiously on the wall facing us during every staff meeting. It was a symbol of management's victory over us enforcement-minded inspectors. It wasn't quite as large as Mao's picture hanging on the Forbidden City walls in Tiennamen Square - but it seemed so. A few days before a highly anticipated visit by a few Senators and Janet Napolitano to our esteemed Port of Entry, an enterprising and audacious inspector drew the dastardly moustache on El Presidente. Several of my buddies asked if I had seen it –to which I immediately and very defensively asked "Why are you asking ME?" "Haysoos" Jerez, our acting port director was apprised of the stunt a day or two before the visit and had it immediately wiped off (lesson learned: the sacrilegious violator should have used indelible ink!). Then he sent out a very caustic memo to everyone casting doubts on our character and our ability to execute our federal responsibilities with professionalism and integrity. He ended his epistle by threatening to fire the person who did it but would give that person two days to give himself up. He really knew how to draw out the penitent – by threatening to fire them right up front! Jerez sealed his threat with the claim that he had the fingerprints of the perpetrator. Well, I knew he didn't have any fingerprints – the perpetrator, wasn't born yesterday. But everyone was angry about Jerez labeling all of us like he did – he was loaned from the Nogales POE – the showplace for the sector. Jerez' response when I surrendered was more reserved than if it had been under soon-to-be indicted (hopefully) Charlie Stemple's regime. Jerez just cancelled my orders to the Federal Law Enforcement Training Center Firearms Instructor Course. I was due to leave for Artesia, New Mexico in a few days. His justification to District was rather weird. He wrote me a memo explaining that he was cancelling my slot because "he wasn't sure I would instruct firearms training in accordance with INS policy." I didn't really care. I had been taught how to shoot by the finest marksmen in the world at Marine Corps Recruit Depot Parris Island, South Carolina. I had been a weapons (and commo) specialist on a Military FreeFall team in 5th Special Forces Group (Airborne). I had travelled to places and done things with foreign troops Jerez didn't even know existed. And I had graduated tied for high shooter from the academy. I didn't have anything to prove to anyone much less a morally bankrupt bureaucrat. But I still would like to have had that red, federal firearms instructor polo shirt in my closet. Life went on ……painfully…. miserably….. at the Port of Entry.

I called Jerez morally bankrupt not just because he told me "there were laws - then there were laws" intimating that I didn't have to enforce the immigration laws so devoutly. I know personally that he is because he had a very public affair with one of our married (as he is) –female- immigration inspectors, Eloisa Schwam. One begins to wonder if you have to be an adulterer(ess) and give drug dealers and

illegals a "pasale" card to get promoted to Port Director at Douglas.
Jerez' wife was back in Nogales (Arizona or Mexico. I don't know)

Jerez and senior inspector (Mrs.) Schwam rendezvoused late one
night on one of the distant holes (pardon the expression) of the
Douglas golf course. That would have remained between them and
the 18th hole had it not been for Schwam's penchant for discussing
their love life via emails on her work computer . Her husband, a
Customs supervisor, was a renowned computer guru. He found the
emails detailing their activities, printed them out by the dozens and
littered them around the Port of Entry. Mr. Schwam posted a bold-
faced note on the Customs' office window addressed to Jerez
warning him to *Leave my wife alone!*" The Schwams divorced
soon after upon which Eloisa followed Jerez back to Nogales where
I'm sure they are totally faithful to each other.

10 January 2003 - Supervisor "J-Low" Lopez has disseminated a
form "Conduct Efficiency Evaluation of Probationary Apppointee."
He directed this form be used by "OJT" (I think he meant "FTO")
officers in evaluating inspectors during their year-long probation.
There are many things wrong with this other than it was ludicrous
that local management would assign this task to a supervisor who
couldn't type polysyllabic words in a sworn statement:

1. The change in appraisal criteria was not
submitted through nor accepted by "bargaining members"
(inspectors and the union).
2. Lopez' intent is to place journeyman
inspectors under this criteria. That's not in our job
description. Field Training Officer (FTO) responsibilities are
defined solely in the senior inspectors' job description.
3. Lopez lists speaking Spanish as the #1 –
and most heavily weighted - performance criteria. This is
back door racial discrimination. Once graduating from the
Immigration Officer Basic Course (IOBC) language training,
INS declares the inspector fully qualified to perform the job.
This is an attempt by supervisor Lopez to handicap white,
non-hispanic inspectors. It would give an unfair –and

unjustified- advantage to Hispanic inspectors. Making cases and completing them satisfactorily for review by the Assistant U.S. Attorney was placed much lower on the appraisal form - almost as an afterthought.

13 January 2003 - at 1120hrs Senior Customs Inspector (SCI) F****** referred a young, Hispanic female to INS secondary as a suspected documented false claim (DFC) to U.S. citizenship. SCI F***** told me she presented an Illinois birth certificate (#112-89 627105) in the name of Daisy Garcia and claimed to be that person. She was a passenger in a vehicle driven by Gilberto Garcia. I questioned the suspect in Customs secondary and also felt she was lying. I then questioned the driver in order to establish conspiracy. Gilberto adamantly insisted the suspect was Daisy. I again began questioning the suspected DFC but was constantly being interrupted by Gilberto. Gilberto was almost shouting (at the DFC but addressing me) that she was Daisy. The DFC was physically flinching from his remonstrations while attempting to answer my questions. I told Gilberto to go sit in a chair about 30 feet away. Once separated, I asked the DFC where she was born. In a low, calm voice I explained the legal consequences of fraud and lying. Her eyes began to tear. I put my hands up in a calming gesture and told her she just needed to tell the truth. I told her I could see she isn't a bad person and that she doesn't really want to lie. I also told her I thought she was afraid of Gilberto. She looked sideways to see if he was in earshot and slightly nodded her head.

I again asked her where she was born. She quietly said "Cuernavaca, Mexico." I told her the answer to the next question was very important. "Did Gilberto know this birth certificate was not yours?" She again nodded her head slightly and quietly said "Yes." At that point I took Gilberto in through the front INS office door and told him to be seated. In order to avoid further harassment of the DFC by Gilberto I brought her through a side door and had her sit in an interview room. Once she was seated, I announced to all the inspectors in our small secondary office – including shift supervisor Ann Glass, shift leader Travis Edwards, senior inspectors Alma Luna and Joe Perez that the suspect is a Documented False Claim to

U.S. citizenship, that she admitted to me as having been born in Cuernavaca and had stated that driver Gilberto had knowledge. Shift leader Edwards asked old she was. I re-entered the interview and, with senior inspector Joe Perez standing almost immediately behind my right shoulder, asked her how old she was. She said she was 15 years old. The date of birth on the birth certificate was dated 1989. I left the room to notify the referring Customs inspector a case had been made. Upon returning to the interview room just minutes later, senior inspector Joe Perez yelled at me in an irritated and accusatory tone of voice – in front of the DFC: "She's saying you are lying! She never told you she was born in Mexico!"

Instead of following normal procedure for completing an Expedited Removal case by completing a biographical sheet, Perez questioned her how I interviewed her. Subjects are quick to pick up on this racial collaboration with prompting from Hispanic inspectors and are quick to recant their admissions. And it wasn't the first time a Hispanic inspector lied to a gringo inspector about what the subject said - -believing we didn't speak Spanish. Perez then accused me of lying about the admission and intimidating the subject. He had done this before on 09/30/99 and 10/23/02. Other members of the Douglas clique had done this behind my back but Perez was the only one to accuse me to my face. Perez' second wife was from Mexico and had lived illegally with him for several years while he was an immigration inspector before marrying her.

If Perez thought yelling at me would cower me into acquiescence he was wrong. I was really angry that someone who took the oath to support and defend the Constitution of the United States, wearing a uniform and badge to enforce the laws of the U.S. was a fifth columnist – and I had to fight him as well as management to enforce the law. Joe Perez was the first one to tell me I couldn't cancel a Border Crosser's card "just" because a Mexican female was illegally receiving Arizona welfare.

Then senior inspector Luna rushed into the room and exclaimed "Let me do this!" She had received some notice during performance appraisals for not having done many Expedited Removal cases.

When I left the room she and Perez closed the doors and began re-interviewing her. I asked aloud why they were re-interviewing her instead of just processing her as an Expedited Removal. Supervisor Glass, said "Maybe they are trying to make a case." "The case is already made! She was referred by Customs inspector F****. I obtained an admission from her that she is not a U.S. citizen and that the driver knew it. This was witnessed by immigration inspector C*****. That has been good enough in the six years I've been here – *or is that only good enough for some inspectors and not others*?" I shouted.

And, regarding the conspiracy to smuggle a Documented False Claim by the driver Gilberto, a memo from the District office dated 01/14/03 required an alien smuggler file be prepared when the subject confirms the smuggler's involvement – establishing the conspiracy to smuggle. Despite my obtaining the conspiracy admission from the DFC and it being witnessed by two inspectors, and both shift leader Edwards and supervisor Glass hearing my statement to that effect, Gilberto, a Resident Alien, was not processed as an alien smuggler but instead released into the United States with his vehicle.

My name was nowhere on the case. Shift leader Edwards physically tried to shrink into invisibility when I asked him to verify that I had made the case. He trembled before the presence of Mexican Moses. In order to avoid a confrontation with her he just became invisible. No action has been taken by management about the clique falsely claiming credit for cases they didn't make (see original complaint dated 02 FEB 99). The smuggler was released DTR – down the road.

The "elephant in the living room" that District was ignoring at the Douglas Port of Entry was that the local Douglas clique of inspectors who were both near illiterate and indisposed to make cases against their Mexican "cousins". They weren't making cases. When the statistics showing who was making cases and who was not became very visible to District the Douglas Clique came up very, very short. When local management had to justify "outstanding" new appraisals with actual performance, the Douglas Clique resorted to hijacking non-clique inspectors' cases.......- when they couldn't subvert making the case in the first place by talking the subject into recanting or accusing the inspector of lying about the admission.

14 January 2003   2345hrs – I arrived at work to see supervisory inspector Lopez "J-Low" and other local Douglas inspectors sitting at the immigration customer counter listening to a CD by a group named WASP. He seemed unoffended by the title song "Fuck Like A Beast" or by another song on the CD mocking the Pledge of Allegiance. Lopez and his ilk explode with (feigned) rage at cartoons mocking Al Qaeda. The Douglas Clique gets District to write me up for jokes about terrorists who kill Americans and yet tolerates songs in the work place about fucking and mocking America. No wonder supervisor Lisa Boatwright told me to "quit thinking of myself as still protecting America." Does my America even exist any more?

I was manning the pedestrian lane one evening when I was discussing this issue with another inspector. She was a female senior inspector who, though not a member of the Clique, also had ties to Douglas. "Well, all the Founding Fathers were corrupt, jailbird bastards anyway!" she said.

18 January 2003   Deputy Assistant District Director for Enforcement Burcham called me at home on a Saturday morning. I was loading my middle son's mountain bike into my van. We were going up to Flagstaff for him to compete in a race. Burcham identified himself and asked if I had written a complaint of some sort against employees at the Douglas Port of Entry. I said I had and asked how he knew that. He told me someone had accessed my computer at work and posted my complaint on the bulletin board. "You might want to think about asking for a temporary "protective" reassignment to Nogales. You've created quite a firestorm at Douglas since it seems everyone's read your complaint. It might not be a good idea for you to report for work there for a while" he said. Great. If things were bad before now the bonfire was really lit. Then I got angry and told Burcham "Know what? The heck with it.

They are the ones who should be reassigned – if not fired. I've told the truth and I'm reporting for work regardless." I showed up for work as usual that Monday.

21 January 2003 - Email to Gregory Burcham and Karyn L. Van Dyck, INS District Headquarters: "All inspectors received an email from Acting Area Port Director Ernestine Morris stating "we will no longer give copies of I-213s to Mexican officials". Is this official INS policy that we give Mexican officials copies of our fraud cases which contain not only the referring inspector but the inspector obtaining admissions – everything about the fraud or drug cases is noted – or is it more "Local Policy"? Where does the insanity stop? This is what happens when INS hires locally! Why is AAPD Ernestine Morris still here?"

I checked with friends at other Ports of Entry and they were stunned to hear "we" were doing this. Apparently the Douglas clique is deeper in the pocket of the Mexican government than even I thought. This behavior is not just "naivete"" or "incompetence". It's called "collusion",

23 January 2003 - Email to Karen VanDyck at NRO-006:

"I received a phone call from Special Agent Bill King of Office of Internal Affairs, 18 January 2003 at approximately 1200hrs. He asked if I had filed a complaint with Internal Affairs. I said "Not recently". He then told me someone had accessed my computer files at work and printed out a 15 page document containing my accusations against other inspectors. I asked Special Agent King if I was in trouble for any kind of computer security violation (knowing Douglas' management penchant for punishing the trivial) and he said no. He said he felt I should know because some of the accusations i.e. "an inspector Acuna letting a load go by" could make it kind of dangerous for me at work. I asked SA King if he felt it necessary that I be temporarily assigned to nearby Naco until things cooled off. He said he didn't want to put me in fear but just to let me know that my complaint had been compromised and "there are a lot of accusations flying back and forth at work now".

I thought about what he said after we hung up then called him back. I asked if he thought I needed protection. SA King again said – without answering my question – he "didn't want to put me in fear" but if I had questions –get this- to speak with Assistant Area Port Director Ernestina Morris! He's encouraging me to ask the one person who leads the opposition to enforcing the law at Douglas if I need protection! Ludicrous!

To prove my point the "Mexican Moses" called me the next day, 19 January, at 1600hrs and tersely informed me I was on "admin leave until further notice. If you have any questions call Greg Burcham" – and gave me his cell phone number . I immediately called Mr. Burcham and told him I was on admin leave. Mr. Burcham, told me it was my choice – I could take it or leave it. This conflicted with both the tone and intent conveyed by "Mexican Moses". I considered the offer for a moment. It was tempting to take paid time off from the constant harassment at work, catch up on some sleep and spend time with my boys. Yet I had done nothing wrong and I was not the one who should be leaving. I also didn't like "Mexican Moses" telling me as if I had no choice. I declined the offer and showed up for work as scheduled.

At 0335hrs 23 January CBP officer A***** told me he saw supervisor Jose Lopez and others of the Douglas Clique gleefully bragging about accessing my computer files and saying things like "We've REALLY got Ligon NOW!" I asked CBP officer A**** if he would be willing to speak with someone else about what he saw and heard. He said, "Of course! Bring 'em on!" This CBP officer also expressed the feeling that Ernestina Morris needs to leave.

01 March 2003   HOMELAND SECURITY be it known that Michael R. Ligon is a Founding Member of the Department of Homeland Security, dedicated to preventing terrorist attacks within the United States, reducing America's vulnerability to terrorism, and minimizing the damage from potential attacks and natural disasters. Signed, Tom Ridge, Secretary, Washington, D.C.

All of us immigration and Customs officers received this certificate. It brought a few grins from us line inspectors. True to form the federal government had built a new bureaucracy and thrown money at the 9/11 incident without really addressing the incipient causes - the border being a sieve. There were two major changes in our operations: the oft-used phrase "don't F@#$ with the 7As" was quietly done away with (since that's how all 19 9/11 hijackers were allowed to overstay their visas); and by repeating the word "terrorism" twice in the above certificate – and ad nauseum in public forums - the more simple-minded (or quite clever) southern border management that wasn't enforcement oriented in the first place now justified overruling our deferrals as "Not a terrorist threat" or "Our mission NOW is anti-terrorism".

George Romney, former governor of Michigan and former president of General Motors (he actually put America on an industrial war-footing during WW II) was interviewed upon his retirement from public service. When asked what he thought of the American public, one of his responses was "Americans don't act until it's too late – and then they over react." This was no truer than after 9/11.

The reason Immigration's previous policy toward "7As" (foreign student visas) was benign was that if a former alien student arrived at a U.S. airport with an expired visa he wasn't eligible for entry into the United States. By law the foreign student is required to be put on the next plane back to his own country where he would be required to re-apply for another visa. Enter the United States airline industry. Expired student visas were fairly frequent (they laughed at how easy it was to obtain a "student" visa and just stay in the United States – I saw them do it in front of us often) and the airline had to pay for the seat on the plane to take the student applicant back home. Airlines don't like paying for seats themselves. That added up to some bucks. So, the airline industry complained to the State Department, who issues the visas in their home country. The State Department told the INS commissioners not to "F@#" with the 7As – and let them enter despite being ineligible to do so. So, America, despite Congress' 9/11 Commission's conclusion that it was a lack of

201

"imagination" that resulted in those peoples' death (typical non-attributable accountability), you can thank the airline industry for a major part in it. I'm surprised this wasn't revealed and used in the subsequent law suits by the surviving family members. Perhaps it was.

Chapter 7. "Domestic Violence"

08 May 2003 Area Port Director Bill Molaski and Asst. Port Director Ernie Morris suspended me from inspectional duties. Molaski stated "It is standard operating procedure. Just get used to working the desk for a year or two." Morris said it was because "you have no gun." Molaski misrepresented my off-duty incident as a "domestic violence issue." You be the judge:

On or about 2 May, a spring Saturday afternoon, my two younger boys and I were doing yard work at the house. I had finished in the back yard and told the boys working in the front yard we were finished for the day, to clean up and we'd go eat and take in a movie. As we were backing out of the driveway in my old Ford truck, my middle son exclaimed "Don't go that way! That's where they are!" Instead of heading down the street as usual I went the opposite way around the U-shaped street. "Who is 'they'" I asked thinking it was some girls giving them a hard time. My youngest said it was Mark Anthony Vasquez and my middle son's ex-girlfriend. My son had broken up with the little slut over a year ago but she was vindictive for the parting. She had told her much older Hispanic boyfriend where my middle son lived. He was driving up and down our street flipping my boys the bird and calling them names the whole time I was in the back yard. "Well now he knows we left home. I'm going back to make sure he doesn't do anything to the house" I said.

Sure enough, when I arrived back at the house he was sitting there in his parked truck. I pulled alongside him and asked why he was parked across the street from my house. He began a long string of denials, profanity and claiming he could park where he wanted. I quicky tired of his name calling, got out of my truck, walked up to his window and said "If you want to talk like a man then get out of your truck and act like a man." The first thing I saw was the ex-girlfriend – about 13 years old - slouching down with her chin on this maggot's forearm – which was lying on his leg. His pants were down halfway to his knees under his T-shirt. Her face was about six inches from this gang wannabe's crotch. I knew her parents from church. "Does your mom know you're out with this loser?" I asked. "She doesn't care" she said. I knew that wasn't true. The maggot didn't man up so I got back in my truck. He began mouthing off again and wouldn't leave so I again told him to get out of his truck. He didn't –probably because his pants would fall down. He didn't leave until I went inside to call the Sheriff's office.

The next evening I was digging a post hole in my front yard to move my mail box from the corner of the yard to the middle. My middle son was riding his BMX bike two blocks away at the elementary school. He came home uncharacteristically late walking his bike. I asked why he was coming home after the street lights had come on. He said his bike had a flat tire. He asked if he could go back to the school after putting his bike up. "You certainly cannot! It's after dark. What makes you think I'd let you go?" I asked. "Vasquez and his gang tried running over me again with his car (apparently he had done that several times in the last few weeks) and told me to meet him and his "boyz" at the school – and to "bring your dad. We're going to kick his ass too." I left my boys at the curb. "We're not going but I've got someone who's got the biggest gang in town to meet them" I said as I went in the house to call the Sheriff's office. While on the phone with the dispatcher my youngest –ten years old- ran into the house screaming *"Dad! They're all here and they've all got baseball bats!"* I quickly told the dispatcher I'm a CBP officer, I'm armed – and to hurry. As I ran out the front door I'm only marginally aware that my German Shepherd is zooming right past my leg toward Vasquez who had a baseball bat high over his head coming down to hit my son on the ground for the second or third time. "Why are you hitting me in my own front yard?" my son cried raising his left arm in defense.

James Soliz, 21, and Marc Anthony Vasquez, 17, were trying to beat my sons with baseball bats. Soliz was cocking a bat at my ten year old son about five feet to the left. They were no more than fifteen yards from me. I could have killed both of those maggots from my front door. I should have. I regret not doing so to this day – and everyone else that showed up on their behalf.

Instead I ran at them with my duty weapon pointed at Vasquez and ordered him to drop the bat. He ran around the back of his car and jumped in the driver's seat. I told my youngest to come to me and away from Soliz who had simply stayed put with his bat cocked. I stuck my weapon through the front passenger window and leaned into the car so my head and shoulders were inside. The muzzle of my weapon was about 12 inches from Vasquez' face when I told him to turn off the car and get out. This idiot just turned and looked me in the eyes. "Fuck You!" he said and began driving away. He was leaving and no longer a threat so I backed out of his window and let him leave. I turned toward Soliz who had by this time raised his bat over his head readying to swing. I ordered him to drop it and he just stood there looking at me like the dullard he is. I was speaking in his language – profanity – and told him I was going to blow his *@#$ head off if he didn't drop the bat. Instead he just let it hang at his side behind his right leg. I grabbed the front of his T-shirt and executed a foot sweep to put his chest on the ground. I jammed the muzzle of my .40 caliber Beretta into his head behind the left ear so hard it pushed the upper receiver back about half an inch. He knew what that was and quit resisting. I told him to put his hands behind his back. As he began to do so, Vasquez returned driving at a very high rate of speed toward me with his bright lights on. I had Soliz's T-shirt in my left hand in the middle of his back and my weapon pointed down and away to my right. When he saw his homey coming back he twisted around facing me and tried to grab my neck. My grip on his shirt instinctively tightened and in sympathetic reflex I squeezed a round off with my gun hand. The boom caused him to stop fighting. I was sitting on him and could feel his butt cheeks tighten under me.

I twisted around and drew a bead at the on-coming Vasquez just above the left headlight. He stopped ten feet from us. He got out with a baseball bat in his hand. Just then another car approached at a high rate of speed from behind me. I spun around and again drew a bead at the same place on this vehicle. It stopped even closer. The last vehicle to race toward me was an old white Cadillac with a diapered baby literally hanging halfway out the back left window. The second vehicle was Vasquez' girlfriend/fiancée/wife (she said all three as she rushed me). The third vehicle was 21 year old Soliz' mommy. Right behind them three Sheriff's deputies arrived and took control of the situation. They cuffed both maggots then one deputy asked for my weapon. He placed my weapon _on the street_ while they talked with everyone involved. That really mad me angry.

After taking the two maggots to jail a deputy came in the house and waited for my middle son and me to write our statements. I called work and told supervisor Chavez (also a firearms instructor familiar with the rules for escalation of force) what happened. Chavez said "Ok, no problem. You can write up a memo when you come in tomorrow." I let him speak with a deputy. After the deputies left I sat in bed with my two boys and asked how they were feeling. Both said they were in shock – they had never seen me that angry or talk like that before. "Would you really have killed them?" they asked. I stayed home for two days to ensure they were ok.

I went back onto the street in front of my house early the next evening after the incident to determine where my spent bullet went. I thought I had it pointed down and behind us. Did it enter one of the homes on the street? The county had just resurfaced our street with asphalt so it took kneeling down to find the impact point. A distinct triangle in the asphalt pointed the direction of the ricochet. It pointed straight at my next door neighbor's front bedroom window. Luckily a few years before, I had installed a low block wall on our property line. The tiny white scar on the wall was about six inches from the top. I was bringing my weapon forward as I fired it.

Other than bruises on my middle son's left arm, neither of my sons suffered any lasting harm – although the more they became teenagers the more I suspected brain damage! My neighbor came out and told me to come get him the next time and he would even up the odds for me. A nurse who lived down the street told me Vasquez had parked his car across the street from my house the previous night – the night of the first altercation. She saw it as she drove to work at 3a.m. I was in Douglas working the midnight shift while that maggot was parked outside my son's bedroom window. Yeah, I should have killed him.

I arrived at work at the Douglas POE three days later with my memo describing the incident in my hand. Molaski and Morris called me into his office and immediately told me I was "suspended from inspectional duties." They never looked at my memo. They never requested it. This proved to me that nothing I ever rebutted was forwarded through them to District.

Morris told me to go "straighten up the file system" in the main office. That was a big mistake on her part. The first thing I looked up was the policy on off-duty shooting incidents. I began outlining my defense case and identified eleven procedures Bill Molaski and Ernie Morris failed to follow in dealing with my off-duty incident. Bill Molaski reported to the District Director that I had recklessly drawn my weapon and fired it during a "domestic violence" event. He also lied about "charges pending against Ligon from the District Attorney." He even took the unusual step of publishing his version on a nationwide Customs data base. Our union rep was useless so I made an end run around Molaski and Morris and appealed directly to the District Director. I was actually very doubtful it would bear fruit because of the thundering silence we all had experienced from Phoenix when we reported the harassment of management.

I could tell when the District Director read my email detailing what actually happened. It was basically my memo that neither Molaski nor Morris would accept. I made it very clear in my email to her that Bill Molaski had lied about the incident. I could tell when she contacted Molaski. His face was beet red all day. I thought he was going to have a stroke. His carotid artery looked like the Alaska pipeline! The District Director confirmed my version with the District Attorney and that there never were any charges pending against me. I was sitting in an office in the main building pretending to sort files when Molaski rushed by and curtly told me to come into his office. Without getting out of my chair, I asked why. He stopped so abruptly that the three sycophants following him almost bowled him over. He stuck his blood engorged head in the office and said "If you want your weapon back come into my office!" I strolled down the hallway and stuck my head in. "As I informed you in my memo, before you and I have any further discussions I want either a lawyer or a union rep present with a recorder." I said. Molaski said "If you want to get back to duty sign this." The memo simply said I was returned to full duty – ten days after being suspended. I signed it and, before I could ask about my weapon, Molaski said "Take the rest of the day off and go get your "gun" from the Sheriff's office". I drove to the Sheriff's office in Bisbee Canyon and approached the counter. The property deputy who retrieved my weapon seemed a bit apologetic and confused. "I don't understand why we even had your weapon!" he said.

Soliz spent one day in jail. The 17 year old maggot, Vasquez, was released into the custody of his mother and his step-dad – a well-known accountant in the County. I attended the trial of both of them. Vasquez' trial was moved up a few hours that day to immediately follow another case against him. He had to appear for another charge of assault against an 8 year-old boy in his front yard as well – also white. I told the judge that the crimes committed by both Hispanic young men were rife with racial epithets against my sons and therefore should be treated as a hate crime. Vasquez' family gasped in horror and disbelief. Hate crimes apparently only apply to whites against minorities!

Vasquez made a deal with the local gang enforcement unit that he would snitch on gang activities in town for them and didn't get any time in custody. I filed civil suits against both of them. The judge dismissed the suit against Vasquez' stepfather because he denied any relationship with him. I won damages against the 21 year-old that made up for loss of overtime and shift differential – almost two thousand dollars. It took close to four years for the court to collect it. Ernestina Morris refused my request to write a letter to the court confirming an amount for my loss in pay.

It wasn't over when I got my weapon back and returned to duty. For some strange reason two months later I was ordered to report to the Nogales Port of Entry to be read my rights and undergo another inquisition by a decrepit immigration supervisor. He had a negative attitude toward me and about the whole affair. Perhaps our former temporary Port Director Jesus Jerez who had returned to Nogales but put a bug in his ear. I was able to get my side of the story out for the record – again- but he didn't like it. One of the assistant district directors called me awhile later and said "Heck Mike, when I read the report I thought you caused us more paper work by NOT shooting those two! What kept you from killing those guys?"

CHAPTER 8. "Q-TIPS", MURDERERS AND MUSIC

One of the few pleasant inspectional duties was to inspect the periodic bus load of "Q-tips." These were tour busses returning from Mexico filled with vacationing, elderly Americans. Most were returning from touring Copper Canyon that is reputed to be larger and prettier than the Grand Canyon. Some well-to-do American tourists drive their RV "land yachts" down to the west edge of the Canyon to piggyback on a railroad flat car. There are Indians in the Canyon who live as they had for centuries past and sell crafts and curios. If I knew they were coming in and I wasn't working on the line I would make an effort to be the first inspector on the bus. Entering the front of the bus I would first say in a loud enough voice for the one's in the back to hear "*Welcome back to the United States of America*!" That always brought a chorus of cheers and applause from them.

During one inspection of a "Q-tip" bus I had made my way toward the rear when I noticed one especially elderly lady visibly upset and trembling. I asked her what was wrong but she was too upset to answer. She was German. Her daughter was sitting beside her and informed me that the passengers had been subjected to a rather rude Mexican military checkpoint inspection an hour from the border. "It brought back some bad memories for my mother" she said. I looked on her left forearm and saw a numbered tattoo – a Holocaust survivor. All I could do was hold her hand and assure her that she was safe now because she was *in the United States*. She had tears of gratitude in her eyes.

Murderer: Another day shift working the pedestrian lane I was joking around with some of the local kids when I felt the presence of someone to my left. I looked around and saw a white, young man standing too close to me. He seemed to want to talk to me so I asked how I could help him. "I need to turn myself in" he said. "For what?" I asked. "Murder" he said. I calmly told him to turn around while I 'cuffed him. "Who did you murder?" "My girlfriend's boyfriend" he said. After a few seconds that made perfect sense considering the charge. This nineteen year old young man had shot his "girlfriend's boyfriend" three times with a .357 Magnum revolver up in Safford. He had run into Mexico and found it definitely not the refuge it appeared in the moment of panic. He just wanted to be back in the United States and get it over with.

Murderer(s): One day a van containing four young people were arrested on the line. They had crossed into Agua Prieta, Mexico then gotten lost and accidently gotten back onto the one-way road leading back into the United States. The Customs inspector saw the van's license plate alert appear on the computer and walked them directly in front of the Customs secondary office. This was just behind the vehicle inspection booths where most of the armed officers could cover the vehicle's occupants. They were taken into custody without any resistance. They had murdered a family of four in South Carolina who were returning from a church revival in Atlanta – A father/husband, wife/mother, a small child and a baby – all shot in the head. In cases like this I sort of agree with Mexican justice.

209

Mexico has no death penalty – local cops just take the bad guy(s) out to the desert and shoot them. In one small Mexican town two men tried kidnapping a small boy and girl from the town square. They were going to sell the children to human organ harvesters. The local citizenry intercepted the men at the outskirts of town and brought the culprits to the town judge. The judge released the two men after a little monetary incentive. The town folk waiting outside put the "habeaus grabbus" back on the men and hung both them *and the judge* in the town square! This occurred in a small central Mexican town in the late 1990s.

Our murderous group was extradited to South Carolina for trial.

Music: I believe it is beyond the capability of any warm-blooded American male to not succumb to the wiles of a beautiful Latina. A few years after my divorce, I met a beautiful Hispanic woman. She gave me her address and phone number in Tucson and we started dating. My first visit to her apartment in Tucson found a room full of "family" – her sister and her family- including her niece a teenage mother who couldn't deal with her newborn baby crying so my date's sister did the mothering. I liked her sister and all the rest of the family. I was invited down to her parents' casa about fifty miles into Mexico where I ate the cooked cactus, refried beans, etc. of a typically humble rancher's meal. Her parents and siblings are good, hard-working people. I assumed she was a Resident Alien if not a U.S. citizen.

I returned the gesture by inviting her sister and her family to my house. I had quite a houseful of Spanish-speaking Latinas of all ages and a brother-in-law at the house when two of my sons arrived for a visit. My boys didn't stay long. They didn't speak a lick of Spanish. Her brother-in-law fixed my kitchen sink while his wife fixed all of us supper. After eating dinner, her twelve year old niece sat at my piano and tentatively began plinking away. I taught her niece the scale on the piano. I'm no great shakes at the piano but I know how to read basic music. My poor grandmother, bless her soul, tried teaching me the piano when I was in fifth grade. I'm one of those multitudes who didn't appreciate grandma's efforts until way later.

The niece insisted on practicing the scale until she had it perfect. Then she learned a first very basic piece. She was a quick learner and showed a lot of enthusiasm for the piano. It was neat seeing her wonder at transferring written notes into sound on the keyboard. It was a magic "Helen Keller" moment for her. I took some pleasure in introducing this earnest young girl to this world of music. I gave her some elementary music books to take with her. The last time I spoke with her mom she was still enjoying her piano lessons in Phoenix.

Then the bomb shell hit. After the piano lesson for the niece I went out on my back patio to sit under the stars with my date - ironically listening to Andrea Bocelli and Sarah Brightman singing "Time To Say Goodbye". It sure was! I discovered my date was not a Resident Alien. She wasn't a U.S. citizen either. She was a Border Crosser living illegally in Tucson.

I didn't call her after that. I was wrestling with how to report her as an illegal. Awhile later her gangster son walked through the pedestrian lane. I was back-up and told the primary inspector that I knew the kid was living and going to school illegally in Tucson. Inspector Cxxxx referred the kid to secondary where his Border Crossing Card was cancelled as an intended immigrant and he was sent back to Mexico. There was a man standing near him at the pedestrian lane whom I recognized as a disreputable local. I asked the kid if the man was with him and he said yes – just as the man said no. I didn't have any proof the man knew the kid was living here illegally – and aiding the kid in his entry so I sent the man down the road after a warrant check. My "ex-date" drove through my lane a week later. She was driving a van full of "cousins". I found out from her son that the disreputable character on the pedestrian lane was her new boyfriend – and from another inspector he was an alien smuggler. I wrote a note on the secondary referral slip detailing how I knew this woman was living in Tucson illegally (even wrote her address and phone number down) and sent her to secondary. I also noted that I suspected her of being an alien smuggler. I finished my rotation on the line a few minutes later and went back to secondary.

The secondary inspector took my note to supervisor "Mexican Moses". Despite my personal knowledge of the woman living illegally in Tucson, Ernestina Morris gave her Border Crossing Card back and let her enter the United States. My ex-"date" walked right past me to the van laughing beside her alien smuggling boyfriend.

Artifacts: I mentioned the Indians' crafts and curios sold in Copper Canyon. Both Customs and agriculture inspectors checked those out for both monetary value and to ensure none of the materials were infested with bugs, etc. and the cash value of the articles. It was not uncommon for Americans to go south and buy some of the world famous pottery for resale in the States. That required a duty. There were other things – besides drugs, etc. -that were prohibited from being brought from Mexico. Ancient artifacts are highly treasured for obvious cultural reasons by the Mexican government. One day I began a secondary inspection of a truck driven by a white, fairly affluent, American man. His wife was a passenger up front and the extended cab of the truck was crammed with full of luggage.

Perhaps it was his talkativeness, overly friendly demeanor or his repeated insistence that they had nothing to declare that spurred me to take everything out of the extended cab. Underneath everything on the floor was what appeared to be a three-foot slab of stone. When I lifted it out and turned it over I saw a snake's head sculpted onto the rock. The driver and his wife immediately began explaining it was just a yard decoration they had found face down in the dirt of a friend's back yard in Mexico. I knew what significance the snake had in ancient cultures in Central America. I didn't know if it was actually an artifact but I knew it hadn't been lying face down in the dirt in someone's yard. It had been recently broken off from something. Lois, our agriculture agent, turned it over to the Mexican Consulate and gave a receipt to the driver. They left very irritated. A week later the Consulate representative came to the Port of Entry and thanked me for retrieving one of their artifacts. It had been broken off one of the pyramids in the Yucatan peninsula.

05 June 2003 - Subject attempted entry into the United States through lane 5 of the Douglas, AZ Port of Entry by driving his 1980

Chevy Citation (MX plated 506SWJ4). He was accompanied by Guadalupe S***M*** DOB: ******. Subject's gestures seemed exaggerated in response to routine questioning. His crossing history revealed he had not been referred to secondary for some time. As a consequence of his exaggerated mannerisms I referred subject to secondary where 212lbs of marijuana was found in the rear of his vehicle.

17 June 2003 – Subject attempted entry into the United States driving his vehicle through the Douglas, AZ Port of Entry. He presented his DSP-150 Border Crossing Card to me. He said he was going to Douglas but he had baggage. I checked his wallet and found a fake U.S. Social Security card in his name. Supervisor Chavez authorized Subject's BCC to be cancelled under 18 U.S.C. 1028 "Possession of a Document with Intent to Defraud the U.S. Government". This was too easy. We seized his entry document and kicked him back to Mexico. After ensuring the guy had disappeared into Agua Prieta, I asked Ray Chavez why we could adjudicate such a simple case so easily with him when Ernie Morris wouldn't consider possession of a fake social security card sufficient evidence to cancel a guy's card. Ray jumped up and ran out the side door to try and get the guy back! I like playing with bureaucratic "mice" when I have the chance. I was disappointed to see Ray act that way. For a moment he acted like a real supervisor.

I was constantly harassed by the Douglas clique for looking in wallets, purses and patting down suspicious Mexicans whose stories or documents didn't make sense. One day a male Mexican came into the INS secondary office requesting a permit. He seemed nervous so I checked his wallet. He had a MasterCard in someone else's name. It was a gringo name. I called the 800 phone number of the security office for MasterCard in New York City listed on the back of the card. I explained who I was and what I had. She told me to hold on a minute. When she came back she told me the card had been stolen from the owner while on vacation at Sun Valley ski resort. She said the credit card owner's vehicle had also been stolen. She described not only the vehicle – which the guy was driving – but gave me the credit card owner's address – which was three blocks west of my house! The security rep called the card owner for permission to give me her phone number. When I called the card owner she was so grateful I recovered her car and credit card. She was a German immigrant married to a retired army officer. In spite of the direct evidence of the stolen MasterCard and stolen vehicle in his possession it still took a long time to convince "Mexican Moses" it was sufficient justification to cancel his Border Crossing Card. She understood it was. She just didn't want to do it. She really didn't like me taking the initiative of calling the credit card company.

An incident that haunted me for a long time was another wallet search in which I found the Oregon driver's license of a 20 year old woman in a male, Resident Alien's wallet. He was a gangbanger and the incident occurred before the gang "Mara Salvatruche (aka: "MS-13") became widely known. In the few encounters I had with them on the border it was hard not noticing there was no soul in their eyes. This gangbanger was one of those returning from Mexico in the middle of the night having visited "grandma" across the line. I called the Seattle police department and asked if they had a "missing person" BOLO on this woman. They had none. There was no phone number listed under her name or that address in the phone book. I couldn't do anything except keep her driver's license and, after (secretly) getting his photos and bio for the gang task force) send the maggot on his way. It wasn't until years later I heard gangs working in concert with cartels often kidnapped young woman. They held onto their drivers' licenses as proof they had them while demanding ransom from the family.

CHAPTER 9.

"Gunfight" With "Pistol" Pete

30 June 2003 - I was manning vehicle Lane 2 when Peter Bachelier, a newly arrived GS-13, scurried out of the main office to tell me "there is no more sitting on primary". He said it was an "officer safety" issue. I wondered how a GS-13 could have enough time on his hands to look out his window and be so concerned with one inspector sitting on a stool on the line. Bachelier quickly had all the stools removed from the line. This really angered a lot of inspectors. Bachelier is a Napoleonic, fraction of a man who epitomizes toxic leadership. When he walked it reminded me of one of Cinderella's mice scurrying around. His earned his nickname "Pistol Pete" while at Nogales POE when he "accidentally" fired a shotgun into the air while guarding seized drugs being prepared for burning. He also mysteriously "discharged" his duty weapon (and probably his "gun" as well) while sitting on the toilet in the men's room. What, you ask, was he doing playing with his duty weapon while sitting on the toilet? I can only guess! He repeatedly bragged to line inspectors about how he still roved vehicles in for secondary inspection as a GS-13. What he failed to realize was that he was no good at spotting suspect vehicles and would only clog up secondary with useless referrals. This kept the secondary inspectors distracted from legitimate referrals and wasted time and energy. He was a little boy playing in an adult world.

Both Customs and immigration inspectors spend a lot of time standing during an 8-hour shift. Many inspectors work double shifts. There were stools placed in each vehicle inspection booth to allow inspectors an opportunity to sit when not requiring drivers to open their trunks or moving to opposite sides of vehicles to check out suspicious passengers. Even the few seconds sitting between vehicles or during the rare times there were no vehicles in our lanes was some relief. Most vehicle traffic coming into the United States is from the Mexican city of Agua Prieta directly across the line. Inspectors quickly become familiar with who requires closer inspection and who does not. Most do not and it is a reprieve to be able to sit down because we also aren't allowed to sit down in the secondary inspection area when there are no referrals there. A lack of basic human understanding and kindness toward the troops appeared to be a prerequisite for promotion to management in CBP.

Additionally, Bachelier and other management were telling me I had to inform them when I had to go to the bathroom. I refused and they threatened to write me up. I told them to go ahead. I'd love to have it in writing. The harassment was getting ludicrous. All inspectors were also being very closely monitored by supervisors to ensure every license plate on every vehicle entering the U.S. was immediately and accurately read by the very-expensive-but-very-unreliable "plate readers". The plate readers were temperamental cameras mounted on posts that read the rear license plates of vehicles approaching the inspection booths. The plate number was then displayed on the computer monitor. It was reading plates incorrectly so frequently it re-focused our inspection from assessing the approaching driver and occupants to our computer monitor and the rear view mirror a few feet in front of our booth to ensure the information matched. This occurred during the critical moment of first contact. This, in my mind, was a real "officer safety" issue. Another problem with focusing on the license plate was the Mexican Department of Transportation re-issued the same license plate numbers to who-knows-how-many vehicles. There is no system in Mexico or the U.S. for verifying Mexican license plates actually belong to that vehicle. Supervisors tracked each inspector's diligence in correcting misread automatically inputted license plates. Inspectors were reprimanded in writing for correcting less than 90%. I don't know if this was an intentional effort to divert our intention from the people entering the U.S. – ergo failing to identify those attempting to enter illegally- or just another bunch of bureaucrats thinking license plate statistics was actually law enforcement. License plates won't kill you. It's the biometrics of the persons in the vehicles that can save your life. An inspector has to prioritize when he has only 20-30 seconds to conduct an inspection.

02 September 2003 - Subject sought entry through the pedestrian lane by presenting his Border Crossing Card saying he was just going to Douglas. He was crossing the line at a time when most crossers were Resident Aliens going to work (living out of status in Mexico). I asked him where he worked. He was very evasive and vague about employment in Mexico. I felt he was working in the fields in Wilcox, Arizona so I told him to return to Agua Prieta and return with proof of residence and employment in Mexico. He was stunned. I had to repeat my instructions several times to get him to return to Mexico. When he finally started to move he headed north!

I had to physically stop him and turn him south toward Mexico repeating my instructions. Not three feet from the turnstile he turned and told another Resident Alien standing in line "tell my boss I won't be at work today." I called him back and took his Border Crossing Card. I again told him he had a week to return with what I expected. I asked the Resident Alien if Subject worked with him in the fields. He immediately said yes then started backtracking.

I logged Subject's Border Crossing Card in the seized document log with my report of the circumstances. Checking the seized document log a few days later I saw it was given back to him by someone who didn't sign the log as the officer returning the document. Based on his Res Gestae – his spontaneous declaration of guilt described in the accompanying I-213 report, it should have been cancelled.

Chapter 10. "Baby Huey"

September 12, 2003 - Not everyone is well-suited for this job. I first saw ****** when a Cochise County deputy stopped by the Port in the middle of a midnight shift. His "ridealong" was an immensely obese law enforcement cadet. The deputy's intent was to leave this cadet at the Port for us to babysit while the deputy performed his "normal patrol duties" – which meant he probably had a girlfriend in Douglas. When the deputy returned and the cadet got in the squad car we could see the wheel wells almost rubbing the passenger side of the vehicle as they left the Port. As he walked toward the car I remember wondering how in the world his knees and ankles bore such weight without exploding.

Two years later I'm manning the pedestrian lane when the shift leader brings in a new inspector. During the introductions I kept thinking the guy looked familiar but couldn't place him. When they left my partner asked "Remember him?" "No". "He was the big kid that rode with the Sheriff's deputies a few years ago." "NO WAY!" I shouted. "Yup. He told me he lost almost two hundred pounds just by running (he had gastro-bypass surgery). And now, HEEERE HE

IS – an immigration inspector!" My partner telling me this horrid news was a Customs inspector and took some glee in rubbing in the fact this dingaling was wearing a white shirt. It didn't take long for the rumors of this kid's off-duty encounters to start circulating. A few days after INS sent out the egregiously inaccurate bulletin that the "American Militia" was a threat to federal officers we heard "Baby Huey" had instigated an unnecessary confrontation with an American Militia member in the nearby Safeway parking lot. No one was hurt but it apparently could have gotten out of hand had not the Douglas PD arrived when it did. Other rumors floated around him regarding similar incidents until I personally experienced his psychotic behavior in the memo below:

MEMO TO: Area Port Director Molaski

THRU: E. Morris, Asst Area Port Director

SUBJECT: Drunk Pedestrian

At approximately 0525hrs. a drunk Mexican national attempted to enter the U.S. by walking down vehicular lane one. Customs Inspector J*** B**** repeatedly told him to go back and come down the pedestrian lane. The drunk continued forward some distance toward JB until he stopped and began yelling obscenities and gesturing profanely at JB. He went back to stand just south of the red line at the end of the pedestrian lane. There he did the same to us including throwing a half-filled, plastic soda bottle at us on the ped lane about 70 feet away. During this somewhat comedic "assault" by the drunk, inspector "Baby Huey (BH)" stood at the south pedestrian door and yelled for the drunk to come here. As he continued to taunt the drunk, "BH" repeatedly placed his hand on his duty weapon as if in preparation to draw his weapon on the drunk. "BH" then asked another inspector if he would walk to the red line with him to take care of the "threat". The inspector wisely declined. JB was the shift leader as well and told Baby Huey in no uncertain terms NOT to walk south toward the red line. When JB returned to vehicular lane 1 just outside Baby Huey immediately walked to the red line at the end of the pedestrian lane and stood there for some minutes with his hand on his weapon taunting the drunk to come back. Before JB came back in to read BH the riot act I told Baby Huey he needed to follow orders on this team – and to keep his hand off his weapon until the situation called for it. This did not. I have worked with inspector BH for approximately two weeks. In my conversations and observations of his conduct I feel he is disassociated from reality. He interprets incidents to fit his perceived fantasies. He unnecessarily magnifies situations. He is an unnecessary shooting waiting to happen. His immaturity and lack of good judgment is a danger to himself, fellow inspectors and a liability to the service." Signed, Mike Ligon,

How did such a nut case get through the immigration academy?

JB and one or two other inspectors wrote memos as well. We finally saw the limit of INS' tolerance for ineptitude when they soon fired Baby Huey. It was probably the potential for a law suit that did it. Incompetence itself would not have gotten him fired from a government job.

02 October 2003   -   Ivan Eduardo G*****- G***** requested entry into the U.S. by presenting his Border Crossing Card at the pedestrian lane. I smelled marijuana on his person and his breath. I asked if he had been smoking marijuana. He first said he had been with friends who had been smoking. When I pointed out to him that the odor was coming directly from his mouth, he admitted to having smoked marijuana. His admission was witnessed by CBP officers W****, H****, and C*****. Any drug use is grounds for inadmissibility, I confiscated his DSP-150 for cancellation by a supervisor.

This young man obviously wasn't connected to the Douglas Clique family tree as his card was actually cancelled! It was probably due to a Customs supervisor being on duty. It was a common joke among the Customs officers that for anyone to be punished for crossing illegally or violating immigration laws immigration supervisors first had to check the Subject's genealogy and see if he wasn't family or friends with the Douglas Clique.

13 October 2003   - I arrived at work for the midnight shift to find
Viviana D**** B***** being processed as an Oral False Claim to
US citizenship. I was the incoming shift leader and asked for the
details of the referral that brought her into our office. One car was
parked in secondary with a young man sitting at the wheel.
Inspector Mora, the evening shift leader, told me the driver, Frank
Zamora of Douglas, brought the Oral False Claim (OFC) across in
his car but "He's OK. He had no knowledge [of her being illegal"
and hurried past me to return the car keys to the driver. As the driver
drove north, I was informed by the referring line officer the driver
claimed his passenger as his US citizen sister. She was neither a
citizen nor his sister. I asked why he was still sitting in his car when
he should have been sitting in a cell or being processed as an alien
smuggler. Mora left quickly without briefing me on the pending
case. Senior Customs Inspector Eli Villareal entered the office and
told me Zamora went to high school with inspector Paul Del Rincon
who was working the shift and told Zamora to stay in the car.
Zamora also owns Frankie's Bar – ergo he knows Mora very well.
Mora told the oncoming shift inspectors who were asking the same
questions as I that the OFC was "family" with Zamora – because we
don't make cases on family members who try to smuggle relatives
in. Senior Customs Inspector Villareal told me Zamora has a
previous alien smuggling record that he knows Del Rincon and Mora
are aware of. VDB, the Oral False Claim, told me during her sworn
statement she never told anyone Zamora was related. Mora lied to
me and allowed his bartender to escape prosecution as an alien
smuggler. VDB was processed for Expedited Removal and returned
to Mexico. Zamora, the driver, avoided prosecution for alien
smuggling with the assistance of his high school buddy, inspector
Del Rincon and a regular bar patron, inspector Mora. One more
reason CBP should no longer allow locals to work at the same POE
where they grew up. But it continues to this day.

20 October 2003 - At approximately 0230hrs an '81 GMC truck
approached the inspection booth on lane 1. A "CAOS" operation
requiring 100% inspection of gas tanks was on-going. Prior to
inspecting the truck's gas tank I asked passenger Mark D*****-
M**** and the driver Derek W**** Garland, both of Douglas for

their IDs. DM made no move to retrieve his ID but instead glared at me in a menacing manor. Observing his demeanor I informed DM I was politely asking for his ID – and I was authorized to do so. DM shouted "I know all about your authority! You don't have to tell me!" I summoned senior customs inspector A**** from the pedestrian lane for back up and to witness the situation. I asked DM how he knew "all about our authority". I asked if he had had any previous problems with Customs or Immigration previously. "I don't have to answer that!" DM shouted again. I turned my attention to the driver, WG, and asked if he had ever been arrested. "What kind of question is that!" WG demanded angrily. I told WG I was authorized to ask that and other questions to determine his admissibility into the United States. WG turned to DM and asked "Aren't we in No Man's Land?" DM told WG "This IS No Man's Land!" WG then produced a card that he shoved in my face. The first sentence read "My attorney has instructed me to not answer any of your questions." I directed WG to pull over for a secondary inspection. "I don't think I'm going to do that" he replied. Placing my hand on my weapon I told WG this was not "No Man's Land" but an international border under federal jurisdiction of the United States government. I told him I was authorized to conduct an inspection of him, his passengers and his vehicle. If he refused to comply he would be removed from his vehicle, handcuffed and taken to jail for failure to comply with the inspection. I told him he had ten seconds. By this time there were at least three other inspectors surrounding his vehicle with their hands on their weapons. Apparently they weren't too high on whatever they were smoking to provoke an armed confrontation with federal officers because he meekly drove his car to secondary – accompanied by four inspectors. Nothing out of the ordinary was found (including their attitude) and they were sent on their way.

11 November 2003 -   At 0226hrs Daniel B****** entered lane 1 of the Douglas Port of Entry driving a recently purchased white, '95 Stratus (VIN:*******). B****** was accompanied by Miguel Angel G**** - Q**** (DSP 150# ******). Senior CBP officer RH requested a declaration of citizenship from both persons. B*** stated he is a U.S. citizen but his wallet had been stolen recently in

Agua Prieta. G**** presented his DSP 150 Border Crossing Card. Officer RH doubted the citizenship of B**** and referred them to secondary for further inspection.

It took me a few moments to recognize B****'s face and voice as the same person I inspected the day before:

During the previous day's inspection B**** was driving an '89 Ford pickup, had also claimed US citizenship and that his wallet had been stolen. B**** told me the passenger in the rear of the truck's cabin was his cousin. I retrieved the passenger's DSP 150 and asked B*** the name of his "cousin". B*** couldn't tell me. Instead, B**** said his passenger was only a friend. So I asked B**** his friend's name. Again, B**** didn't know his name. B*** told me he had just come from Tucson to drop a friend off in Agua Prieta and was returning immediately. B**** told me he was taking his "friend" to Douglas. I saw an overnight bag on the floor in the rear of the truck's cabin at the passenger's feet and several overnight bags in the bed of the truck. I also saw a pallet of blankets in the bed of the truck that appeared to have had someone lying on it recently. The blankets were shaped like a human and I pushed on them to ensure there was no one underneath. I asked B**** who else had been in the truck. B**** said "No one. I make a lot of trips back and forth between Tucson and Agua Prieta giving friends a ride". I extracted the passenger and asked CBP officer B*** to IDENT him. I referred B*** to secondary for a more intensive inspection of his vehicle. G*****, the passenger, was returned to Mexico with his DSP-150 and told to return with proof of residency and economic solvency in Mexico. B****was allowed to proceed into the United States.

Today I reminded B**** of yesterday's inspection. He denied having entered. Further interviewing resulted in B**** admitting to me in the presence of CBP officer RH that he was born in Mexico. He stated a specific state of Mexico and stated he was definitely a citizen of Mexico. He also admitted to having driven the Ford truck the previous day. When supervisor Eli Villareal entered the room, B**** recanted his admission and claimed to be a U.S. citizen.

222

IDENT revealed an apprehension of B**** by the Border Patrol in San Ysidro on July 6, 1998 for alien smuggling. That entry indicates B*** told the Border Patrol he is a U.S. citizen. While searching B*** prior to putting him in the holding cell, I found an AZ vehicle registration for the '89 Ford truck. I asked B*** if that was the same truck he was driving the previous day. He said it was and that he was on his way to pick it up in Douglas. The truck is registered to a Cruz A**** - C****, with a residential address in Douglas.

B****'s true name and citizenship is in doubt. He has told BP he is a U.S. citizen yet told the two of us he is Mexican. Passenger G***** is the same passenger I returned to Mexico the previous day. He returned again today without having complied with the previous inspection. His DSP-150 Border Crossing Card has been notched by the Border Patrol (meaning he has been caught either jumping the line or smuggling). His card is cancelled.

CBP supervisor Villareal allowed B*** to enter the United States despite his questionable citizenship. What should have happened was B*** returned to Mexico and required to return with proof of citizenship and set up with an NTA (Notice to Appear) before an immigration judge to prove his citizenship. Either way, he should have been charged with alien smuggling and prosecuted. He's gleefully playing both sides of the fence because supervisors don't want to take "risks" in offending a US citizen or suffer the wrath of Mexican Moses.

09 February 2004 - At approximately 0755hrs I took declarations from M**** Romo and Maria S*****. Romo was driving a green, '93 Chevy Suburban (TX Kxx Zxx). They both claimed U.S. citizenship. Romo said he had just driven 12 hours from Durango, Mexico. I asked Romo to open the trunk of the vehicle. When I saw five backpacks I asked if everything in the car was his. He said everything was his and Maria's. Opening one of the backpacks I found a Mexican voter registration ("tarjeta de votar") card. As I began looking through each backpack Romo told me he was bringing clothes back from Mexico for his children who were in Texas. Romo first told me the Mexican voter card belonged to his nephew – whose name he couldn't recall. When he saw me taking adult clothes out of the backpack Romo told me it was his uncle's card – and also didn't know his uncle's name. Being relieved on the line I escorted Romo and his vehicle to secondary where I conducted a more intensive inspection. I found a Resident Alien card in the name of X….. Angeles and a business card of Texas parole officer Leslie Perkins. I called Ms. Perkins and explained the situation. She informed me Romo had violated his parole by leaving the state of Texas and driving a vehicle. Romo was told to return all items not belonging to him to Mexico. This report is being faxed to Romo's parole officer for a report of status violation. Romo's license plate is being entered in our database as a suspected alien smuggler.

17 February 2004 - At approximately 1555hrs today I observed Gorge A**** M***** approach primary pedestrian CBP Officer N**** and claim U.S. citizenship. Gorge appeared to be under the influence of a mind altering substance. His speech was slurred and his eyes failed to focus. His body weaved back and forth while being interviewed. I did not smell alcohol. I felt he may be under the influence of drugs and may also have contraband narcotics on his person. Gorge also had gang-related tattoos on his arms and neck. I conducted an immediate pat-down for weapons and summoned a supervisor. While awaiting the arrival of the supervisor I found two boxes of "Rophynol" in Gorge's back left back pocket. Each box was still sealed and contained 30 tabs each of the "date rape" drug. Gorge did not have a prescription for this controlled narcotic. I also found several identification cards in the name of Udiel C*** S**** in Gorge's possession. The pills and ID cards were seized. A want/warrant check came back negative. Supervisor Glass determined there was no evidence either way regarding Gorge's citizenship so allowed him to enter the United States. Yeah supervisor, that's right, error on the side of the alien - to quote Mexican Moses "Why would they lie?"

14 March 2004 - Contreras- L***, M***, a 25 year-old, female Mexican with a Border Crossing Card had been crossing the line at the same time for several weeks – 0730hrs. She said she was going to Gaytan's Duty Free Store on the corner to make a phone call or exchange money – even though she never had any money. Instead, she would always meet someone, get in their vehicle and head north. I received approval to seize her Border Crossing Card and require her to bring in proof of residence and economic solvency. Her BCC was returned by an inspector who didn't sign the log as required when returning the card. Customs supervisor Harnett authorized me to seize her document again pending proof of presentation of the required documents. She is suspected of working illegally in the U.S.

19 April 2004 – R****-Z****, Jose Luis, a Mexican national presented DSP-150 (Border Crossing Card) #******* was referred to secondary for a K-9 inspection. Subject was nervous and immediately requested to use the latrine. I felt he may have concealed weapons or contraband on his person so conducted a cursory pat down for safety. I found a Michigan driver's license issued in subject's name in his wallet with subject's address listed as **** Briggs Blvd. NE. Grand Rapids, MI. I also found a business card in the name of Ver Wys Bros. Inc., Doug VanderMeer as the owner. It is an insulation, windows, and siding business. I called this business and spoke with the owner who said subject is a family friend who had worked for him for about two years two years ago. Subject is inadmissible per Section 222(g) of the INA. Rather than cancelling his Border Crossing Card for working illegally in the U.S. Ernie Morris "deferred" the man by letting him keep his card and go back to Mexico – only to allow him to return later through a friendlier inspector or at another Port of Entry.

The National Chamber of Commerce is complicit in Congress's demographic subterfuge of the United States by heavy "lobbying" (translated: $$$$) of politicians for every piece of legislation opening the borders of the U.S. . During WW II the federal government established the "Bracero" program allowing Mexican farm workers to harvest the crops in the U.S. – presumably to make up for the lack of American manpower diverted to fighting the war. What began as a response to a war-time manpower crisis evolved into an agricultural guest worker program that lasted into the '60s. It ended only when neither the U.S. nor the Mexican government could agree on conditions regarding the program. The Mexican government wanted control over issuance of the work permits (and the bribes that went with them) and improved working/living conditions for the migrant workers such as better housing, sanitary facilities, medical care, and education for the children.

The U.S. government would not surrender the permit process knowing of the Mexican government's proclivity for corruption and because the ranch and farming lobby didn't want to pay for better living conditions and medical care for the migrant workers. There is actually a photo of a Border Patrol agent in Texas trying to pull a Mexican man *into* the United States and a Mexican police officer trying to pull him back to Mexico. All three are standing in a paved portion of the Rio Grande River. A Chief Border Patrol Agent testified before a congressional committee in the '60s that it was his responsibility to gather up migrant workers for the local ranchers and farmers.

19 September 2004 - Ricardo R**** - G****** requested entry into the US through my lane driving a '95 Chevy Lumina (AZ 5**L**). He declared his US citizenship and gave me a California identification card. I felt he was being evasive regarding ownership of articles in his car so I asked him to open his trunk. While opening it everything suddenly became his sister's. I asked where his driver's license was and he said he didn't have one. I asked if it was suspended and he said he had never had a driver's license – at 28 years old. He was also unfamiliar with the U.S. Selective Service registration requirements at age 18. I felt he was not a U.S. citizen and was probably smuggling illegal aliens. I referred him to secondary where he was determined to be an Oral False Claim to U.S. citizenship and a prior deported alien with a U.S. Marshal's active warrant for narcotics trafficking. He was using his dead brother's identity. He was detained for prosecution.

CHAPTER 11. "DIRTY" HARRY

Harry Bailey was one of my most trusted fellow inspectors. The moniker "Dirty Harry" comparing him favorably to the Clint

226

Eastwood character. He was from Douglas but he didn't play their games. He is honest as the day is long. On one evening or midnight shift he was manning lane 1 when the driver of the elevated Suburban he was inspecting put the car in reverse. The driver jammed on the gas pedal and immediately became climbing onto the hood of the low-slung sports car full of teenagers behind him. If he had continued he would have crushed everyone in the sports car. He was obviously fleeing the inspection and putting several lives at risk. Harry fired a .40 caliber, hollow point round through the driver's door and nearly took of the punk's testicles. I don't know how the driver got back to Mexico but the word from the Mexican police was the driver nearly bled to death from the severed artery in his leg. Even the Agua Prieta police chief said it was a "good shooting". Harry saved a few lives that night. It also proved a .40 caliber, fully jacketed, hollow point will penetrate a car door and do some damage.

About a year later, again on the evening shift, the Port received a call from the Border Patrol that a driver of a pickup truck was fleeing from Border Patrol agents and heading toward the Port to escape to Mexico. The lanes into Mexico were choked with traffic. Instead of veering away from the Port, the driver aimed his truck at the inspectors forming a line at the Port's north end. He jumped an island and floored it toward the inspectors. It must have looked like a bull fight as the truck passed Harry and rammed into a southbound inspection booth. The booth is made of thick steel and bullet-resistance glass. The truck driver hit it squarely and bent the booth into a 45 degree angle. He must have been wearing his seat belt because he backed up and again aimed his truck at the inspectors to get through the Port secondary area and into Mexico. As he sped past, Harry fired one shot. A fire-plug of an inspector, wife of a Border Patrol agent, also fired. The truck stopped. As he fell back against his seat he grunted. When Harry and others extracted him from the truck he appeared unconscious. They couldn't find an obvious bullet wound and didn't see any blood. "Fire plug's" bullet hit the radio in the dashboard. Harry's bullet tore the top half of the driver's heart off. The doctor said the driver could have been shot on the operating table and he still couldn't have been saved.

I learned about the shooting at the staff meeting the next morning. I got the details from other inspectors. Ernestina Morris conducted the staff meeting and, in somber, regretful tones, sadly reported that the "patient" died. The maggot was a drug smuggler who tried to kill federal officers and he paid for it with his life. Score one for the good guys. Morris' and her clique's mourning over the death of a local blight on society made me sick to my stomach.

I'm not sure if that's when Morris' harassment of "fire plug" began but it soon became obvious to all of us that she was on Morris' "hit list" of people she was trying to fire or make quit. I was in good company!

Inspectors who have been involved in a shooting incident resulting in the death of the suspect were usually reassigned to just about any other Port of their choosing. This removes the inspector from an environment where vendettas can be brutal. Douglas and District management gave Harry a hard time about transferring him. They took a year to allow him to transfer to the northern border. I can only imagine what it was like for his wife and kids to live in Douglas after the shooting. Harry continued to be enforcement-minded. He became so fed up with immigration he resigned and went back to work in a mine. I lost contact with Harry after he left. I wish him well in life. Harry was also a fellow former Marine.

The evening after the fatal shooting, I was driving through Bisbee on the way home. Just west of the traffic circle in Bisbee is an abandoned lumber yard. It is located just east of the huge hole in the ground that was the Bisbee Copper Mine. As you approach the traffic circle from the west there is a wide gap in the curb that had been a driveway into the lumber yard. It had been fenced off for years but was a convenient place to pull over and be off the main road. It was 00:27 am when I drove past the lumber yard and saw a Bisbee police officer interviewing the driver of a white sedan in the old driveway. He was alone and I saw a bunch of heads in the back seat of the sedan. I pulled up behind him and asked what he had.

"These guys are down from Phoenix and they have a shotgun in the trunk" he said. He had closed the trunk since I pulled around. I could see the backs of four heads in the back seat and a front passenger. That made six. "I don't know if they have any more weapons in the car with them but there reason for going to Douglas doesn't make sense" he further informed me. "How do you want to handle it?" I asked. "Well, we need to get them out of the car" he said. I agreed and moved to assume the number 2 officer position for a felony stop of multiple suspects. I thought he was going to go back to his side of his patrol car and begin instructing them how he wanted them to get out of the car. This is a high risk situation that requires an absolutely commanding voice and visual control of what the subjects are doing.

Instead of returning to his side of the patrol car, he walked right up to the front passenger side of the sedan and opened the door. I caught up with him wondering if he had changed his mind and hadn't told me. I didn't know what he was going to do. He talked to the front passenger a moment then told him to get out of the car. As the passenger stood up I heard the officer utter "What's *this*!" and began fighting the passenger for control of something apparently in the belt of the passenger's pants. Instead of yelling "GUN!" to let me know he was in danger, he continued to grunt and grasp and he continued trying to wrest something from the passenger. I shoved my weapon around the right side of the officer and considered a contact shot on the passenger but something made me hesitate. I couldn't see exactly where the passenger was in front of the officer. I was concerned about the driver and the back seat passengers. I ran around the back of the sedan, rested my arm on the opened window sill of the driver's door to sight in on the passenger wrestling with the officer and yelled for the back seat passengers to put their hands behind their heads. It wasn't the best tactical position to be in considering. The officer gained control of the passenger and pulled him back toward the hood of the patrol car. I assumed a kneeling position behind the officer's driver door and proceeded to get the others out of the car, patted down and seated on the curb one at a time. Their attitude was that this was an enjoyable lark. When I finished patting down the last one I turned toward the squad car to see about four Border Patrol agents and the officer's Bisbee back-up standing behind the first officer's car. "How long have you guys been there?" I asked. "Long enough to see you do a great job?" they said grinning. "Thanks for the help!" I said. Cop humor – gotta love it.

It turned out the front passenger had a gun in his waistband – a toy gun. If the officer had yelled "Gun!" I would have immediately shot that 18 year old kid dead with no questions asked. One of these white teenagers had taken their father's shotgun and driven down to the border to sell the shotgun to "someone." The front passenger brought the toy gun to "keep anybody from ripping us off." The officer called the driver's dad then told them -in so many words- to turn around and get their asses back to Phoenix. Before they left I let the passenger know how close he came to dying that night. I showed him a .40 caliber, fully-jacketed, hollow point round and asked if he knew what that would do to him. His attitude became appropriate for the situation. He started stuttering.

I was lucky too that night. I spent the next few nights trying to get to sleep wondering "What if?" Harry didn't have that luxury. Harry told me he felt justified in shooting the drug smuggler – and he was. His biggest worry, he said, was what INS management was going to do about it. The FBI conducted the shooting investigation and quickly cleared him.

CHAPTER 12. HITLER'S COUSIN

Jueves, 30 de Septiembre del 2004 - "Marcando el Paso Por Jorge Gino Flores: ……..**Testigo Ocular…** de una demostracion de me vale madre por parte de un emigrante que parece primo hermano de Hitler y que se avento' 25 minutes platicando mientras nosotros nos estabamos derritiendo de calor   de coraje y aguantandanos, no asi una senora que abandono' su carro y fue y le' leyo' parte de la carilla, ademas de una reverenda llamada de atencion y nosotros los de la cola le dedicamos una serenata de madrazos…."

Arriving at work one day I was congratulated by several inspectors for being named "Hitler's cousin" in a local newspaper across the line. They showed me the above editorial in the anti-American, Agua Prieta newspaper, "Plan de Agua Prieta" that also contained several photos of me conducting an inspection of a vehicle. The editorialist said I took twenty-five minutes to inspect one vehicle while many others waited in line in sweltering heat. It was over a hundred degrees that day. No inspector is allowed to take more than 30 to 45 *seconds* –at the most- to conduct a primary inspection on the line at any time. Supervisors spend most of their careers ensuring we are not "abusing" the public by taking too long on primary inspections. If it takes longer than half a minute or so we're expected to send the vehicle to secondary where officers have the leisure of time and space to conduct a thorough, controlled, intensive inspection. I agree with this and was always aware of the impact the heat had on people waiting in line. Strangely I wasn't written up or given days off by management for earning the title "Hitler's cousin". I'm sure it was placed in my personnel file......the one Ernestina Morris didn't want me to see because "it has stuff in there we don't you to see".

Charity (?)

Christmas was approaching and the annual collection of food and toys for the home for abused wives and children was under way. Surprisingly I was asked to help load the donations into the government van and go to the shelter – a few blocks down 1st Street for unloading and delivery. I gladly went along believing it to be just that. After unloading the gifts I returned to the van for the trip back to work but was informed by inspector Luna that "pictures" would be taken by the local newspaper. I politely declined. As I watched the Douglas Clique getting their pictures taken with those poor, abused women and children I was embarrassed for those who didn't have the sense -or decency- to be embarrassed themselves. I could see the embarrassment of the shelter's residents when they realized their pictures would be on the front page of a very small community's newspaper. The immigration Douglas Clique apparently had no class – as well as no morals. I seemed to remember the Lord telling us "let not thy right hand know what thy left hand doeth" and "those who doeth their good deeds in secret I will reward in secret".

About the same time the Combined Federal Campaign was going on. I had seen on the news where the director of this organization had been indicted for fraud and embezzlement. He had been living high on the hog with Rolls Royce's, mansions, etc. while managing a national charitable organization. I read the catalogue of organizations federal employees were "allowed" to choose to "donate" to by having a one-time or monthly allotment drawn from our pay. Many showed an average of 40% of the contributions going to "overhead". I never contributed. I gave my own way and I kept it to myself – except for this one time.

At the end of this "charitable" fund drive Port Director Charlie Stemple proudly announced that the "Port" had contributed a grand total of a little over two thousand dollars toward the fund. Stemple then commented to the assembled twenty or so inspectors that "we all gave – except one person …..and we know who he is." Returning from my weekend, a buddy told me what Stemple said.

Well, I succumbed to pride in response to this accusation of being a cheapskate – and in doing so probably lost the blessing. Later in the shift I managed to work in the subject of Mormons' practice of paying tithing in a conversation with a supervisor. I knew he would blab it back to Stemple. I informed the supervisor that I have been a full tithe payer since joining the Mormon church in 1968. That meant I've been paying 10% of my gross income every month for most of the last thirty or so years. I didn't mention Stemple's sarcastic remark. I let the rat line work. As opposed to many organizations listed on the Combined Federal Campaign register with high living leadership and varying degrees of high overhead, I know my tithing is spent on good causes around the world – to benefit all of God's children by volunteers with little to no "overhead" – and very, very little public recognition. And that's fine with me.

Mathew 6: 1-4: "Take heed that you give not your alms before men, to be seen of them: otherwise you have no reward of your Father who is in heaven. Therefore when you give your alms, do not sound a trumpet before you, as the hypocrites do in the synagogues and in the streets, that they may have glory of men. Verily I say unto you, They have their reward. But when you give alms, let not your left hand know what your right hand does: That your alms may be in secret: and your Father who sees in secret himself shall reward you openly." (King James Bible). I can only testify that the Lord has kept his promise to me by blessing my family abundantly for keeping this law.

Malachi 8:3 "Will a man rob God? Yet ye have robbed me. But ye say, Wherein have we robbed thee? In tithes and offerings. Ye *are* cursed with a curse: for ye have robbed me, *even* this whole nation. Bring ye all the tithes into the storehouse, that there may be meat in mine house, and prove me now herewith, saith the LORD of hosts, if I will not open you the windows of heaven, and pour you out a blessing, that *there shall* not *be room* enough *to receive it.* And I will rebuke the devourer for your sakes, and he shall not destroy the fruits of your ground; neither shall your vine cast her fruit before the time in the field, saith the LORD of hosts. And all nations shall call you blessed: for ye shall be a delightsome land, saith the LORD of hosts." (King James Bible)

21 October 2004 - 0800hrs. Manning the pedestrian lane Luis Nain G**** - C***** approached and presented his Border Crossing Card. It was time for kids his age to be in school –on one side of the border or the other – and he was traveling alone. GC told me he went to school in Agua Prieta in the afternoon and was just crossing now to help clean his aunt's house in Douglas. Under his shirt he had an "Omega Alpha Academy" sweatshirt – a tax supported charter school. He was carrying a spiral notebook and a change of clothes for PE. I also found a school lunch ticket with one hole punched in it. Senior inspector Joe Perez approached and immediately told me GC was "OK". Without asking me what I had found, inspector Perez began asking the young man where he was going in Spanish. I heard him tell Perez he was going to school – at

233

Alpha Omega. Perez told me in English the young man was going to the private Catholic school Loretto – which was legal because it was not tax payer supported. I was, again, dumbfounded that an immigration inspector would lie to a fellow officer to allow a Mexican young man attend a state-supported (tax payer) school illegally. It turned out that Perez and another inspector had told him twice before to bring in proof of going to Loretto. I guess they couldn't read the bright yellow sweatshirt. Or maybe that wasn't "enough evidence". His card was cancelled – at least that day.

Another ludicrous example of the "service" mentality of the INS management: Periodically a representative of the Kickapoo Indian tribe would arrive at the Port of Entry. INS management provided them office space to register people as members of their tribe. The tribal boundaries lay across the U.S.-Mexico border. In addition to the State Department's oft-quoted "Don't F*** with the 7As!" referring to foreign students, INS used the same expletive phrase regarding the Indians – "Don't F*** with the Indians!" The problem with this registration process was that any Mexican could claim –and gain- membership in the Kickapoo tribe and receive entry documents into the United States. This also qualified them for government assistance. This fraud was so sacrosanct we could only shake our heads. I'm sure some enforcement-minded inspector wrote his/her congressperson complaining of the gaping breach in local management's interpretation of the law. Finally, after about five years, a senior ranking Border Patrol representative arrived to tell our management that he had the official rolls of the Kickapoo tribe and if the applicants weren't related to those on the rolls they didn't qualify for membership. Suddenly the Kickapoo rep quit coming. Most other recognized American Indian tribes don't recognize Kickapoos as legitimate American Indians. Well, several thousand (Mexican) "Kickapoos" are American citizens now. "Local Policy" is such a powerful weapon to yield in the demographic subterfuge of America.

11 December 2004 - An American citizen told me he has seen two Mexican citizens from Agua Prieta with Border Crossing Cards taking their daughter to the public school in Tucson every day for the last two years. He gave us their names. When we referred this couple who were obviously living in Tucson illegally, inspector Geronimo Grijalva gave them their entry documents back to them and allowed them to proceed on to Tucson. They laughed in our faces as they drove away.

15 December 2004 - An I-551 holder (Resident Alien) was referred to INS secondary. His criminal record revealed he had been arrested for kidnapping and possession of narcotics with intent to distribute (a drug dealer). An immigration judge told him "You'll never receive U.S. citizenship but you can keep your Resident Alien card". What kind of sense does that make? Obviously the man is a clear case of moral turpitude (a category for deportation) and the judge admits this by denying him U.S. citizenship – but allows him to remain in the U.S. as a Resident Alien? Give me a break!

A DSP-150 holder (Border Crosser) was referred to INS secondary for a more intensive inspection. It was discovered that this young Mexican citizen was receiving psychiatric counseling in the United States. A self-written poem seething with violence and hatred was found on his person in which he wrote "Hatred…..F@#$ YOU!.....Ain't GONNA TAKE IT NO MORE!" Supervisor Ann Glass overruled our recommendation to lift his border crossing card [(212)(a)(1)(A)(iii) – Physical or mental disorder with associated harmful behavior] and let him enter the U.S.. I hope he didn't go to school illegally in the U.S. as well. He was a border crosser. Who was paying for his psychiatric counseling? The U.S. taxpayer.

This reminds me that the Social Security Agency continues to refuse to allow INS to crosscheck the citizenship of everyone receiving Social Security. There are newspapers in every "Little Asia" in every major city advertising places that will instruct newly arrived aliens –legal or illegal- on how to qualify for Social Security.

30 January 2005 - At approximately 2355hrs, a young woman driver approached lane one. She was holding a lemon in her hand. After taking everyone's declaration I asked her if that was a lemon and not a lime. She said it was a lemon. I informed her that lemons were prohibited from being brought into the United States. She yelled sarcastically "No Way! Is my godfather working tonight?" She told me she bought the lemon at the gas station in Douglas and had the receipt for it. Since she showed me the receipt and had apparently just made a quick trip into Mexico I gave it back to her. Since she tried "name dropping", I thought she may be needing protection for other reasons so I asked for her driver's license and asked her to open the trunk of her car. While I was inspecting the trunk, she walked over and threw the lemon into the trash can. I told her the lemon had to be thrown into an agricultural waste bin and asked her to retrieve it. After doing so she asked me for a pen so she could write my name down. I've made it standard procedure that whenever a person crossing the border asks for my name I immediately refer them to secondary to speak with a supervisor. I did so in this case. For all I know the shift supervisor could be her "godfather." It's pretty handy to have a "godfather" who is a supervisor at a U.S. Port of Entry when you are a Mexican citizen.

01 March 2005 - I didn't note whether the man entering the U.S. through the pedestrian lane was a Border Crosser, Resident Alien or U.S. citizen but he was suspicious enough for me to conduct a quick pat-down for contraband. I found the following penciled "briefing notes to aliens being smuggled" in his pocket:

"Welcome Abourd. OK this is how Figured out iF you have never been a that Little be town of douglas, Arizona borders of U.S. a Mexico Country's divide their territories by a self fish of bunch of guys predigised but anyways let them be happy we all 're animalitos of gots   on Mexico side is locaited the beautiful city. OK city not a town we all his beutifull people is name is Agua Prieta Sonora Mexico one state of the states of Mexico.

Make sure to tell people that is cane of help each other doing this we help em to get safe to any point They're disteny should be we are just given you a ride to get red of the could tempersure on the side of the road we picked 'em up

This is going to a little incoterble ride but try to keeping down at least by the sides of back sit & don't lower down the windows to much in case that you have to let air come true the window to fog off back windows to much breeding [sic!] OK on our coming back will be seeing a few US borders on our right hand sides parked up to me the best way to do it early in the morning around 6 to 6307 when traffic it should be cane of heavy traffic or when is coming down the SUN's up comes at darkness or dask so any Questions? Thatkyou Let's make out of this one a good habit Fwy 51 souht 10 EAST F80 south E191 south"

The author includes a hand drawn map of roads from Douglas to Bisbee and Benson and a detailed drawing of where each person in the vehicle should sit. The man who wrote this is so far behind the power curve of literacy he probably had to turn to smuggling and other criminal enterprises to rise above the poverty level.

01 July 2005 – <u>Customs and Border Protection Officer Competency-Based Assessments for Promotion Feedback Report</u>: Total Score For: First-Line GS-12 Supervisory CBP Officer – 93; Total Score For: GS-12 CBP Officer (Course Developer/Instructor) – 93.

This test was weird – it included a section on ascertaining the meaning of statements containing double negatives. I had never seen such a test before – but it didn't matter. No one used the test results to promote anyway. This was the test rumor had it that Mexican Moses took twice and failed both times – to eventually be promoted to Assistant Port Director. Every supervisor position that was announced between Douglas and Naco was filled by a family member of another supervisor.

NOTE: This could be remedied by CBP very easily. Supervisors serve at the whim of higher management. Supervisors can be reassigned based on the "needs of the service." The Service certainly "needs" to break up the nepotism and failure to enforce the law at Douglas by reassigning every home grown supervisor to another Port of Entry far, far away from the U.S./Mexican border – if they can't be fired for malfeasance. I don't think the FBI agent interviewing me in the hotel room understood "malfeasance" when he asked me "But have you seen any *real* incidents of corruption?" There are more kinds of corruption than taking money from drug dealers and letting drug loads through your lane. It was like trying to push a string getting anyone to understand what was wrong with the management at the Douglas Port of Entry.

Prior to this test CBP had sent out a career assessment survey that gave points for schooling and experience related to duties and responsibilities on the border. When a few of us veterans were heard discussing including our military experience on the forms, the "Perfumed Prince" exclaimed "They don't want anything on it that you've done ***prior*** to your employment with INS!" You could hear the fear in his voice that every one of the veterans was better qualified in life experience, schooling and work than he was. I pointed out that if that were true his degree from New Mexico Military Institute wouldn't count either. Despite his and the other members' of the clique protests our previous experience and education did count. That made every one of us more qualified than any inspector working at the Port of Entry who was from Douglas and had never left. Despite the comparative dirth of qualifications, the Perfumed Prince was the first to be promoted to senior inspector and supervisor. One of my peers conducted a survey while a union steward and prepared a pie chart depicting the allotment of training opportunities for the last few years. The "Perfumed Prince" – Paul Del Rincon- was Stemple's "boy" and received 80% of all training opportunities – most of which weren't announced to the general officer population in violation of the management/union Agreement.

During a staff meeting one morning the subject of volunteers to be INS recruiters came up. I raised my hand and expressed an interest in being a recruiter. Charlie Stemple and Mexican Moses muttered among themselves that recruiting was a "SEP" program. I overheard them and asked a co-worker what "SEP" was. "It stands for Special Emphasis Program" he said. "It's for minorities." A light went on in my head then. That explained why INS was over 70% Hispanic. If only Hispanics were allowed to recruit immigration inspectors then it would naturally follow – based on what I was seeing in Douglas- that pretty much only Hispanics would be hired. The SEP program gave enough gratuitous extra points to minorities who failed the written entry test to pass the test regardless. Immigration inspectors also received promotion points for recruiting duty. Hispanic recruiters were telling gringo applicants they had to be able to speak Spanish in order to be hired by INS. I saw the two female INS recruiters from Douglas POE say that to an audience of military personnel at Ft. Huachuca. It was a lie.

[In 1976, while I was attending graduate school at Cal. State L.A., Hispanic secretaries were telling only Hispanic applicants to the L.A. County Sheriff Department about the opportunity for "mock" oral interviews. These provided a significant advantage on the actual interview. Professor Bristow, a nationally renowned criminal justice author, filed a law suit on behalf of non-hispanic applicants and won.]

No one had to speak Spanish in order to be hired. At the end of the basic immigration academy training those who passed a fluency test could go home and start working. The language training for those who didn't test out consisted of memorizing five or six pages of Spanish phrases. I didn't think anything of it during the recruiters' briefing at Ft. Huachuca because I had six months of Spanish language training at the John F. Kennedy Special Warfare Center, Ft. Bragg, N.C. and had taught military blocks of instruction in Spanish to troops in Central America. I didn't test out of the five weeks of language training because I didn't answer the tester's questions verbatim from the list. A former Mormon missionary who served a two-year mission in Latin America didn't test out either. Figure that one out.

My Spanish "instructor" at FLETC was an airport senior inspector from Panama. He had three gold caps on his front teeth with stars cut out. I spent most of the five weeks of language training teaching him how to read the instructor manuals so he could teach the class. The review for the final test consisted of two days of constant repetition of those five pages from a Puerto Rican supervisor who had retired from the New York transit department. His first comment to us was "I will guarantee none of you will fail this test." Incredibly, after the exam he asked each student one by one what we thought of his preparing us for the test. Of course everyone said it was very good – excellent! I was next to last to be asked. I told him I thought it was cheating and an integrity violation. I had to go explain that to the deputy director of the academy. He didn't want to hear it either.

So therein lies why INS was over 70% Hispanic - only Hispanic inspectors were being selected for recruiting duty.

30 July 2005 - Sometimes your radar may suspect one thing only to find something else by chance: At approximately 1415hrs I received a secondary referral from CBPO G***** requesting I interview the occupants regarding possible child smuggling and an intensive inspection of the vehicle – a white, 1996 Chevy Suburban. I immediately recognized the driver, Omar M******* (DOB: **/**/**) as having crossed through the pedestrian lane a few days prior. At that time OM did not appear to have a credible reason for having gone to Mexico. He was also memorable for having unique, gang-type tattoos on his neck, shoulder and forearms. OM had a female passenger, Brandi C****, (DOB: 02/**/**) in the front seat and a very young girl with lots of curly black hair in a child's car seat in the back seat. Although appearing too young to talk, the young girl was surprisingly articulate and able to convince me that BC is her mother and that she is a U.S. citizen. BC told me she is 17 years old and from New Mexico en route with her boyfriend to Phoenix via Agua Prieta. The reason for their detour to Mexico and her accompanying a suspected gang member caused me to suspect she may be a runaway. Further interviewing convinced me she is not. I asked everyone to exit the vehicle. While searching OM's wallet for zero tolerance drugs, CBP Canine Officer, JH walked by with his K-9, Jessy. I asked him to run the car while I continued interviewing OM. Moments later, K-9 officer JH signaled me to take OM into custody after Jessy alerted to the vehicle. A total of 563 pounds of marijuana was found concealed throughout the vehicle.

09 August 2005 - No inspector is 100% alert all the time. Being angry about someone you catch red-handed being released into the

U.S. by management can occupy much of your thoughts on the line. This one almost got by me: At approximately 1035hrs. Subject attempted entry into the U.S. driving a 1996 Grand Am (MX plate: 7** S***). Subject presented his DSP-150 Border Crossing Card as did his female passenger. I perceived nothing amiss and waved them through. Something about the female's facial expression changing upon being waved through caught my attention so I continued to watch them as they drove away. A few feet further away she smiled broadly as if asking the driver "Is that all there is to it?" I radioed secondary to verify her print with that on the Border Crossing Card. They didn't match. Further interviewing in secondary established conspiracy between the driver and the imposter. Both were processed for deportation and returned to Mexico.

10 October 2005 - Subject approached the pedestrian lane and asked if he could enter the United States with the letter (below) since he "lost" his visa. He informed us very solemnly he had received it from the U.S. government. The below is written exactly as the letter is written:

"By virtue of having fulfilled the requirements that the law imposed you, checking that their record is already clean, this Department Justice and the name the Government of the United States, it grant you the pardon, exhorting it to that conduce in the successive inside of the right road.

Sincerely, Gary F. Kelley, Chief, Law Appeals Unit"

Once we stopped laughing we deported him. He paid $500 for the letter. He's not the only one being ripped off by his fellow Mexicans. We see "spotters" every day standing on the sidewalk on the Mexican side of the line paid by the drug smugglers to see which inspector is passing cars through like an expressway. We see them use a cell phone to call the drug safe house which lane to get into to stand a better chance of getting through without a rigorous inspection. Some of the spotters get "off duty" and walk the block south to the Agua Prieta bus station where they prey on naïve crossing hopefuls getting off the bus from further south in Mexico –

241

even from countries further south than that. They are easy to spot because they look different and have that "deer in the headlights" look. The maggots approach the newly arrived with assurances that they can get them across the line without being caught – no problem. But it costs money. These destitute survivors of an unimaginably arduous trip are, of course, eager to make the last final obstacle – the border of the United States- and gain the Promise Land. They can see the American flag flying over the Port of Entry from the bus station. The maggots are experts at extorting the last secreted cash from these people and then walk them toward the line. The maggots get them close enough to raise their hopes even further, point toward the southbound sidewalk and tell them to simply walk north on the southbound sidewalk at the maggots' signal. The inspectors will never see them. The maggots then walk away to a point "where they can see better" and give the conned traveler the signal. Of course in broad daylight we see them and arrest them – at which time the maggot disappears to the nearest bar for a tequila and a pocket-full of cash. It's almost impossible to do at night as well – unless you are a fit young male willing to low crawl along the guardrail. It became such a problem our management told inspectors we couldn't arrest them anymore. Management told us to quit apprehending illegals running north on our southbound traffic lane in plain sight. They said it was a "Border Patrol problem and if they didn't see fit to have a unit here then – oh well". We continued to arrest them anyway until Customs management arranged for a BP unit to "sit the X" on the southbound lane.

Aaaah yes, the X! A successful concept distorted to paralysis. The "X" concept was started by a Chief Border Patrol Agent in Texas whose community leaders were haranguing him about the hordes of illegals crossing the Rio Grande, committing crimes and wreaking general havoc within several communities. He devised a plan to place a Border Patrol agent in a vehicle every 100 or so feet along his sector. This was obviously man-power intensive as well as eating up a lot of overtime money. But it dropped the crime rate dramatically in the area. The community leaders were pleased and the citizens could sleep safe at night. However – comma- INS management told him to stop doing it. No one knows why. The

Mexican government probably complained. When he told them he wouldn't stop unless they put the order in writing, they simply starved him of funds until he couldn't man the Xs anymore. He eventually ended up retiring and being elected to Congress.

Most of the BP agents we encountered hated sitting the X. The concept had been distorted by management to the point that when agents could see hundreds of illegals stampeding across the line within a stone's throw from their vehicle they were prohibited from leaving their assigned "X" to pursue them. They had to radio in the number and direction – and hope back up arrived before the coyote got them to their ride. That's one reason why BP only catches about 25% of those jumping the line. Another reason is that Border Patrol Chief Agents manipulate the figures to satisfy their politically appointed masters. There's been at least one investigation by the Inspector General about that in the San Diego sector.

22 October 2005 - Jesus Alberto LOYA-Grajeda approached the pedestrian lane and attempted entry into the United States by claiming to be a U.S. citizen. I was roaming the primary line area and happened upon CBP officer M***** conducting his inspection of LOYA-Grajeda. CBPO M***** was still relatively new and apparently unsure of LOYA-Grajeda's citizenship. I was observing from a distance until CBPO M***** waved me over to assist him with the inspection. LOYA-Grajeda told me that he had an Arizona birth certificate at his mom's house in Agua Prieta – then it was in Douglas – then it was in Tucson. He had no other form of identification. I informed LOYA-Grajeda that we could either take him into the office and run some checks on him to determine his citizenship or he could withdraw his application for entry and go back to Mexico and retrieve his birth certificate. LOYA-Grajeda volunteered to return to Mexico. This was common practice with persons whose status is in doubt. I simply used the information he gave me to provide him a choice. It's called "allowing the alien to withdraw his application for entry". This option is exercised hundreds – if not thousands - of times a day on the southern land border.

It is not uncommon for young U.S. citizens to have their U.S. birth certificates across the line in a border Mexican city – particularly with so many Resident Aliens being "allowed" to live in Mexico and the number of Mexican women having babies just inside the U.S. at "birthing mills", gaining automatic U.S. citizenship for their newborn then returning to live in Mexico until the child turns 18 – at which time he/she can immigrate a plethora of relatives without ever having lived in the United States.

About fifteen minutes later one of the Customs inspectors informed me that, rather than return to "grandma's house" to retrieve his Arizona birth certificate, LOYA-Grajeda circled around the inbound traffic lanes and attempted to enter the U.S. by running north on the southbound sidewalk on the opposite side of the Port of Entry. CBP officer T*** apprehended LOYA-Grajeda and brought him into immigration secondary. He was then turned over to the Border Patrol for processing as an Entry Without Inspection (EWI). During processing it was discovered that LOYA-Grajeda was a prior deported criminal alien. He came up positive on all five criminal data bases. LOYA was arrested by Tucson PD on March 19, 2003 and charged with three counts of Armed Robbery, two counts of Aggravated Robbery, and one count of Aggravated Assault. Loya was arrested by Douglas Border Patrol on February 5, 2003 and charged with Alien Smuggling. Loya was charged with being an Oral False Claim to U.S. citizenship on December 1, 1996 in Phoenix. Field Office Supervisor Jeffrey Richards authorized an Expedited Removal on Loya as per Section 212(a)(7)(A)(i)(I) of the Immigration & Nationality Act. LOYA was expeditiously removed to Mexico through the Douglas (AZ) Port of Entry on October 23, 2005.

So. I "allowed" LOYA to return to Mexico. The Border Patrol spent a few hours creating another useless file on LOYA – and, declining prosecution for being an alien attempting to enter the United States after being deported (a significant prison sentence), then escorted him back to Mexico through the same Port of Entry he had just come from. This was the typical "revolving door" experienced every day by CBP officers and Border Patrol agents.

Ask any Border Patrol agent of the practice of using illegal aliens' "other" index finger on IDENT so the alien won't come up as a recidivist whose number of attempted illegal entries qualifies for the hours-long Expedited Removal process – just to get kicked back to Mexico. We both did our jobs and had the same results. A copy of Border Patrol's I-213 Record of Deportable Alien/Inadmissible Alien was faxed to the Douglas Port of Entry on November 15, 2005.

On an evening shift in either January or February (two months after the incident) supervisor Jose Lopez, "J-Low" beckoned me into Customs secondary. He was holding the Border Patrol's I-213, my memo explaining my part in the incident and memos from officers T***** and C**** who had witnessed it. C***** had asked LOYA if he was drunk and he replied "No, I'm crazy". "J-Low" asked me if I knew what "Weingarten" was. I said it was our version of Miranda. Lopez affirmed that then informed me I was going to be read my Weingarten Warning tomorrow morning. "For what?" I asked. "For deporting a U.S. citizen" he replied. "Fine! I've _never_ deported a U.S. citizen!" I answered. J-Low – and the Douglas management directing this witch hunt couldn't even make up a decent charge against me. The Border Patrol's report clearly stated Loya was not – nor ever was- a U.S. citizen.

So bright and early the next day, I showed up for work and was summoned into an upstairs room in the main office. Our "perfumed prince", inspector Paul Del Rincon, read me Weingarten - which includes a threat of dismissal – and began interviewing me regarding Loya. My first response was a request to see all the documents pertaining to the incident to include my memo. Del Rincon said they "weren't available". I told him I saw them in "J-Low's" hands the night before. Del Rincon said "They'll be made available at the "right" time." I asked Del Rincon to clarify when the "right time" was and he refused to answer. He continued asking me questions about Loya and I continued to answer that I couldn't remember. It was two or three months ago and I needed to refer to my memo.

Del Rincon's mission from Stemple and Morris was to get me to admit that I ordered Loya back to Mexico without first checking with a supervisor. Douglas management had instituted another "local policy" and taken line officers' statutory authority to determine an alien's admissibility away from us a few years back. Officers had to refer applicant's questionable eligibility for entry to a supervisor. Line officers were –in the words of Donna De la Torre, District Director – "deferring too many applicants". We all knew from experience that supervisors *always* allowed "questionable" applicants entry into the United States. They wanted to make GS-13 and got the message from District to "pasale".

The notice to suspend me for forty five (45) days showed up five months later on May 6, 2006.

29 October 2005 The incident today raised more than a few inspectors' eyebrows: Subject was caught drug smuggling – whereupon she immediately started dropping inspector Paul Del Rincon's name. She obtained her Border Crossing Card July 16, 1999. She was caught drug smuggling a little over three months later on October 22, 1999. Her Border Crossing Card was returned to her shortly after that offense allowing her to continue smuggling drugs until today. Inspector Mora gave several reasons for her card being returned to her: "per Phoenix", "per Del Rincon" – even "to make it easier on her!" This time she was ER'd and sent back to Mexico without her card –where she waited for an opportune time for a member of the Douglas Clique to give it back to her.

CHAPTER 13. CHE' GUEVARRA

7 December 2005 Subject presented his Resident Alien card requesting entry into the United States. He was referred to secondary for a more intensive inspection. I was backing up the secondary inspector when I observed a picture of Che' Guevarra in subject's rear window. Subject had previously crossed the border wearing a Che' shirt. I asked Subject if he knew who Che' was. He did. I asked Subject if he knew Che' was Castro's man in charge of La Cabana Prison in Cuba and had murdered hundreds of innocent people. He didn't but asked "So?" In fact, Che' was asked by one of his former guerrilla comrades just before his execution, why Che' was doing this and Che' replied "I don't tolerate anyone who doesn't think like I do." Subject said "So what?" I asked Subject if he knew Che' was a communist revolutionary who actively advocated the overthrow of the United States government. "Yeah, so what?" he said again. I asked Subject if he ascribed – or followed- Guevara's philosophy of overthrowing the U.S. government. "Yes I do! I can think whatever I want! I have free speech!" he proudly claimed.

I escorted him into the immigration office and informed him he was being processed for exclusion from entry into the United States under Title 8, Code of Federal Regulations, Volume 1, Section 313 "Membership in the Communist Party or any other Totalitarian Organization". This statute prohibits entry into the United States anyone who "advocates, advises, recommends, furthers by overt act, *or admitting a belief in a doctrine*....of the Communist Party..." That took the cockiness out of him. I turned him over to an inspector that was a member of the local clique who proceeded to coach him through the sworn statement and avoid being deported. Subject was wrong twice: He was a Resident Alien –meaning he's supposed to be living in the United States. He was living in Agua Prieta, Mexico. But I'm just being picky.

The issue of "Mexican-american" Resident Aliens living across the line in Mexico is pandemic along the southern land border. This allows them to avoid many duties of citizenship like paying state and local taxes, etc. yet enjoy most of the benefits of citizenship. Immigration law requires a Resident Alien who surrenders his status by no longer living in the United States to request a readjustment of status and receive an accurate entry document – like a Border Crossing Card. This is universally ignored by Port Directors along the southern land border.....and Americans wonder why Hispanics aren't assimilating into the American culture.

29 January 2006 At approximately 1230hrs. Subject requested entry into the United States through Lane 2 of the Douglas, AZ Port of Entry. She told me she, the ten year-old boy and the baby accompanying her are all U.S. citizens. Subject presented Arizona birth certificate #xxxxx in the name of (xxxxxx) as proof of the baby's citizenship and relationship as her daughter. I immediately noticed the baby didn't look like Subject. The baby was crying in the car seat as if suffering separation anxiety from its' real mother. I asked Subject to open her trunk where I found only one small suitcase. Subject told me there were only the baby's clothes in the suitcase – then quickly added there were her and her son's clothes in it also. There didn't appear to be sufficient clothing or other paraphernalia in the vehicle to justify a weekend trip from Phoenix. Subject constantly snapped her chewing gum and tapped her fingers on the steering wheel. Even when warned of the possibility of arrest, Subject continued to insist the baby was her daughter. I referred her to secondary where, under intensive questioning, she admitted the baby was neither hers' nor a U.S. citizen. The baby was turned over to a member of the Mexican consulate. Subject was processed for prosecution as a baby smuggler.

Baby smuggling is an especially egregious offense to most inspectors. In some instances Hispanic Resident Aliens are smuggling babies of relatives in Mexico across so the child can grow up in the United States. In most cases women (usually) are smuggling babies across for money. This more than just about anything else reveals how desperate life is for a woman (or family) is in Mexico for a mother to voluntarily separate herself from her baby, entrust the child into the arms of a total stranger to be brought across an international border through the Port of Entry while the mother/family attempts to sneak across the line cross-country at night. This desperate act is fraught with potential problems. When the alien smuggler is caught and processed for deportation, the baby is turned over to the Mexican consulate. That breaks the connection of the smuggler to the mother. If the mother makes it across how does she know where her baby is if the smuggler has been deported back to Mexico? Vice versa if the mother is caught and "VR'd" back to Mexico by the Border Patrol and the smuggler makes it across with the baby. How is contact re-established? If the smuggler makes it across with the baby regardless of what happens to the mother, the family is contacted and more money is demanded. This is called extortion. At the same time such media furor was being made over the Cuban boy in Florida, Elian Gonzales, an 18-year old young Mexican mother died of thirst in the Arizona desert after giving her baby the last of their water – and being abandoned by the smugglers. The baby survived and was returned to family in Mexico. I'm amazed baby corpses aren't found by the dozens in the Arizona desert.

For quite a few years management refused to prosecute baby smugglers until a woman was caught doing it a third time. A sharp inspector on the line noticed blue stains on the baby's bib. The unconscious baby was unresponsive to stimulus so the driver and everyone in the car were sent to secondary. The female Mexican driver had overdosed the baby with DimeTap to keep it from crying with separation anxiety. The woman was finally processed for prosecution. She got four years in prison. This was a case that resulted in the Assistant U.S. Attorney's office in Tucson actually prosecuting baby smugglers for a while.

One night while I was on the pedestrian lane a young woman ran up screaming that her baby was dying. I took the child out of her arms and held its' mouth to my ear as I looked for the chest to rise. Nothing. I yelled for someone to call 911. When the paramedics arrived they discovered the mother had over medicated the baby in an attempt for the both of them to be "rushed to the hospital" without being inspected and thus gain entry into the U.S. .

At one of the mini-musters management told us to just wave Mexican ambulances through and we would send an inspector to the hospital. Word "got out" about that loophole real quickly –somehow- and the frequency of ambulances multiplied immediately. After there weren't patients in the emergency room when we arrived management said we could establish that there was indeed a medical emergency, the identity of the patient and the EMTs had entry documents prior to allowing the ambulance to enter.

16 February 2006   Letter to: Dorothy Pullo, FOIA Office of Field Operations, Room 5.5C, 1300 Pennsylvania Avenue, Washington, D.C.:

"I am a CBP Officer at the Douglas, AZ Port of Entry. I was just informed by Assistant Area Port Director Rick Spring that I had a "red jacket" with the Office of Personnel Management. Mr. Spring had just returned from temporary duty in D.C. and told me he saw my "red jacket". I am formally requesting a copy of all records on me with CBP Field Operations. I am also formally requesting an answer to why I was "un" selected for duty in Iraq."

Silly me. It was probably just a red divider placed in my file that was easily taken out when FOIA came a callin'. Mr. Spring told me it wasn't a flag for any kind of on-going investigation and intimated it was there permanently – which meant I would probably never be promoted to supervisor. He had only heard of one or two of those before seeing mine. This type of labeling is illegal and a violation of 'The Agreement" with the union. All I received from FOIA was a computer generated copy of basically my biographical data and pay rating. So it's official. All the way to D.C. - I'm a trouble maker.

Here I am 55 years old and still believe in "Truth, Justice and the American Way." I feel like I've deluded myself for ten years thinking I was helping win battles against illegal immigration, drug and alien smuggling and gangsters taking over America. The "red file" made me realize our government had surrendered without a fight. My idealism evaporated and for the second time in my life I felt my country had betrayed me (Vietnam was the first).

CHAPTER 14.
AMERICA'S FRONTLINE

01 March 2006   Message from Acting Commissioner Spero [ACSADMIN.COMMSG]: SUBJECT: Anniversary of CBP:

"Three years ago today, four separate agencies in three departments of government were combined to form U.S. Customs and Border Protection (CBP). The creation of CBP within the Department of Homeland Security (DHS) was truly historic: for the first time in our nation's history one agency was charged with managing and securing the borders of the United States. As we all know, CBP is responsible for carrying out our priority, anti-terrorism mission of preventing terrorists and terrorist weapons from entering the United States. Every day, we, as employees of CBP, serve and protect the United States, our citizens, and our economy. Twenty-four hours a day, 7-days a week, over 42,000 CBP employees......protect nearly 7,000 miles of our border with Canada and Mexico. Together, we are America's frontline."

First, the hypocrisy of higher echelons proclaiming "Every day ....serve and protect. We are America's frontline" makes me want to puke. I was told by supervisor Boatwright specifically to quit thinking of myself as 'America's frontline'. Secondly, this is a celebration of a reorganization that isn't working. Combining immigration specialists and Customs specialists into a CBP generalist by simple fiat does not work – and the supposed "comprehensive cross-training" they boast of is woefully, inadequate. Creation of DHS was a fulfillment of a prediction of mine – and every other thinking individual - that the administration and Congress would try to solve a problem they long ignored by creating another government bureaucracy and throwing money at it. Thirdly, it shows how the "crisis of the moment" diverted management's even minute attention to catching illegal aliens and drug smugglers. All we really needed to do was to close the "7A" (foreign student) gap and for the politicians and immigration management to get serious about backing up the inspectors on the line who were actually trying to enforce the laws already on the books that got America in the mess it became.

16 March 2006 01:57hrs OFFICER ALERT / SOUTHERN BORDER

"The Office of the Assistant Special Agent in Charge, Calexico, California has received information from a source of unknown reliability indicating that a trafficking organization in the Algodones, Mexico area is offering a bounty of $7,000.00 to anyone who kills a Border Patrol Agent or CBP officer. The threat applies to the international border and Ports of Entry near the border between California and Arizona. ASAC Calexico agents are working to determine the validity of this information."

11 May 2006 – Subject XXXX, Address: xxxx Street, Douglas, AZ entered the United States through the Douglas, AZ Port of Entry driving a red, 1994 Buick Skylark accompanied by XXXXX (DOB: xxxxx). I first observed subject speeding recklessly into the crowded secondary area. I immediately ordered him to stop. CBP officer XXXXX approached with a referral slip informing me subject could not open the trunk of the vehicle, that it was his mom's car and that she is the only one who can open the trunk. I asked subject to open the trunk. Subject's speech was slurry as he repeated he couldn't open the trunk. As I was going to ask him if he could get into the trunk through the back seat, subject grabbed his crotch and said "I've got your fucking trunk right here mother fucker!" I asked subject to exit the vehicle. Upon exiting the vehicle subject began raising his arms in an offensive manner. I told him to turn around and face the vehicle but he began resisting even more. With assistance from another inspector I used an approved arm restraint on subject and began escorting him to a holding cell. Upon reaching the raised walkway in front of the secondary office subject dropped to the ground and refused to get up. The secondary inspector assisted me in lifting him off the ground but he again began resisting even more. I took subject to the pavement and handcuffed him. A pat down was approved by Customs supervisor XXXXX during which subject continued to physically and verbally resist. Emptying subject's right pants pocket two "buds" of green, leafy substance fell from his pocket onto the ground. This later tested positive for 3.2 pre-test/2.9 post-test ounces of marijuana. Subject was a juvenile so his mother was called and he was released into her custody. I'm sure she grounded him…..

13 May 2006 A young Mexican male entered Immigration secondary office stating he had lost his "pasaporte". He also stated he wasn't sure he had lost it at the Port of Entry. After a search of the customer counter area we couldn't find it. Instead of letting us inform him his passport wasn't here, Supervisor Jose Lopez accused inspector Ray Goode of keeping the passport. "Jay-Lo" then assisted the young man in completing and filing a $700 tort claim against the immigration service.

This was by far not the only time Jose Lopez actively participated in thwarting inspectors' efforts to do their job.

I caught a male, U.S. citizen smuggling two people he claimed were his U.S. citizen relatives in a rental car. In fact they were unrelated. I had been calling rental car offices to notify them that their vehicles were being used in alien or drug smuggling. Most responded with an urgent request for us to hold onto the vehicle until they could get a representative down to pick it up. Only one national rental car company said they didn't care. Every rental car contract states the vehicle is to be used only within the confines of the United States. Not only did INS stop seizing smuggler's vehicles but "local" policy prevented us from prosecuting American citizens who were earning money smuggling Mexicans into the U.S. . Usually if a U.S. citizen was caught with illegals in his car all he had to do was tell a supervisor "I didn't know they were illegal (when I picked them up just across the line) and the supervisor would release them with absolutely no consequences. Most, if not all, supervisors were incapable of learning (much less willing) to implement criminal law principles like "presumption of knowledge" and "constructive possession".

I was between a rock and a hard place. "J-Low" Lopez told me to release the car back to the smuggler if the rental company didn't have someone here in ten minutes. The car rental company representative in Tucson where the vehicle was rented pleaded vigorously with me on the phone for us to wait half an hour so a representative just down the street from us in Douglas could finish with a customer and drive over to the Port and retrieve the vehicle. I didn't want the smuggler to laugh his way out of the Port of Entry. I brought up a legal question about the case that required Lopez to seek further knowledge from the Mexican Moses. Luckily she didn't know either which took more time. Just as Lopez came back into secondary to release the smuggler and the rental car, the rental car rep arrived and I gave her the keys. The smuggler was pleading with her to give them back as she walked out to take possession of the car. Supervisor Lopez wrote me up for giving her the keys instead of the smuggler. The smuggler lost money on this deal. By using the vehicle for illegal means he lost his deposit, etc.

Supervisor Lopez also told us he didn't want any deferred inspections when he was the shift supervisors. This prevented inspectors from deferring an inspection for an applicant into the U.S. when his admissibility was in doubt but without direct evidence. For example if a Mexican citizen wanted an I-94 six month permit but didn't have proof of residence or economic solvency. In addition to telling us we had to give them the permit despite the lack of "comprobantes", we could no longer tell them to go back and bring such proof prior to issuing them the permit. In other words we were to give permits to anyone asking for them. It took our discretion away and opened just another floodgate for illegal entry.

Supervisor Lopez actually told us that the six-month I-94 Permits were a Mexican citizen's "right" to have – and repeatedly asked inspectors "How many WHITE people are questioned about their citizenship?" The answer is: EVERY ONE of them! His ignorant question ignores the fact that 98.5% of those entering the southern land border are Hispanic. DUH!

Tourists traveling on I-10 twenty miles north would look at their maps and see Douglas right on the border. Thinking to do a quick souvenir shopping trip into "Mexico", they would park their cars on the U.S. side and walk into Mexico for a few blocks before realizing there was next to nothing (legal) for them to buy in Agua Prieta. I can't count how many times American tourists walked through the pedestrian turnstile complaining "there's nothing there!" Most of them don't know that every person entering the United

States is required by law to state their citizenship orally to the inspector. That's a legal requirement so that if the person lies about it he is prosecutable. Occasionally a few ethnocentric American citizens complain in a huffy "Don't I LOOK like an American?" "What does an American LOOK LIKE?" we ask. This gives them pause and a moment to think about what they said. On the other hand we would occasionally have some – mostly young, Hispanic people cross the pedestrian lane and intentionally not declare their citizenship so they could say "Are you asking me because I'm Hispanic?" and make a racial discrimination innuendo. They learn this hostility from the border schools teaching "hispanic studies" classes. The reason Douglas, Naco and Nogales are the three cities in Arizona that use the lowest amount of educational funds for the English as a Second Language (ESL) program is that they teach their students in Spanish – up through high school. I met a Hispanic parent who withdrew her child from school in Nogales because she didn't want her son handicapped in an English-speaking environment by being taught Spanish in the public school. Not all do but many.

One bright sunny day I was standing out in the secondary vehicle inspection area with the Customs guys. I noticed a group of people walking north on the pedestrian lane. They had just been inspected inside and been admitted into the United States. Amongst the gaggle of black-haired pedestrians was a head of blonde hair that really contrasted with the crowd. As I looked to see who that might be I noticed she took a couple of half steps to take her further toward the back of the gaggle. That caught my eye. Then I noticed her trying to adjust her step in those spiked high heels to stay in the same position relative to the group.   It looked like she was trying to avoid observation by us inspectors in secondary. I walked across the northbound lane and opened the gate to the pedestrian lane. "Where are you from?" I asked. When I asked that the whole group hurried on except for a white male who was standing about three feet behind her. "New York" she said. "Where are you from originally?" I asked. "Germany" she replied. I had lived in Germany albeit only a year when I was nine years old but I have an ear for languages. "That doesn't sound like a German accent to me" I said and asked her to come into immigration secondary. This woman was in her 20s, dressed in a very short, black mini-skirt, and a see-through blouse. In other words she was "dressed to distract" – and it worked at the pedestrian lane. The white guy started to disavow any knowledge of her so I asked the guys on the pedestrian lane if these two had come in together. He told them she was his girlfriend and vouched for her citizenship. So I brought both of them in. It turned out they had "met" on the internet. She had purchased a plane ticket to Mexico City and a bus ticket to Douglas, AZ because "I was told it was the easiest place to sneak through." She was from the former Soviet Union state of Georgia. Her accent was Russian. She was processed for expedited removal and returned to Mexico. He, as the alien smuggler, of course, was set free to try getting her in at another Port of Entry.

The media and politicians calling illegal aliens "immigrants" is incorrect. The term "illegal alien" is a specific legal term applying to a non-US citizen within the borders of the United States. Calling them "immigrants" gives a "win" to the liberals who control the debate by intimidating key figures into granting aliens quasi-legal status by using the term. Even the Arizona Supreme Court Chief Justice has ordered lawyers to desist from using the term "alien". Balderdash!

25 May 2006   Subject requested entry into the United States through the Douglas, AZ Port of Entry as a passenger in a white, 2001 Pontiac Grand Am driven by (driver). Subject claimed to be a U.S. citizen "through his sister." He either refused to answer or gave incorrect answers to the immigration process he claimed to have been through. The driver stated she has known Subject for two years and knows him to be a U.S. citizen. I referred all occupants to INS secondary for a more intensive inspection. CBPO R***** obtained an admission from subject that he is a Mexican citizen and processed him for expedited removal.

The driver who attempted to smuggle the illegal into the U.S. was released with her car.

25 May 2006 (Same Day) Subject requested entry into the United States as a passenger in a 1982 Toyota driven by (driver). She presented a DSP-150 Border Crossing Card (#xxxxxx) and claimed to be that person. Subject told me she didn't work, attend school or was married. She quickly told me she lived with her parents when she realized she lacked means of support. I referred Subject to secondary as a possible intended immigrant (out of status as a Border Crosser). CBPO P****** immediately noticed a fingerprint disparity and ER'd Subject as an imposter. Subject admitted to CBPO R***** that she paid $120 for the document in Agua Prieta. In fact, officer P***** noticed that there were TWO female imposters in the car! Well, at least I knew something was wrong. And P***** and R****** were good inspectors who wouldn't send the car down the road just because I was the referring officer.

12 June 2006 The most amazing act of honesty I ever saw at the border occurred today. A 39 year- old woman from Guanajuato, Mexico entered the immigration secondary office – not to request a six-month permit- but to apologize for being "illegal". She explained that she was visiting her daughter in Tucson and decided to fly to Georgia to visit a suddenly sick sister. She was there only one week of a planned 30-day vacation before realizing she didn't have the required I-94. She immediately bought a bus ticket back to Douglas for $175.00 so she could be "legal." D**** and I conducted the interview, her comprobantes were sufficient (and legitimate) and we issued her a permit – our mouths still agape as she walked out the door. It reminds me of a quote by J. Edgar Hoover: "Self discipline is the best form of law enforcement"

21 June 2006 An I-551 holder (Resident Alien) living in Agua Prieta (making him "out of status") admitted to me that he had been convicted of drug smuggling. There must have been a "perfect storm" of supervisors (Customs) that night because we set him up for deportation.

Part of his expedited removal forms states:

1. You are not a citizen or national of the United States.

2.   You are a citizen and native of Mexico.

3.   You were admitted to lawful Permanent Residence on 02/28/91 in Tucson, AZ.

4.   On February 03, 2006 you attempted to enter the Douglas, AZ Port of Entry by presenting your Alien Registration Card.

5.   At the time of your application for entry you were driving a vehicle which was found to have 25 packages of marijuana concealed in the back seat with a total weight of 18.53 kgs.

6.   In a sworn statement you admitted that you agreed to smuggled (sic) the marijuana into the United States and that you were going to be paid $900 to $1,000 dollars.

On the basis of the foregoing, it is charged that you are subject to removal from the United States pursuant to the following provision(s) of law:

Section 212(a)(2)(C) of the Immigration and Nationality Act, as amended, in that a consular of immigration officer knows or has reason to believe you are an alien who is or has been an illicit trafficker in any controlled substance or who is or has been a knowing assister, abettor, conspirator, or colluder with others in the illicit trafficking in any such controlled substance."

It is crystal clear from the above legal verbage that the U.S. government wants drug dealers out of the United States (at least that is what the law says). He should have been required to stay in Mexico until his hearing before an immigration judge on August 4, 2006. Instead, Ernestina Morris issued the drug smuggler a Multiple Entry Permit so he could "visit friends in Tucson."

21 June 2006 Subject attempted entry into the United States through the Douglas, AZ Port of Entry as a front passenger in a vehicle. She presented DSP 150 #........(border crossing card) in the

name of .... and claimed to be that person. The driver
..........told me he worked with the Subject and the female rear
passenger at a factory in Agua Prieta for the last seven months and
called Subject and the other female by the names on the DSP 150s.
The driver jokingly told me they were both his girlfriends. Subject's
photo face seemed slimmer than the Subject's so I conducted a
fingerprint comparison. I saw a mismatch on both Subject and the
female rear passenger. I referred them to secondary with the driver's
statement supporting a conspiracy.

Well the two female imposters were ER'd but the smuggler was
given back his car and sent merrily on home in Douglas, Arizona.
He walked because the Douglas immigration management never
enforces the law against the smugglers. In my opinion when a non-
clique inspector sends such cases back to the secondary office and
the smuggler is related, a friend of the family or is known socially by
the clique inspectors/management, regardless of the substantial
evidence to make a case against him, he is let go. Customs
inspectors mockingly called this immigration process "Checking the
genealogy tree".

Chapter 15.

Into the Maelstorm

The January charge of "Deporting a U.S. citizen" hadn't been
resolved yet. However, the proverbial feces really hit the fan upon
the impending departure of Assistant Port Director "Pistol Pete"
Bachelier in February 2006. He sent an email to all inspectors and
staff praising the "team work" and "high morale" of us all. It was a
pure whitewash of his Napoleanic and paranoid management style
the whole time he was at Douglas. His intended audience was really
his higher chain of command rather than a sincere appreciation to the
troops. I couldn't let it pass without providing the "ground truth" in
response:

04 March 2006 -   Email to APD Bachelier, RE: Thank You Email from APD Bachelier To All Inspectors Upon His Departure May 2003 – February 2006:

"To APD Bachelier, I don't understand your letter – except as it glosses over reality to look politically acceptable. I never felt you supported us in any way. In fact, I had the uncomfortable impression that in your spare time you fantasized about ways of "catching" us doing some perceived wrong – like telling the Special Enforcement Team (SET) to "keep an eye on us" and wanting to take the chairs on primary away from us. During staff meetings you – and the rest of management – felt self-important by standing in front of us and talking down to us, always finding a reason to disagree with anything we said or offered up as a solution. Whenever one of us objected to some of the inane BS distributed by management all of you circle the wagons – even physically moved closer to each other– and began berating us. Not once did I hear any logical response to anything any of us said in "staff" meetings. We troops aren't stupid. Just about any inspector at this port could do a better job of managing than you or any other management-level employee at this port could – with the exception of De La Ossa who holds his own. We know what you and management say about us behind our backs. We know when you screw up or screw us and lie to De La Torre about it. Because of the type of "management" you and your conspirators oppress us with the morale at this port is lower than whale feces – and that is at the bottom of the ocean. Not one officer at this port is impressed with the lack of intelligence exhibited by management here. Not only lack of intelligence but lack of life experience – which would have made a world of difference. You prevent us from enforcing the laws and make us public door mats. You encourage and promote sychophants to protect the secrecy of your incompetence. I consider it a tragedy that so many good officers are so poorly led. Instead of firing one supervisor who was demoted and returned here at another port he is dumped on us to take out his vengeance. With the quality of officer at this port management could have the easiest job in CBP. Just let us do our job and support us. Instead, management has instilled fear and loathing – and you take great pleasure in that knowledge.

Theory X management went out with the end of the industrial revolution.

We are "thanked" for sliding cards through the card reader – like we are doing it for you! ? Not even close. We are doing it because you said you "almost vomited" when you saw the stats then threatened us with bad paper if we didn't slide every persons' card. Your concern with stats and promotion over enforcing the laws and backing up the troops is nauseating.

One last indicator that you and management are out of touch with reality here – You think the morale of the troops here is very high? You must be smoking crack if you think so. Why do you think so many officers are begging to leave? Why did Rick Harmon take deferred retirement – as I am?

I have been on a "team". I commanded a team. This port is not a team. Mike Ligon"

This email was sent to all addressees that Bachelier sent his farewell to. It soon reached one of our officers on temporary duty in Japan. It was discussed at a national union meeting in Las Vegas. And of course it created a firestorm within Douglas management. They immediately began the process to fire or suspend me – again. This time they had been publicly humiliated (with the truth) and were bringing to bear all their "big guns"…… evidenced by the following:

19 December 2004[sic]: (It should have been dated 2005 – more proof of the Peter Principle by the author)

MEDMORANDUM FOR: Mari Yonkers, Director Employee Relations

FROM: Todd Boucher, LER/BTV

SUBJECT: DRB Case Request

"I've attached a case that I believe merits DRB consideration.

In this case, CBP Officer Michael Ligon failed to perform his job and refer an individual to secondary, rather, the [sic] he allowed the individual to return to Mexico. Approximately one-half hour earlier, the U.S. Border Patrol caught the individual as he entered the country.

I believe the seriousness of Officer Ligon's failure to perform his assigned duties is compounded by the fact that the OFC (oral false claim to US citizenship) he encountered occurred at the end of his shift and he was apparently too lazy to process the individual properly. As well, the individual had an extensive criminal history.

I would be pleased to present this case to the board if you wish.

Signed, Todd Boucher, LER/BTV"

05 May 2006 - "Dear Mr. Ligon:

This advises you, in accordance with the provisions of Title 5 of the Code of Federal Regulations, Part 752, that I am proposing to suspend you for forty-five (45) calendar days from your position as Customs and Border Protection (CBP) Officer, GS-1895-11. A final decision concerning this proposal will be effected not earlier than thirty (30) calendar days from the date you receive this notice. The reason for this proposed action is as follows:

CHARGE 1: NEGLIGENCE IN THE PERFORMANCE OF DUTY

Specification: On October 22, 2005, at approximately 2000hrs you were acting as the secondary officer in the Pedestrian Only Designated lane at Douglas, Arizona. You were working with CBP Officer Gary Oldberg, who was functioning as the primary officer in the POD lane. On this occasion, Officer Oldberg was processing a pedestrian in the POD lane, Mr. Alberto Jesus Loya-Grajeda, a Mexican alien and prior deportee, who was attempting to cross from Mexico into the United States. When Officer Oldberg began questioning Mr. Loya-Grajeda it became apparent that the subject was making an "oral false claim" (OFC) of United States citizenship.

For this reason you then began questioning Mr. Loya-Grajeda who again presented himself to you as a United States Citizen. During this questioning, you told Mr. Loya-Grajeda that he wasn't being truthful and you in fact suspected that he was a Mexican National making an OFC of U.S. citizenship.. Instead of referring the subject for additional secondary inspection, as required by local CBP policy, you escorted Mr. Loya-Grajeda back into Mexico and told him he would need to provide appropriate documents in order to enter the United States.

Approximately 30 minutes after you escorted the subject back to Mexico, he was apprehended by Officer Bork while attempting to walk north through the southbound lane in order to enter the United States. It was then necessary to call the Border Patrol who took over the case and apprehended Mr. Loya-Grajeda. A subsequent check of Mr. Loya-Grajeda's records revealed that he has an extensive criminal history including arrests for alien smuggling, armed robbery and aggravated assault and prior deportation from the United States which occurred on November 10, 2004.

CHARGE 2: DISRESPECTFUL CONDUCT

Specification: In an electronic mail message responding to a message from outgoing assistant Port Director Peter Bachelier, which you sent to all personnel at the port of Douglas Arizona on March 4, 2006 at 3:21A.M. you made numerous disrespectful comments regarding port management in general and outgoing APD Bachelier in particular. Among other things you accused APD Bachelier of not supporting employees in any way, and of looking for ways to get employees in trouble. Specifically you stated: (repetition of my email contents).

In your message you went on to accuse outgoing Assistant Port Director Bachelier and other members of port management OF [sic] exhibiting a lack of intelligence, preventing CBP from enforcing the laws and making them public doormats. You also stated that believe management encourages and promotes sycophants to protect the secrecy of its incompetence and instills fear and loathing in the work force. You concluded your message by stating that in your opinion the port is not a team. Instead of sending your comments only to those managers to whom they were directed you chose to share them with all personnel at the port.

In proposing this action, with respect to conduct chronicled in Charge 1, I have considered that your lack of vigilance when processing travelers, is extremely serious and cannot be tolerated from a Customs and Border Patrol (CBP) Officer. The subject of returning pedestrians to Mexico has been addressed at several prior briefings and muster meetings of CBP Officers. During these meetings, it was stressed that no one gets sent back to Mexico without supervisory approval. Your failure to follow these established local policies for processing travelers is inexcusable in the post 9-11 era. In this case had Mr. Loya-Grajeda been a terrorist and had he been able to enter the United States, the result could have been catastrophic. Your actions in this regard were in direct conflict with some of the principal missions of U.S. Customs and Border Protection, which includes preventing terrorist suspects, criminals, and illegal aliens from entering the United States. Your conduct has diminished my confidence in your ability to perform your duties as a Customs and Border Protection Officer.

With respect to Charge 2, I have also considered that by sending electronic mail containing derogatory comments about port management to all of the employees in the port you caused a considerable disruption in the port which detracts from accomplishment of the CBP mission. While you have the right to express your opinion to port management regarding its effectiveness and efficiency, you do not have the right to portray management in a disrespectful manner to other employees in the port. To do so causes disruption in the work place which cannot be tolerated.

I have also considered your previous disciplinary record which consists of a suspension for 2 calendar days which you served in July of 2000 (telling immigration assistant Bonnie "The Italian" Velasco to go to hell for interfering in my case). Therefore, based upon the foregoing, I find that this proposal is warranted and, if effected, will promote the efficiency of the service.

This is only a proposal. You have the right to reply to this proposal orally, in writing, or both, and to furnish affidavits and other documentary evidence, including medical documentation, in support of your reply. If you disagree with this proposed action, your reply should set forth the reasons for your belief that this action should not take place.

The Deciding Official, Donna De La Torre, Director, Field Operations,, Tucson Field Office, must receive any written reply to this proposal within ten (10) calendar days beginning the day after you receive this notice. Your written reply, if you choose to submit one, should be addressed to:

Donna De La Torre, Director, Field Operations, Tucson Field Office

c/o Mr. Chris Ramsey

U.S. Customs and Border Protection

Labor and Employee Relations

1300 Pennsylvania Avenue, NW, Room 7.2C

Washington, D.C. 20229

Of course once I was served with the notice from District Headquarters that they wanted my head, word spread among all the inspectors. Immigration and Customs had been combined into CBP by now. I received a surprise letter of endorsement from a Customs senior inspector:

To: Donna De la Torre, Director of Field Operations, Arizona CMC

From: CBPO Steven Lynn, Douglas Port of Entry

Subject: In Defense of CBPO Mike Ligon

Date: 05192006

"I am taking this opportunity to make a few comments in support of CBPO Mike Ligon, who I have worked with for about 10 years at the Douglas, Arizona POE, and who I consider to be a very professional and reliable CBP Officer.

CBPO Ligon has always been a very enforcement-minded officer, which I observed when he formerly worked for INS, and which I notice on a daily basis today. He knows his job and he understands the mission of the Department of Homeland Security down here on the Arizona-Mexico border.

His memo of 03/04/2006, wherein are contained some very accurate criticisms of the management style here in Douglas, is not exactly the memo I would personally write. But there are clearly some salient points that CBPO Ligon makes, particularly when he mentions in a few spots the poor leadership of Douglas management. I have seen leadership in a number of different settings, and what we generally have in Douglas is not it. APD Bachelier was a particularly a poor leader. Maybe good PR and a good visual image, but day to day on the ground? No.

I do not put an exaggerated stake in morale. My general view of people today is that they want to have their hand held. But the Douglas officers, particularly the new and younger hires, are not that happy about what they are being shown down here, and many are trying to leave.

Veteran officers like CBPO Ligon are an excellent example to them of what it means to stay the course and do the job every day in a workmanlike fashion. Thank you for this opportunity, CBPO Steven Lynn."

CBP Officer Lynn was a veteran Customs officer with a lot of experience who was as disgruntled with Douglas management as I was. We weren't particularly close friends but we were both very law enforcement oriented about our jobs. I appreciate his unsolicited support in the face of highly placed, legacy immigration bureaucrats lowering the proverbial "boom" on me.

I responded to the notice-to-suspend with a five page rebuttal citing two U.S. Supreme Court cases involving government employees right to free speech and repeating the many specious and exaggerated management inquiries conducted against me for the last ten years.

Joining the "union" was supposed to be optional. You could either join and pay union dues or not. Either way each officer was still eligible to receive representation by the union representatives. That's what the union contract said – The Agreement. I mentioned before that many, if not most, immigration inspectors at our Port didn't join because we saw inspectors vying for the union rep position in order to travel on boondoggles to Las Vegas and other places around the U.S. . Most line officers thought of union reps as just inspectors bucking for fast track promotion to GS-12 supervisor. That's how management co-opted the union reps.

I notified Joseph Martin, President of AFGE Local 2859 in Yuma about management's notice to suspend me for forty-five "(45)" days. He had to check with "national" union headquarters to see if they would represent me. When he called me he said they would …….but it would cost me almost two thousand "(2,000) dollars. So much for "The Agreement" covering both dues and non-dues paying officers. It was still less money than a lawyer but I didn't know how well I would be represented. I had done pretty well on my own and the quasi-local union reps who sat like bumps on a log during management's frequent inquisitions on me I wasn't optimistic on this one. During a previous battle with management, national union reps came down to Douglas to talk to me. They looked like "collectors" for New York loan sharks. They told me the same thing Port Director Jesus Jerez told me "There's laws….then there's laws. You don't have to look so hard!" I told them they wasted a lot of union dues money flying from D.C. to tell me that. I told them they were part of the problem.

The previous Nogales union rep had come over to Douglas when Molaski and Morris suspended me for the fabricated "domestic violence" incident. What he told me he said to them differed significantly from the kiss ass approach documented in the final report – the hypocrite.

Martin eventually told me "Look, they're going to suspend you for 45 days regardless of what "we" say. But I want you to appear in person to give your rebuttal to the charges." I asked why I should subject myself to their grilling if they were just going to suspend me anyway. "First, you did a great job finding those U.S. Supreme Court cases regarding federal employees' right to free speech. Your very public email to Bachelier is really why they want to suspend you. You embarrassed them big time. Second, There are going to be two court recorders there from Headquarters, D.C. to transcribe your reply. In addition to your rebuttals to the two specific charges, I want you to read verbatim your 27-page complaint of what's been going on in Douglas for the last ten years. Donna De La Torre is going to have to sit there and listen to it. The court recorders will take your testimony back to D.C. where it will become an official record . That's why I want you to appear" he said.

Martin's rebuttal included comments to the effect: _**"..this type of discretionary RTM (Return to Mexico) is a long standing past practice and is very common along the southern border; .....the Service has cited a policy concerning the referral of applicants for admission, but did not present this policy with the information provided to Officer Ligon. Furthermore there is no policy concerning who you can or can't refer to secondary. Or if you can or cannot allow an applicant for admission to return to Mexico.**_

The reference to "what if" the guy had been a terrorist was humorous. When I caught a German man heading the wrong way south into Mexico at two in the morning "looking for information" – about what he didn't detail- with several different names on several different documents, management wasn't interested – the FBI was. Nor were they when I received a thanks from the immigration intel officer for giving him such information on incoming Middle Easterners who were allegedly "Phds in nuclear biology."

Chapter 16.

Bearing Witness

My sworn testimony before the Director of Field Operations, Tucson District Office, Donna De La Torre was scheduled for around the second week of June 2006. A week before my appearance I received a letter from the Department of the Army. My March request for a return to active duty as a mobilized retiree was accepted. I would be receiving orders to active duty soon. I faxed a copy to Douglas Port management and the union rep that day.

I drove up to Tucson dressed in a blue suit and arrived on time. I and my union rep were escorted into a conference room and sat to the right of the head of the table. The two D.C. court reporters were already set up on the other side of the table. They had two microphones taped to the middle of the table. Ms. De La Torre entered a few minutes late accompanied by two male bureaucrats. One was her legal advisor. She never looked directly at me.

She had reason not to. Two of her staff members and the union rep had told me she had recently been caught "getting it on" on her office desk with our previous port director Molaski who had recently been transferred up to Tucson. The day before my testimony one of the real old-time inspectors showed me an old photo of De La Torre sitting in the middle of a booth between Stemple, Ernestina Morris holding up glasses of beer in a bar. From what I was told, De La Torre was of the same bolt of cloth as my morally bankrupt management.

After the required preliminaries, I began reading my 27-page complaint. De La Torre interrupted twice but was told both times by legal counsel she had to let me speak. I was only interrupted a few times by the court recorders to remind me to speak louder and to reposition the microphones. When I finished De La Torre made an inane comment about "not knowing" what was going on in Douglas. I told her I had sent her direct emails and repeated memos telling her what was going on and had never received an answer from her. I don't know if the court recorders got that on tape but I saw them write those statements down. So now everything I complained about is part of an official document and public record. It had become public knowledge at the Port of Entry when Mora accessed my computer and tacked my complaint to the bulletin board.

On the drive back home, the union rep called and said he had gone back to talk with De La Torre to reach some kind of agreement. He reminded De La Torre that I would soon be going back into the "service of my country". Her response was "Well, if he's going into the military, we'll just wait to suspend him until he gets back."

10 June 2006 Upon arriving at work today one of the new, non-local/clique female inspectors –an excellent inspector- asked aloud why there are two small Mexican flags stuck onto the immigration office window. I went outside to verify this and, seeing them, took them off the window and threw them in the trash – then retrieved them and put them in my pocket to remind me of what I and other American enforcement-minded inspectors were up against at the Douglas, AZ Port of Entry. This was just prior to my departing for mobilized retiree recall to active duty in the army. It was an appropriate farewell message from the Douglas Clique. I still have those flags. They still "drive the bus".

I received my orders back to active duty in the mail on Saturday, July 12, 2006. I was to report to Ft. Jackson, South Carolina for "re-greening" on Sunday, July 13, 2006 – my oldest son's 23rd birthday. The first of all three sons to join the Marine Corps. Although I had asked for assignment at Ft. Bragg with Special Forces Command, I was instead reassigned to the Military Intelligence Captain's Career Course, Ft. Huachuca, Arizona – my home town and the same office I had retired from in 1996. Since, as was typical for the army, I had to report the next day I had to get some things done for the house to be empty while I was gone a few weeks. I called the evening shift leader at Douglas, George De La Ossa, to tell him I was taking admin leave tonight and had to report for active duty in South Carolina the next day. I contacted him on his cell phone while he was golfing with 'Perfumed Prince" Paul Del Rincon at the Douglas Golf Course. I told him of the last minute receipt of my orders and requested admin leave for this evening. He told me to give my duty weapon and a copy of my orders to my local union rep (who didn't live far away) and he would ensure I was listed on admin leave for the shift tonight. I emphatically told him I would be on active duty and therefore on military leave from CBP. He said he understood.

I went through three weeks of "re-greening" at Ft. Jackson, S.C. in over 100 degree heat and famous southern humidity. I realized how much older I had become since I retired from active duty ten years ago. A few weeks after reporting for duty at Ft. Huachuca, I received another pay statement from CBP. De La Ossa had listed me as "AWOL" the Saturday I called him to take admin leave. My pay was reduced accordingly and it was listed as such in my personnel records. I called him the next day. He started claiming he didn't remember talking to me – until I reminded him that the union rep had personally handed him my duty weapon and my orders to active duty. In other words there was a witness. I realized we were on speaker phone and I could hear Ernestina Morris whispering in the background. De La Ossa began stammering like he was caught between the truth and Morris. I told him if he didn't correct the error on my pay check I was going to the union and the Judge Advocate General's office and file a claim of harassment against him and Douglas management for punishing me for going on active duty. It was quickly corrected. They just never quit sticking their knives in my back and twisting them.

Epilogue

The ten years that I was reading everything about counterinsurgency, revolutionary warfare, etc. on the midnight shifts at the Douglas, AZ Port of Entry thinking it would somehow benefit me teaching it someday proved to be true. I continued teaching the same subjects I taught to the Military Intelligence Captain's Career Course, 2006-07 as I had from 1994-96. I enjoyed teaching immensely. As my year of active duty drew to a close I could envision the Douglas management sharks smelling blood in the water upon my return to duty with CBP. I qualified for early retirement so I didn't have to go back. But I didn't have a decent job waiting for me in lieu of CBP. A few weeks before my tour ended, Chief Warrant Officer James Hess, a fellow instructor, had been selected to be the Chief of the All-Source Analyst Committee. His cubicle was next to our conference table around which I and another activated CBP officer from nearby Naco swapped horror stories. Chief Hess and I had been instructors on the same committee for the last year. He knew I spoke my mind. When I conveyed my indecision about whether to retire from CBP –and avoid the piranha frenzy- or go back to Hell and continue building retirement in Douglas, Chief Hess, like Michael the Archangel, offered me a job as a contract instructor on his committee teaching intelligence to new enlistees.

I gratefully accepted. I submitted my retirement papers to CBP via fax and began my new job a few blocks away from my active duty office the end of August. I had been driving 102 miles from my home to Douglas each day and back almost every day (often working 28-32 days in a row), working under constant managerial harassment, working twelve (12) different shifts that changed every two weeks. Now I was working eight (8) hours a day five days a week with paid holidays off nine miles from home. My kids said it was the first time I had smiled in years.

Douglas management was incensed that I had "escaped" punishment for the embarrassing email. They thought that I had simply "called the army and asked to come on active duty to avoid punishment at Douglas". And, of course, the army -being so responsive- sent me the orders that day. Their lack of sense of the real world still amazes me.

It's been five years now. In my new job I was promoted three times in the first six months, put in charge of establishing and supervising a new section then selected for my current position which I am enjoying immensely.

Over the years working on the border I often wondered why Mexico was so messed up that its' citizens had to flee north to obtain a decent living. They certainly had enough revolutions in their history to make a decent democracy. I learned that 20 families owned over 80% of the land and resources in Mexico. There was no middle class to speak of. While writing this book and detailing the corruption of the Douglas, AZ Immigration management I had an epiphany. Douglas immigration management was a microcosm of Mexico.

Recommendations

Out of curiosity I called the CBP information office to ask if contiguous border citizens were required to obtain I-94 Permits and what the prerequisites were for obtaining the permit so one could travel more than 25 linear miles from the border. I spoke with Janice Mosher at 1420hrs on 18 February 2011. Her response was revealing. She said I-94s are not required for either Canadians or Mexicans travelling more than 25 miles into the United States. Ms. Mosher told me the aliens' visas issued by the American consulates in those countries sufficed for travel anywhere in the United States! I asked her if there wasn't a statute in 8 CFR Section 212(a) Documentary Requirements for Mexicans entering the United States requiring them to provide proof of residence and employment or economic solvency to obtain a six month I-94 Permit. Ms. Mosher replied incredulously "Most Mexicans crossing the border are just going "day shopping" and going back home *so they rarely ask for I-94s*!" She continued to say that *most Mexicans who enter the United States with the intention of going more than 25 linear miles from the border fly in*! So I asked her what documentation they presented to the airport CBP officers when given the I-94s to complete prior to deplaning. She said all they needed was the American- consulate issued visa. "But the consulate visa is issued only once for ten years. What documentation is required to show they are still living and working in Mexico upon entering the U.S. during those ten years? In other words, what inspection requirement ensures their return home and prevents them from staying in the U.S.?" I asked. Ms. Mosher, CBP Information Officer, said "That rarely happens."

I don't understand how Ms. Mosher interprets "rarely" but conservative estimates' list approximately *12-14 million illegal aliens living illegally in the United States*. There are probably closer to 18 million – and growing rapidly. *It is estimated that about half of these are visa overstays*! When I recovered from my shock of her incredibly naïve statement all I could say was "Really?" Ms. Mosher became irritated and said "Look, I'm not going to argue with you about this. I have 19 callers in line waiting to ask what documents are required to enter the United States". "I understand.

Could you direct me to an office or person who is knowledgeable about this?" I asked. "No" she said "and I'm not going to argue with you." - and hung up.

As incredible as it seems, I suspect – cancel that- *I know* - Ms. Mosher is not the only CBP employee operating under the deluded, naïve or intentionally deceptive assumption that Mexicans living and working illegally in the United States "rarely" happens.

In March 2011 I visited with a friend who still works at the Douglas Port of Entry. I asked him if things had gotten any better. He said they had gotten worse. The inspectors are still coerced into not asking for any recent proof of residence or economic solvency – and they've quit doing so. He also said the new inspectors report being intimidated *at the academy* into not doing so. They've quit teaching them to do so. So, America, the floodgates are wide open.

Unless the residency and solvency requirements are re-codified and mandated by top leadership on down, the flood will continue ......and the American culture will continue to disappear.

The following recommendations are made in hopes of regaining control of our Ports of Entry:

1.***Establish an "exit inspection" program***. The computer system was actually approved and funded by Congress on more than one occasion but was always taken out of the final bill at the last moment. We have the technology and capability to determine who is NOT leaving the U.S. That in conjunction with enforcing a law permanently banning those overstaying their visas from ever again receiving any kind of entry permit (and freeing ICE agents to pursue them) alone would have such a ripple effect on the illegal population in the U.S. as to cut the number in half .

2.Return the authority to defer inspections back to the line inspectors. Allow them to do the job they are paid to do – determine admissibility of aliens into the United States. ***This includes the authority to deny admission if the applicant fails the inspection.*** This authority is currently denied inspectors. ***In other words, almost***

no one is denied admission! If management overrules an inspector's deferred inspection require justification by the supervisor by memorandum to District.

2. Rescind the 6-month I-94 permit. Re-implement the "duration of stay and location only" permits. Make issuance of duration-of-stay I-94s dependent on presentation of sufficient proof of residence and economic solvency in the applicant's native country for the last 12 months. This is an excellent way for law enforcement officers to be able to track those who have entered our country and determine if they are out of status.

2.Eliminate the practice of "local policy" at Ports of Entry. The law is the law. It reminds me of a quote I saw on a wall behind a police chief's desk: "No one is above the law. Nor is anyone beneath it. Nor do we ask anyone's permission to enforce it. – J. Edgar Hoover". This is a leadership issue. It is also applicable to Arizona's tough immigration law SB 1070. Several administrations and special interest groups chose a knee-jerk reaction to Arizona's law before reading it. ***It is almost verbatim the same as the federal law!*** I wrote a training manual for state and local law enforcement officers to facilitate their ability to determine status of suspected illegals. It is the same process we CBP officers use on the border. It takes 20 seconds and is not based on racial profiling.

3. Permanently Prohibit local citizens from working at the same Port of Entry where they grew up. This will drastically reduce the potential for corruption, conflict of interest and "local policy".

4. Start seizing smuggler's vehicles again. Donate the smugglers' vehicles to charity to avoid "handling costs" by CBP.

5. Lengthen time required for imposters and other fraudulent applicants at Ports of Entry to regain their entry documents to five years (now at one year) – if there is no political will to cancel them permanently for breaking the law.

6. If a Border Crossing Card (I-586) holder is caught having entered without inspection (EWI'd – jumped the line) permanently cancel his card. This "12, 15, 20 chances" before being cancelled is ludicrous. It's called 212(a)(6)(A) in the Immigration & Nationality Act.

7. If a driver of a vehicle is found to have an illegal alien or drugs in his vehicle, whether he claims to have known it or not, seize his vehicle and cancel his entry document – he's an alien/drug smuggler. It's a legal concept called "constructive knowledge/possession". The driver is responsible for assuring he has nothing illegal in his vehicle like drugs or illegal aliens.

8. Make promotions dependent on level of education and experience (including military) instead of the "good 'ol boy" nepotism now in place.

9. Move supervisors to another district once they are promoted to a managerial position.

10. Establish an organization similar to Corps of Retired Executives (CORE) consisting of retired immigration inspectors (CORII). This Corps would be available to assist state and local law enforcement in the identification of illegals within the United States.

11. Change federal immigration policy to reflect the "traditional" policy as described in Beck's "NumbersUSA" rather than current, ruinous policy now in existence. In other words, go back to the limited, controlled immigration policy rather than the million per year allowed now. Or stop legal immigration altogether for a decade to "allow" recent immigrants time to acculturate into the American culture.

12.Shorten the Expedited Removal (ER) process. Currently we are extending constitutional rights to aliens who haven't even successfully entered the United States! Once we catch oral or documented false claims to U.S. citizenship, imposters, aliens in possession of fraudulent documents, etc. we should be able to complete a simple, one-page Form I-213, enter the information into the appropriate data bases, and return them to Mexico – like we did before the ER process and just as the Border Patrol still does.

13. Mandate an "enforcement" philosophy from the Director of Homeland Security down to the lowest levels of management. The 9/11 Commission Report to Congress revealed the "service" mentality was responsible for 9/11. If the immigration managerial "service" philosophy doesn't change another 9/11 is just a matter of time.

14. Enforce the law prohibiting Resident Aliens from living outside the United States. RAs who live in Mexico and commute should be required to surrender their Resident status.

15. Stop issuing U.S. birth certificates to alien children born in the U.S. to alien parents. Eliminate the incentive for the lucrative "birthing mill" market.

16. Mandate the Social Security Agency –and all state social service agencies - cooperate with DHS agents who are looking for illegal aliens utilizing state and federal social services. This requires an increase in the numbers of investigators looking for fraud The program would pay for itself in recovering revenue wasted through fraud.

17. Stop paying obeisance to the Mexican government in enforcing our immigration policy. That's a leadership issue at the top of DHS and the State Department. The last time a former Marine commandant (Gen. Chapman, 1980s) was commissioner of INS he lasted only two years.

17. Stop federal funds to sanctuary cities and organizations providing safe haven for illegals and subverting the immigration laws of the U.S.

18. Enforce the laws regarding Resident Aliens violating the laws of the United States. They should be deported and permanently denied citizenship in the U.S.A. It's not that hard to be a law-abiding resident.

Grounds for Inadmissibility

Note the bold print notations!

212(a)(1)(A)(i) Communicable disease of public health significance

212(a)(1)(A)(ii) Lacks immunization against vaccine-preventable diseases named by statute

212(a)(1)(A)(iii)Physical or mental disorder with associated harmful behavior

212(a)(1)(A)(iv) Drug abuser or drug addict

212(a)(2)(A)(i)(I) Crime involving moral turpitude

212(a)(2)(A)(i)(II) Controlled substance violation (includes US and foreign laws)

212(a)(2)(B) Multiple criminal convictions with aggregate sentence of 5 years

212(a)(2)(C) Controlled substance trafficking

212(a)(2)(D) Prostitution or commercialized vice

212(a)(2)(E) Asserted immunity from prosecution

212(a)(3)(A) Espionage, sabotage, or export of sensitive technology or information

212(a)(3)(B)(i)(I) Aliens who have engaged in terrorist activity

212(a)(3)(B)(i)(II) Aliens who are likely to engage in terrorist activities upon admission to the U.S.

212(a)(3)(B)(i)(III) Aliens who have incited terrorist activities

212(a)(3)(B)(i)(IV) Representative of terrorist organizations designated by Department of State pursuant to section 219 INA

212(a)(3)(B)(i)(V) Members of terrorist organizations designated by Department of State pursuant to section 219 INA

212(a)(3)(C) Adverse foreign policy considerations

212(a)(3)(D) Immigrant membership in totalitarian party

212(a)(3)(E) Nazi Persecution or genocide

212(a)(4) Likely to become a Public Charge (welfare)

212(a)(5)(A) No approved labor certification

212(a)(5)(B) Graduate of a nonaccredited medical school seeking to enter the US to practice medicine and does not meet licensing and English language requirements

212(a)(5)(C) Any alien seeking admission to work as a health care worker who does not meet certification and English language requirements

212(a)(6)(A) Any alien present in the U.S. without being admitted or paroled or any alien arriving in the US at a time or place not designated by the Attorney General *(jumping the line)*

212(a)(6)(B) Aliens who did not appear for or remain at removal proceedings within the previous five years

212(a)(6)(C)(i) Willful misrepresentation of a material fact *(Lying to a CBP officer – never, NEVER, enforced!)*

212(a)(6)(C)(ii) False claim to US citizenship

212(a)(6)(D) Stowaways

212(a)(6)(E) Alien smuggling

212(a)(6)(F) Alien subject of [sic] final order for violation of 274C INA

212(a)(6)(G) Any alien classified as a nonimmigrant student (F-1) who violates a term of that status under 214(1) INA ***(if this had been enforced 9/11 may not have occurred)***

212(a)(7)(A)(i)(I) Immigrant ***not in possession*** of valid, unexpired visa, reentry permit, border crossing card and a valid passport of [sic] other travel document

212(a)(7)(A)(i)(II) Immigrant with visa issued without compliance with section 203 INA

212(a)(7)(B)(i)(I) Nonimmigrant ***not in possession of*** passport valid for at least 6 months beyond period of initial admission

212(a)(7)(B)(i)(II) Nonimmigrant ***not in possession*** of valid nonimmigrant visa or border crossing card

212(a)(8)(A) Immigrant who is permanently ineligible to citizenship

212(a)(8)(B) Anyone who has left the US or stayed outside the US to evade training or service in the armed forces during the period declared by the president to be a national emergency

212(a)(9)(A)(i) Any alien ***previously removed*** after being ordered removed at the time of arrival is inadmissible for 5 years (20 years if subsequent removal or aggravated felon)

212(a)(9)(A)(ii) Any alien previously removed after being ordered removed after proceedings initiated at a time other than the time of arrival or an alien who departed the US while an order of removal was outstanding is inadmissible for ten years (20 years of subsequent removal or aggravated felon)

212(a)(9)(B)(i) Any alien (other than "LPR" – Resident Alien) who was unlawfully present in the US for more than 180 days but less than one year who voluntarily departed the US is inadmissible for 3 years. ***(this also means those with Border Crossing Cards who were living illegally in the U.S. – and we found out when the requested re-entry into the U.S. This was routinely ignored)***

212(a)(9)(B)(ii) Any alien (other than LPR) who was unlawfully present in the US for more than one year who voluntarily departed the US is inadmissible for 10 years *(ditto the above note)*

212(a)(9)(C)(i) Any alien who has been unlawfully present in the US for an aggregate period of more than one year and who enters or attempts to enter the US *without being admitted (jumping the line)*

212(a)(9)(C)(ii)   Any alien who has been ordered removed under Section 235(b)(1) or section 240 INA, or any other provision of law, who enters or attempts to enter the US without being admitted

212(a)(10)(A) Immigrant coming to practice polygamy

212(a)(10)(B)   Any alien accompanying a helpless alien

212(a)(10)(C)   International child abductor

212(a)(10)(D) *Any alien who has unlawfully voted*

212(a)(10)(E) Any alien who has renounced US citizenship to avoid taxation by the US

www.ingramcontent.com/pod-product-compliance
Lightning Source LLC
Chambersburg PA
CBHW060237290526
45789CB00001B/84